THE PTSD WORKBOOK

Simple, Effective
Techniques for
Overcoming
Traumatic
Stress Symptoms

Mary Beth Williams, Ph.D., LCSW, CTS
Soili Poijula, Ph.D.

New Harbinger Publications, Inc.

Publisher's Note

This publication is designed to provide accurate and authoritative information in regard to the subject matter covered. It is sold with the understanding that the publisher is not engaged in rendering psychological, financial, legal, or other professional services. If expert assistance or counseling is needed, the services of a competent professional should be sought.

Distributed in the U.S.A. by Publishers Group West; in Canada by Raincoast Books; in Great Britain by Airlift Book Company, Ltd.; in South Africa by Real Books, Ltd.; in Australia by Boobook; and in New Zealand by Tandem Press.

Diagnostic criteria for PTSD and Acute Stress Disorder adapted with permission from the *Diagnostic and Statistical Manual of Mental Disorders, Fourth Edition, Text Revision.* Copyright 2000 American Psychiatric Association.

Copyright © 2002 by Mary Beth Williams and Soili Poijula
New Harbinger Publications, Inc.
5674 Shattuck Avenue
Oakland, CA 94609

Cover design © by Lightbourne Images
Edited by Clancy Drake
Text design by Tracy Marie Powell-Carlson

ISBN 1-57224-282-5 Paperback

All Rights Reserved

Printed in the United States of America

New Harbinger Publications' Web site address: www.newharbinger.com

04   03   02

10   9   8   7   6   5   4   3   2   1

First printing

I would like to dedicate this book to the families, friends, and colleagues of the victims of the terrorist attacks of September 11, 2001. I would also like to dedicate it to the numbers of responders and traumatologists who have provided services to those who have been traumatized by those events. This workbook is also dedicated to survivors of many other types of traumatic events as they travel their own healing paths.

Contents

Preface

Let's Roll

When this workbook was first conceptualized and was being written, life in the United States of America was moving along according to the rules of comprehensibility, security, and sameness. There was no hint of the destruction, and death—and the paradigm shift—that would occur on September 11, 2001. Suddenly, life is not the same and never will be the same for thousands of families and the friends of those families; for thousands and thousands of rescue workers, crisis debriefers, firefighters, law enforcement officers, EMTs, and military personnel; and for the American nation as a whole. The illusion that most Americans had of invulnerability, that "it could never happen here," is gone. Yet the American spirit is not gone. It may be shaken, but the words of Todd Beamer of Cranbury, New Jersey and United flight 93 have become the motto for many.

The horror of trauma that has been lifelong for many is now more familiar to others than it has ever been. As airplanes fly overhead and we look to the sky to make sure that they truly are flying and not crashing, Vietnam veterans express the sentiment, "Welcome to our world." As child abuse survivors relate their reactions to the tragedies and hear the stories of the masses, they, too, say "welcome to our world" of terror.

As an American who is also a crisis intervenor, I have listened to the stories of many during the past few weeks—firefighters on the scene and off at the Pentagon; nurses who watched the collapse of the World Trade Center towers from the thirty-third floor of their own office building, unable to help or do anything to prevent the mass casualties. They spoke of their own flight down the thirty-three flights of stairs to the dust and debris that surrounded them. There were the stories of Arab, Muslim, and even Sikh and Hindu families who were afraid to leave their homes because of possible retaliation. Yet, in the midst of these stories are also the stories of persons who want to help. There is the story of one trauma survivor who made a sign that said "Bless Our Fallen Heroes," covered it with plastic wrap, and took it to the local fire station in the dead of night. There is the story of another survivor who made 200 tricolor bows and handed them out at her church. There is the bank employee who organized a community-wide forum for her church so that others could hear messages about trauma and its impacts and about hope for healing.

It is my hope that this workbook will be helpful to many of those who have been traumatized by the horrors of September 11, 2001. Keeping Todd Beamer's words in mind as a new motto for healing, "Let's roll," and face the future as our ancestors did when they said, "We have not yet begun to fight."

—Mary Beth Williams, Ph.D., L.C.S.W.
September 2001

Introduction

Trauma survivors need to find ways to work through their experiences and get a sense of meaning and understanding is great. While the majority of those who have experienced direct trauma or who have witnessed trauma will heal, even persons who do not develop full-blown post-traumatic stress disorder, or PTSD, will experience a number of the symptoms of post-traumatic stress: flashbacks; intrusive thoughts and memories; hyperreactivity; avoidance of persons, places, things, and other triggers; jumpiness; and other symptoms. Other persons have experienced lifelong traumas that are character changing; many of these people suffer from a syndrome that researchers are just beginning to describe, called complex PTSD. This workbook was conceptualized as a resource for the survivor who experiences a few or many of the symptoms of PTSD or complex PTSD.

When we were first asked to develop this book, we asked colleagues to share exercises that might help survivors do the work themselves. We also began to focus on the exercises we use in our own clinical work. Indeed, our clinical experience is what makes us qualified to author this book. Both of us are primarily grunt workers in the trenches of the field of trauma. We have met with many clients on a regular basis for both short-term and long-term therapy. That extensive experience allows us to say that though the road of healing may be long and difficult, healing can and does happen.

In this workbook, you will have the opportunity to complete numerous exercises that will give you insight into your symptoms, your beliefs, your behaviors, and your feelings about the trauma or traumas you endured. Many of these exercises can be completed in the book itself, so that the book becomes a record of your recovery from trauma as well as a resource for you to turn to again and again throughout that recovery. Other exercises can be completed in a separate notebook or journal, which can also be used to expand upon the exercises you complete in the book or to record your other thoughts and feelings along your journey to healing.

We hope that this book will help you on that journey.

1

A Look at Trauma: Simple and Complex

What is trauma? What does it mean to survive it? To work through it? How many times have you thought that life was understandable and was going along smoothly when something happened to change its entire course? One morning you wake up and the sun is shining, or drizzle is falling around you, and you feel love. However, three hours later, nothing is the same. Maybe it is because of a conversation; maybe there is a car accident that kills someone you love. Maybe a tornado swoops down and changes everything. Everything. There you are, hanging on the edge of a precipice. What do you do? Do you quit? Do you run away? Do you decide you want to just die and not face it anymore? Do you even want to go on?

Prior to the occurrence of a traumatic event or events, there are generally certain basic assumptions that guide your life. You probably believe that the world is kind, that there is meaning to your life, and that things make sense. You believe that you are good and worthy of having good things happen to you (Janoff-Bulman 1992). Then trauma strikes. You are suddenly no longer in control of what has happened around you. You're vulnerable and your world is no longer safe and secure. Furthermore, you can't make sense of what is left over. The meaning of life that was present just a short time before is gone. Life is no longer fair and just.

The first step in dealing with trauma is to recognize its impact. A traumatic event has many possible impacts. It can impact your feelings, thoughts, relationships, behaviors, attitudes, dreams, and hopes. However, it can also be a way to find a new direction and purpose in life. The title of this book was originally *Schlogging beyond Trauma*. That title evokes a journey. To start that journey, read the following description and see if you can picture it in your mind.

A Trauma Story

You have experienced something terrible. Perhaps you were in a car crash and the car is a mass of tangled metal. Perhaps you have begun to deal with your history of child abuse and feel as if you are coming out of a cave of torture and pain. Perhaps you have been a refugee and have escaped a land of hurt and loss. Now you want to get on with your life. You know that, across the bog that lies in front of you, is a life that is more safe and secure, peaceful and calm. You also know both that no life is ever totally safe and that the only way to gain some sense of security is to walk across the bog.

You have a backpack full of things to help you on your journey to the other side; these things include the techniques in this book. The backpack is heavy, but you can't discard anything because you don't know what you might need. You start on your journey, and shortly you realize that the bog is actually made of tar. As the sun begins to shine, the surface gets sticky and vapors begin to swim around your head. You get dizzy. You are thirsty. Each step is like pulling a weight.

What do you do? You remember all of the things you have with you. You have a water bottle with a spray mister. You have binoculars so that you can see the other side of the bog. You have a pair of hiking boots that will prevent you from sinking and getting stuck. You have a small oxygen bottle. You have a choice: you can turn around, going back to the world of trauma, or you can go on. Your trip may take time. You may be exhausted when you get to the other side. You may sweat and smell and feel as if you can never take another step. But you can go on. The closer you get to the edge of the tar bog, the more clearly you will see the trees and waterfalls on the other side. If you use what you have and what you've learned and will learn in this workbook, you will schlogg through; you will survive; you will make it.

Defining Trauma

The word *trauma* is a familiar one. You have heard it on the radio, on the TV news, in conversations. "Trauma" may describe the effect of a massive earthquake in El Salvador that has killed thousands, a tornado in Alabama, a plane crash, a murder down the street, or even an unexpected death. You've seen the pictures and you've heard the stories about how people feel when they've been victimized by auto accidents, hurricanes, floods, tornadoes, assaults, robberies, rapes, plane crashes, school shootings, fires, abuse, and other catastrophic events and situations.

Now it has happened to you. Or perhaps it happened to you years ago and for an extended period of time. You are either the direct victim (it happened to you) or the secondary victim (it happened in your world or you were a bystander or observer) of a traumatic event. Or you may be someone who works with the victims of traumas but has not directly experienced a traumatic event. However, you have seen enough to know that your exposure to awful events has impacted you significantly.

Reacting to Trauma

What happens when you experience a traumatic event or series of events? There are many reactions you might have. Initially, you may feel shock, terror, or a sense that what happened is unreal or surreal. You may feel numb, as if you've left your body (a phenomenon called *disassociation*). You may not even remember all the details (or any of the details) of what just happened. If you are a survivor of lifelong traumatic events, your reactions may be different. You may feel as if you have lived in a war zone your entire life, you're always watchful, always ready to be attacked or hurt at any moment. You may not even know who you are as a person. As Tedeschi, Park, and Calhoun (1998) write, stress can have complex aftereffects resulting in an enhancement of growth.

Many factors impact how you react to a traumatic event. Your age (younger persons often react more significantly than older persons); the amount of preparation time you had prior to the event (for example, a hurricane may have several days' notice, while an earthquake has no forewarning); the amount of damage done to you (physically, emotionally, and spiritually) or to your property; the amount of death and devastation you witness; the degree of responsibility you feel for causing or not preventing the event: these are just some of the factors that can impact your reaction to a traumatic event.

In fact, three major types of factors influence the development of *post-traumatic stress disorder* (PTSD). They are *preevent factors, event factors,* and *postevent factors.* PTSD is the best known of the long-term consequences of trauma. (This disorder will be described in detail shortly.) Between 10 and 80 percent of people exposed to a traumatic event develop PTSD at some point in time. PTSD is treatable.

Pre-event Factors

Although there are situations in which exposure to trauma is so great that these factors are less influential (e.g., surviving a major airplane disaster in which almost everyone dies), certain pretrauma factors often influence how a person reacts to traumatic events. Among them are the following:

- previous exposure to severe adverse life events or trauma or childhood victimization, including neglect, emotional abuse, sexual abuse, physical abuse, or witnessing abuse

- earlier depression or anxiety that is not merely situational and that impacts brain chemistry

- ineffective coping skills

- family instability, including a history of psychiatric disorder, numerous childhood separations, economic problems, or family violence

- family history of antisocial or criminal behavior

- early substance abuse

- trouble with authority, even in childhood, including running away from home, school suspension, academic underachievement, delinquency, fighting, or truancy

- absence of social support to help out in bad times

- multiple early losses of people, possessions, home

- gender: women seem to be twice as likely as men to develop PTSD at some time in their lives

- age: young adults under age twenty-five are more likely to develop the disorder (Friedman 2000)

- genetics: members of some families seem less able to withstand trauma than others (Meichenbaum 1994)

Event Factors

There are also factors related to the victim during the event that contribute to the possibility of developing PTSD. These may include:

- geographic nearness to the event

- level of exposure to the event: greater exposure leads to a greater likelihood of developing PTSD

- the event's meaning to you

- age: being young at the time of the event

- being a victim of multiple traumatic incidents

- duration of the trauma

- the existence of an ongoing threat that the trauma will continue (e.g., war)

- being involved in an intentional, man-made traumatic event

- participation in an atrocity as a perpetrator or witness (an atrocity is a very brutal, shocking act; for example, purposely killing women and children)

Post-event Factors

The final category of PTSD risk factors include those that exist after the traumatic event. These may include:

- the absence of good social support

- not being able to do something about what happened

- indulging in self-pity while neglecting yourself

- being passive rather than active—letting things happen to you

- inability to find meaning in the suffering

- developing ASD (acute stress disorder). (ASD occurs in a certain percentage of people who experience trauma; it is described later in this chapter)

- having an immediate reaction (during the traumatic event or shortly after) that includes physiological arousal (high blood pressure, a startle reaction) and avoidant or numbing symptoms (Friedman 2000)

To learn more about these factors, you may want to read Meichenbaum's book, *A Clinical Handbook/Practical Therapist Manual* (1994). Tennen and Affleck (1998) and McCrae (1992) believe that there may be personality traits that help a person cope with adversity. People who are high in extraversion (they seek out others) and openness, are conscientious in working toward goals, and have a sense of agreeableness (an ability to get along) are more likely to draw strength from adversity and trauma as a way to cope with what happened.

Other important factors that might impact how you react include having an *internal locus of control* (you are able to reward yourself for behavior and you believe that control of what happens lies with you, not with sources outside you); *self-efficacy* (a sense of confidence in your own coping ability); a sense of *coherence* (the recognition that even seriously traumatic events are understandable, manageable, meaningful); and hardiness, or strength (Antonovsky 1987; Kobasa 1982). You may also do better in coping with traumatic events if you are motivated to do so, if you have an optimistic attitude, if you have an active coping style, and if you've successfully resolved other crises.

Exercise: My Ability to Cope with Trauma

Check those of the following statements that you believe apply to you.

_____ I have a high degree of extraversion (I like to be with people).

_____ I am open to new experiences.

_____ I am conscientious in the work I do (I follow through).

_____ I am an agreeable person.

_____ I believe that my source of personal power lies within me.

_____ I am confident in my own abilities to cope with situations.

_____ I try to find meaning in what happens to me.

_____ I try to break down bad situations into manageable parts I can handle.

_____ I am motivated to solve the problems that occur in my life.

_____ I am generally an optimistic person—I see things more positively than negatively.

_____ I take control in situations whenever possible, or at least try to take control.

_____ I like a good challenge and I rise to the occasion.

_____ I am committed to overcoming the bad things I have experienced in life.

_____ I have a good social support network—there are people I can turn to.

_____ I understand my life's circumstances and what I can and cannot do about them.

_____ I have faith.

_____ I have a good sense of humor.

_____ I have a sense of hope.

_____ I like to try new things or look at things in new ways.

_____ I am open to how others feel.

_____ I am an action-oriented person—I would rather do something than sit back and let it be done to me.

_____ I actively try to structure my own life and make plans.

What do you observe about yourself from reading these statements: _____

_____

_____

How many of these items did you check? Do you notice any pattern of those you did or did not check? _____

_____

_____

The more you checked, the more likely you are to take action and to work through the trauma that happened to you.

* * * * *

Before you learn more about yourself and how you respond to traumatic events, it is important for you to have more information about the numerous possible reactions to trauma. The first of these is called a *normal stress response*. In times of stress, people react in a variety of ways: they may have physical reactions—their pulse may increase, they may sweat; they may have anxiety, fear, anger, or other emotional responses; they may shut down and freeze; they may go into a rage and try to fight; or they may run from the situation. These are all normal responses. Stress that is positive is called *eustress*. It could involve life-saving or other positive reactions to an emergency situation; a eustress reaction would allow you to rescue yourself or someone else from danger. Negative stress is called *distress*. It's debilitating and may cause you to function poorly in a dangerous situation—or one that feels dangerous. Stress can impact your body, emotions, thoughts, and relationships. This book will deal with severe, disruptive distress reactions—specifically the reactions associated with post-traumatic stress disorder, or PTSD.

Acute Stress Disorder (ASD)

If your reactions to the event or events developed within the first few days or weeks after the traumatic incident, you may have developed what is known as *acute stress disorder* (ASD). According to the *Diagnostic and Statistical Manual of Mental Disorders*, Fourth Edition, or DSM-IV (American Psychiatric Association 1994), you were exposed to a traumatic event in which:

- You experienced, witnessed, or were confronted with an event or events that involved actual or threatened death or serious injury, or a threat to your own physical integrity or that of others.

- Your response involved intense fear, helplessness, or horror.

Either while experiencing or after experiencing the distressing event, you had three or more of the following *dissociative* (zoning out, spacing out) symptoms:

- You felt numb, detached, or emotionally nonresponsive.

- You had reduced awareness of your surroundings (you were in a daze).

- You experienced *derealization*—a sense that the world is unreal or that you are detached from or not a part of your environment; you experienced an unfamiliarity with what were previously familiar places.

- You experienced *depersonalization*—a disoriented perception of your body, identity, or self, perhaps with an out-of-body experience or feeling of "being in two places."

- You experienced a type of dissociative *amnesia*—the inability to recall one or more important aspects of what happened to you.

Furthermore, you persistently reexperienced the traumatic event in at least one of the following ways: you had recurrent images, thoughts, dreams, illusions, or *flashbacks* (reliving the experience), or you felt distress when exposed to reminders of the event.

The following are also true:

- You persistently avoided any stimuli that led to your remembering the trauma.

- You had marked symptoms of anxiety or increased arousal (problems sleeping, irritability, poor concentration, increased startle reaction, and body restlessness).

- The condition caused you marked, clinically significant distress or impairment in social, occupational, or other areas of your life—that is, you couldn't do the tasks you needed to do.

- The condition lasted for at least two days and at most four weeks and occurred within four weeks of the traumatic event.

Post-Traumatic Stress Disorder (PTSD)

Max is a Vietnam veteran who was in many combat missions. He was wounded twice and eventually had to be medevaced to a hospital before returning home. While Max was being flown out by helicopter, there was gunfire and the medic caring for him was killed. Max has nightmares of the death of this medic. He avoids airplanes, guns, helicopters, and air shows and has problems with anger and sleep. Max has PTSD.

Symptoms of PTSD

If your reaction to traumatic events persists for a period of time, or if it occurs at least six months after the event occurred, you may have developed post-traumatic stress disorder.

The following description of PTSD is adapted from the DSM-IV (American Psychiatric Association 1994).

1. You have been exposed to a traumatic event in which both of the following were present:

   - You experienced, witnessed, or were confronted with an event or events that involved actual or threatened death or serious injury, or a threat to the physical integrity of yourself or others.

   - Your response involved intense fear, helplessness, or horror, or your perception of the event led to these emotions.

2. You reexperience the event in one or more of the following ways:

   - You have recurrent and intrusive distressing recollections of the event, including images, thoughts, or perceptions.

   - You have recurrent distressing dreams of the event.

   - You act or feel as if the traumatic event was recurring, and you may have a sense of reliving the experience through illusions, hallucinations, and active flashbacks.

   - You experience intense psychological distress or bodily reactions when exposed to internal or external cues that symbolize or resemble an aspect of the traumatic event (e.g., sights, smells, sounds, dates); these are called *triggers*.

3. You persistently avoid things or events (triggers) associated with the trauma and numb your response using three or more of the following:

   - You make a great effort to avoid thoughts, feelings, or conversations associated with the trauma, or to avoid activities, places, or people that would cause you to remember the trauma.

   - You can't recall an important aspect of the trauma.

   - Your interest or participation in activities is much less.

   - You feel detached or estranged from others.

   - Your ability to feel emotion is restricted, as is your range of emotions (e.g., you are unable to have loving feelings).

   - You have a sense of a foreshortened future—you can't see ahead into a far-off future (e.g., you do not expect to have a career, marriage, children, or a normal life span).

4. You also have persistent symptoms of increased physical arousal that were not present before the trauma, as indicated by two or more of the following. You experience:

- difficulty falling or staying asleep

- irritability or outbursts of anger

- difficulty concentrating

- hypervigilance (being overly watchful)

- exaggerated startle response (you're jumpy)

5. All of these symptoms have lasted more than one month.

6. Because of these symptoms, you are significantly distressed or impaired in social, occupational, or other important areas of functioning.

The PTSD is *acute* if your symptoms have been there less than three months, and *chronic* if your symptoms have lasted three months or more. It is *delayed onset* if your symptoms began at least six months after the stressor event or events.

The first half of this workbook is designed to help you if you've been diagnosed with PTSD or if you have symptoms of "partial PTSD"—that is, you have some symptoms but not enough to qualify for the *DSM-IV*'s clinical diagnosis.

What Is PTSD?

Terr (1994) has written about two distinct types of trauma: type I and type II trauma. PTSD is more likely to be a reaction to experiencing or witnessing type I traumatic events, which are single, catastrophic, unanticipated experiences. A sexual assault, a serious car crash, and a natural disaster are all type I events. These type I events also can be called *critical incidents*. If you have experienced a type I trauma, you often have a detailed, clear memory of what happened. Your memories remain alive unless you work through them. You may find yourself frequently looking for a way to explain what happened or a way you could have prevented what happened.

Roger Solomon, in his unpublished manuscript "Dynamics of Fear" (2001), writes that it is possible to describe such an incident in the following way:

1. Here comes trouble. (You become aware of a threatening situation.)

2. Oh, shit! (You become aware of your vulnerability; you may feel weak and not in control.)

3. I've got to do something. (You realize you have to act to survive or gain control over the situation; you acknowledge the reality of the danger. You make a transition from an internal focus on vulnerability to an external focus on danger. But if you focus solely on this danger, you tend to feel even weaker and more out of control.)

4. I have to survive. (You focus on the danger in terms of your ability to respond to it. You consciously or instinctively come up with a plan, start to react, and begin to feel more balanced and in control. It is more important to focus on this thought than on the previous one.

5. Here I go. (This is your moment of commitment: you have the resolve to act, whether instinctual or planned; you mobilize tremendous strength; your mind becomes focused and clear and you have increased awareness and control. (You act, often without thinking further.)

6. Oh, shit! (After the event is through and you've survived, it is normal to return to feelings of "oh, shit!" Don't let yourself get stuck here. Give yourself credit for all that you did do to respond in the other stages.)

Use this description when thinking about Larry's experience. (Note that, like Larry's story, many traumatic events are complex, and you may cycle through some or all of the steps more than once during the course of the event.) Larry was having breakfast at a restaurant when a waitstaffer ran in and yelled, "Run, run. He's got a gun!" (steps 1 and 2). Larry did not even pick up his glasses, but took off across the restaurant, out through the lobby (where he saw a dead body) and down a hall (steps 3, 4, and 5). About ten others ran ahead of him. In the middle of the hall was a woman lying facedown, terrified. Everyone, including Larry, either ran over or around her. Suddenly, Larry turned and went back to try to help her (step 3). She was a large woman, a dead weight, and would not move or help Larry help her. As Larry tried to pick her up, the shooter rounded the corner and was less than six feet away from Larry (step 2). Larry instinctually thought, "I want to live." He dropped the woman's arm and ran (steps 4 and 5). He did not turn around to look at the shooter's eyes for fear that the connection between them would make him the next victim. Seconds later, Larry heard two shots. He thought one was for him, but both were for the woman—the killer shot her twice in the head. Larry kept running and escaped death by mere seconds (step 6).

Complex PTSD or Disorders of Extreme Stress, Not Otherwise Specified

If you have experienced prolonged, repeated, extensive exposure to traumatic events, you may be suffering from a disorder that has not yet been named in the DSM-IV, the clinical manual used by treatment providers to determine diagnoses. This disorder, first described by Judy Herman (1992), is called either complex PTSD or disorders of extreme stress, not otherwise specified (DESNOS). Persons who may suffer from complex PTSD include prisoners of war, hostages who were held captive for long periods of time, concentration camp survivors, war zone survivors, cult survivors, battering victims, domestic violence survivors, sexual abuse survivors, and children who have suffered years of other types of trauma. Help for symptoms of complex PTSD is presented primarily in the second half of this book, although some of the symptoms are similar to those of PTSD.

Some people exposed to prolonged trauma have a better chance than others of *not* developing complex PTSD. Children who are particularly resilient may be able to survive traumas better and continue to do well throughout their lives, especially if they have healthy support systems around them. Females who experience early trauma are less vulnerable to stress than males, and are at less risk to act in a disruptive way after the events. If you have above average or higher intelligence and you generally did well at school, you probably have higher self-esteem. This sense of self-esteem can help you cope with a lifetime of abuse. If you have always been easygoing, you may be less vulnerable to depression and anxiety and have higher *self-efficacy* (the ability to make effective plans and follow through on them). If you had protective adults in your life as a child, you may have been shielded from some of the bad effects of trauma that can appear in your adult life. If you are and have been more *resilient*, or able to recover from or adapt to setbacks, you also tend to build on your strengths and use them to make good decisions; you avoid blaming others; you dwell less on the past; and you may now work hard to build a good, healthy family unit (Tedeschi, Park, and Calhoun 1998).

Symptoms of Complex PTSD

You are more likely to experience symptoms of complex PTSD if your traumatization occurred early in your life, was prolonged, and was interpersonal. According to Herman (1992), the seven symptoms groups of complex PTSD include:

1. Alteration in regulation of affect (emotion) and impulses
   - chronic affect dysregulation (your emotions have a life of their own)
   - difficulty modulating (managing and regulating) anger
   - self-destructive or suicidal behaviors
   - difficulty modulating sexual involvement
   - impulsive and risk-taking behaviors

2. Alterations in attention or consciousness
   - amnesia
   - transient dissociative episodes (short periods of zoning out)
   - depersonalization

3. Somatization (how your body holds your trauma)
   - digestive system problems
   - chronic pain
   - cardiopulmonary symptoms
   - conversion symptoms (psychological problems that get converted into physical symptoms—e.g., hits with a hammer on the back of a child become unexplained back spasms for the adult)
   - sexual symptoms
   - panic

4. Alterations in self-perception (how you see yourself)
   - chronic guilt, shame, and self-blame
   - feeling that you are permanently damaged
   - feeling ineffective
   - feeling nobody understands you
   - minimizing the importance of the traumatic events in your life

5. Alterations in perception of the perpetrator (this is not needed for a diagnosis of complex PTSD)
   - adopting the distorted beliefs of the perpetrator about yourself, others, and what happened as true
   - idealizing of the perpetrator
   - preoccupation with hurting the perpetrator

6. Alterations in relations with others
   - inability to trust
   - revictimizing yourself
   - victimizing others

7. Alterations in systems of meaning (how you see life, others, and spirituality)

- despair, hopelessness
- loss of beliefs that previously sustained you

(adapted from Meichenbaum 1994)

What Is Complex PTSD?

If you have complex PTSD, you may have some or all of these personality issues:

1. You may have problems with your ability to regulate emotions, especially anger.

2. You may find it hard to "stay present" without becoming amnesic (unable to remember), dissociative (spaced out), depersonalized, or preoccupied with the trauma.

3. You may not see yourself as a functioning individual who can avoid feeling helpless, shameful, guilty, stigmatized, alone, special, or full of self-blame.

4. You may not have the ability to separate yourself from your abuser or perpetrator without either being preoccupied with revenge, feeling gratitude, or accepting the perpetrator's introjects as true. (*Introjects* are someone else's beliefs that you take into your head as your own and then believe.)

5. You may not have the ability to have positive, healthy relationships with others without being isolated, withdrawing, being extremely distrustful, failing repeatedly to protect yourself, or constantly searching for someone to rescue you (or for someone you can rescue).

6. You may not have the ability to find meaning in your life and maintain faith, hopefulness, and a sense of the future without feeling despair and hopelessness (Meichenbaum 1994).

Remembering Trauma

You have various types of memory. You have short-term memory (items remembered quickly, such as a phone number, and then lost just as quickly), long-term memory (permanently stored information), explicit or declarative memory (facts, concepts, and ideas, including your ability to recall the traumatic event in a cohesive way), and implicit or nondeclarative memory (acts, descriptions, or operations based on thought and automatic internal states). The traumatic events that have happened to you or to those you know seem to be recorded more easily in implicit memory (Rothschild 2000). Implicit memory includes behavior that you learn through *conditioning*, or exposure to various stimuli. During a traumatic event, many sights, sounds, smells, or other cues get associated with that event in your mind. These cues become triggers that can lead you to have the same intense reaction to them that you had during the original event. Thus, your post-traumatic stress disorder appears to be "a disorder of memory gone awry" (Rothschild 2000, 35). Sometimes you will know how closely connected these triggers are to the trauma and what you remember about that event. At other times the connections are harder to recognize and you may have a hard time making sense of your PTSD symptoms and their triggers.

"True" or "False" Memories

There is a great controversy about whether or not memories of trauma are "true" or "false," "repressed" or not. If and when you go to therapy and begin to talk about your trauma history and your memories, it is important to remember that your therapist does not have the power to know whether or not your traumatic experiences occurred in the way that you remember them occurring. The ethical, knowledgeable trauma therapist will listen to your story without either challenging it or asking leading questions or reassuring you that everything you remember happened in exactly the way you remember it. It is easier for you to reassure yourself and others that what happened was "true" when you have independent corroborating information, e.g., newspaper reports, medical records, personal accounts, or witnesses. Some traumatic events are indelibly burned into your mind. Others may be repressed and hidden to you, yet available to others. Your memories are not stored as video-tapes with total retrieval possible. To be sure, it may be possible to retrieve a great deal about an event, but some aspects of an event may have been lost to your mind's ability to remember.

For example, Shirley remembered being molested by her father between the ages of two and five and again between the ages of twelve and fourteen. She had no memories of other sexually abusive experiences. In a well-planned confrontation during a therapy session she told her father about her memories. He admitted his abuse of her and then proceeded to tell her of other abusive acts he had committed toward her—acts of which Shirley had no memory at all. In spite of his revelations, she continues to have no memory of them.

Meichenbaum (1994) offers some other important points about remembering trauma:

1. Remembering is a reconstructive process, not merely a retrieval of a record of past experience. You generally forget more than you remember.

2. Your memories can be influenced and distorted over time.

3. Reconstructing a memory does not bring up everything in exact detail.

4. It is possible, at times, to believe strongly in memories that are inaccurate.

5. It is not necessary for you to remember everything about a traumatic event exactly as it happened. What is important is to recover enough information so you can process the memory and put it and its accompanying emotions, body sensations, and thoughts into your past.

Psychoeducation

Learning about memories, trauma, and the impacts of traumatic events is called *psychoeducation*. Before you begin to work on what bothers you about your traumatic experiences, you should know at least some of the language trauma professionals use and have some information about trauma. The first few chapters of this book are intended to help you with your psychoeducation. You now know that the symptoms you experience in the present are related to the traumatic events you've experienced in the past. You are not going crazy and you are not presently crazy. Many others have experienced similar events and have similar symptoms, although in different degrees or combinations. Your reactions are normal in the sense that you are experiencing the normal human response to overwhelmingly stressful events.

Why Remember?

An important reason to try to remember what happened to you is to decrease the fear associated with the traumatic events. Memories of trauma are not dangerous in and of themselves, even though they may feel dangerous. Confronting your memories in a safe environment—writing about them, describing them out loud, drawing them, or finding other ways to deal with them—helps you to work through, or *process*, your traumatic history. Processing memories helps you to integrate them into your past. Continuously avoiding memories of trauma keeps those memories in your present, with all their associated pain, fear, rage, depression, shame, and self-blame (Astin and Rothbaum 2000). Through the process of remembering, you may come to understand what happened to you. You also may become angry at the way you were violated. Remembering safely will give you a sense of control over the experience and the terror you felt.

If you choose to work on memories of trauma, talk about it in the past tense, not in the present tense. Much of the work this workbook asks you to do is on reminders of the memory rather than on the actual trauma story. If you are not willing or able to remember your traumas, if you don't want to work on your trauma narrative with a therapist or (if you are safe to do so) by yourself, do not criticize or blame yourself. This workbook can still help you control the symptoms of PTSD and complex PTSD.

If you are willing to do some work on intrusive memories but you doubt either their relationship to your life or their truth, ask yourself the following questions, answering in the spaces provided (adapted from Adams 1994):

1. Does your intuition tell you that what you remember is or was real, no matter how hard you try to disbelieve it? _____

_____

2. Does the memory keep returning, even after you try to forget it? _____

_____

3. Does the memory "fit" with your habits, fears, behaviors, symptoms, health problems, or the facts of your life as you know them? _____

_____

4. Is your memory of certain aspects of the traumatic event clear? _____

_____

5. Are certain aspects of the event cloudy? _____

_____

6. Does your memory come in fragments? _____

_____

7. Does remembering anything about the event bring you a sense of relief, understanding, or increased strength? _____

_____

8. Can you find corroboration of what you remember from other sources (people, newspaper articles, medical reports)? _____

_____

9. Do you get more or less distressed when you think or talk about your memory? _____

_____

Look at your answers to these questions. What have they told you about what and how you remember? (Use your journal to write more if you need to.) _____

_____

_____

_____

_____

Who Am I?

Before you look at the traumas that have impacted you, it is important for you to look at who you are. Your sense of yourself serves as the reference point for who you want to become and what you want to do with your life. Traumatic experiences can rob you of your sense of self. If you find the questions in this exercise difficult or impossible to answer, it may be that much of your self-knowledge is missing, and you may need to look to others to help you. You may need to find a therapist skilled in trauma treatment to help you do the work in this workbook and reestablish your sense of self. The following exercise is designed to help you look at what you know about your own core self—your basic identity—and whether that self is healthy, partially healthy, or unhealthy.

Exercise: Am I a Healthy Person?

Answer the following questions and complete the following statements to get a sense of yourself (use your journal to write more if you need to):

What about me gives me a positive sense of who I am? _____

_____

_____

What facts describe me? _____

_____

_____

I feel competent about (or in control of): _____

_____

_____

I have worth because: _____

_____

_____

I am able to be intimate with: _____

_____

_____

My basic values are: _____

_____

_____

I have a positive sense of humanity and the meaning of life because: _____

_____

_____

I make the following appropriate, reasonable demands on myself: _____

_____

_____

I make the following inappropriate, unreasonable demands on myself: _____

_____

_____

The following "shoulds" govern my life and are inflexible:

I should _____ .

I should _____ .

I should _____ .

Which of these "shoulds" would you be able to discard or throw in a trashcan?

_____

_____

Mark with an "X" where you lie on the following continua:

Rigid ———————————————————— Flexible

Harsh ———————————————————— Gentle

Critical ———————————————————— Accepting

Inappropriate ———————————————— Appropriate

Overcontrolling ———————————————— Undercontrolling

What did you learn about yourself by doing this exercise? _____

_____

_____

Now that you have done this exercise, how would you describe your core self? _____

_____

_____

* * * * *

Trauma and Errors in Belief

All human beings hold certain beliefs or expectations about themselves, others, and their world; those expectations are called *schemas*. The ways you think about yourself, others, and your world can impact how you behave and the choices you make. Listed in the following exercise are a number of beliefs that may result from exposure to traumatic events. The occurrence of traumatic events can change your beliefs related to your five fundamental psychological needs—needs for safety, trust, power, esteem, and intimacy. Recognizing how trauma changed your beliefs is one way to identify the impact of trauma on your life to get information about what beliefs can be challenged or changed.

Exercise: My Trauma-Related Beliefs

Check the beliefs that apply to you and then write about a situation or situations in which that belief was created or in which it determined your actions or decisions. Try to be specific when describing these situations. Are any of them trauma-related?

Belief #1:

_____ I think I am a victim and that my troubles are the fault of others.

Situations in which this belief determines my actions: _____

_____

Belief #2:

_____ I believe that I can't do things. (By the way, I don't realize or don't accept the fact that "I can't" generally means "I won't" or "I don't want to." I *can't* is really a statement of refusal.)

Situations in which this belief determines my actions: _____

_____

Belief #3:

_____ I believe that my actions don't impact others. My actions won't bring injury or harm to them or cause them emotional pain.

Situations in which this belief determines my actions: _____

_____

Belief #4:

_____ I can't put myself in others' places.

Situations in which this belief determines my actions: _____

_____

Belief #5:

_____ I am unwilling to do something that is disagreeable to me.

Situations in which this belief determines my actions: _____

_____

Belief #6:

_____ I usually feel I have no money, time, etc., to spare when others ask me to do things.

Situations in which this belief determines my actions: _____

_____

Belief #7:

_____ I develop aches and pains to avoid doing things I don't want to do, and then believe I am sick.

Situations in which this belief determines my actions: _____

_____

Belief #8:

_____ I don't often have energy to do things—particularly when I don't want to do them.

Situations in which this belief determines my actions: _____

_____

Belief #9:

_____ I don't believe that I have to live up to obligations—I think it's okay to say "I forgot" or just ignore what I am supposed to do.

Situations in which this belief determines my actions: _____

_____

Belief #10:

_____ I believe that others should do what I want them to do.

Situations in which this belief determines my actions: _____

_____

Belief #11:

_____ I believe I am entitled to use others' property as if it were my own, and to borrow things without permission.

Situations in which this belief determines my actions: _____

_____

Belief #12:

_____ I believe that my "wants" are really my "rights."

Situations in which this belief determines my actions: _____

_____

Belief #13:

_____ I believe that others betray my trust; the truth is that I don't trust.

Situations in which this belief determines my actions: _____

_____

Belief #14:

_____ I believe that things must happen because I think they must.

Situations in which this belief determines my actions: _____

_____

Belief #15:

_____ I believe that I can make decisions without finding out the facts.

Situations in which this belief determines my actions: _____

_____

Belief #16:

_____ I believe that I am right and that my point of view is right, even when evidence says that it's wrong.

Situations in which this belief determines my actions: _____

_____

Belief #17:

_____ Even when I am proved wrong, I believe I must cling to my original position.

Situations in which this belief determines my actions: _____

_____

Belief #18:

_____ I do not believe in thinking or planning ahead.

Situations in which this belief determines my actions: _____

_____

Belief #19:

_____ I believe that I am not supposed to fail.

Situations in which this belief determines my actions: _____

_____

Belief #20:

_____ I believe fear is a weakness and I deny that I am afraid.

Situations in which this belief determines my actions: _____

_____

Belief #21:

_____ I believe that expressions of anger, like direct threats, intimidation, sarcasm, or passive aggressiveness, are good ways to get what I want from people.

Situations in which this belief determines my actions: _____

_____

Belief #22:

_____ If something doesn't turn out the way I expect it to, I believe I will be criticized and found wanting.

Situations in which this belief determines my actions: _____

_____

Belief #23:

_____ I believe I will be let down by others.

Situations in which this belief determines my actions: _____

_____

Belief #24:

_____ I believe that I will win in any struggle. I have power.

Situations in which this belief determines my actions: _____

_____

Belief #25:

_____ I enjoy a fight in and of itself.

Situations in which this belief determines my actions: _____

_____

Have you learned anything new about yourself by completing this exercise? Has it confirmed anything you knew previously? What does it say about how your traumatic experiences have impacted you? (Use your journal to write more if you need to.)

_____

_____

_____

_____

✳ ✳ ✳ ✳ ✳

Exercise: My Healing History

In the next chapter you will look at how you can provide safety for yourself before and during doing the work in the workbook. Before beginning that work, though, it is important to look at where you believe you are in your own healing process.

The list below begins with statements of disbelief that you were traumatized and follows the steps you'll take as you work hard at healing. How many of these steps have you worked through?

_____ 1. I believe that whatever happened to me in the past was of no consequence, or that nothing actually happened at all.

_____ 2. I believe something terrible happened to me and I am not just imagining it.

_____ 3. I am aware at some level that I am a trauma survivor.

_____ 4. I am aware that I am a trauma survivor and that I choose life over self-inflicted death.

_____ 5. I am aware I am a trauma survivor and I am ready to deal with my feelings of being damaged goods or unworthy of love and attention.

_____ 6. I am angry that I am a trauma survivor.

_____ 7. I feel rage toward the perpetrator of the trauma that happened to me (including God and other people or forces).

_____ 8. I have discussed my traumatic experiences with support persons not in my family.

_____ 9. I have discussed my traumatic experiences with members of my family.

_____ 10. I have reexperienced at least some of what happened to me during the traumatic events and have begun to deal with my feelings.

_____ 11. I have begun to give up undeserved guilt or feelings of my personal responsibility for what happened, since it was not my fault. I have assumed appropriate guilt or personal responsibility for what happened if I was to blame to any degree.

_____ 12. I recognize that I acted appropriately, in the only way I could act at the time of the trauma; it was the traumatic event itself that was not appropriate.

_____ 13. I am beginning to understand how the traumatic events have impacted my current relationships and ways of acting.

_____ 14. I am beginning to develop some control around those aspects of myself and my life that are impacted by or connected to the traumatic events.

_____ 15. I am beginning to recognize what I want from all my relationships.

_____ 16. I have a successful intimate relationship.

_____ 17. I have a positive sense of self and my self-esteem is consistently improving.

_____ 18. I have made a choice whether or not to forgive those who traumatized me.

_____ 19. I recognize that by forgiving, I am reclaiming my own personal power.

_____ 20. I am in touch with my anger and rage and am no longer controlled by them.

_____ 21. I have a positive, healthy relationship with my Higher Power or with my own sense of spirituality.

Given my answers to the above questions, this is how I would describe my healing history:

_____

_____

_____

* * * * *

Feeling Safe

As we just stated, before you look at the traumas that happened to you, it is important that you feel safe. It is also important that you are able to recognize when you need to take breaks to take care of yourself. Chapter 2 will help you with making these choices about your safety.

Exercise: Committing to the Work

If you are willing to do the work, now is the time to make an initial commitment. Where are you in regard to your desire to change? By picking up this book, you have shown that you are not denying any need to look for change. You may still have some resistance, but at least you are willing to begin to look. So, are you:

_____ contemplating the need to change: developing a desire to take action through seeking information?

_____ preparing to move ahead in your work on trauma: beginning to focus on what you need to do?

_____ taking action, with some anxiety?

_____ maintaining your already developed action plan?

_____ finishing up your healing process or coming back for a "booster session"?

Journal Exercise: Drawings

The final exercise in this chapter is a series of drawings that will give you information about who you are. These drawings were originally designed by Spring (1993), and we will ask you to complete them now, at the beginning of the workbook, and again at the end of the workbook. Comparing them will give you an idea of the progress you have made. We have suggested that you keep a separate notebook or journal to use to do some of these exercises. The five drawings listed below should go in that journal.

Don't worry if you have no artistic ability. In drawings 1 and 5 when you draw yourself, how large are you? What facial expression do you have? What are you doing? In drawing 2, draw what is important to you in your world and how your world is to you. What symbols are present? What emotions? In drawing 3, show the ups and downs of your life in a linear way. Is your road straight, curvy, full of hills and valleys? Drawing 4 is self-explanatory.

1. This Is Me, I Am. This drawing shows you what you think about yourself. It is your self-portrait.

2. This Is My Space. This drawing shows how you see your world, your position in it, and your reaction to it. Do you believe you have a space in your world? What are your relationships with significant others? Where do your fears, wishes, anger, depression, and personal strengths and weaknesses fit in? How do you tolerate your world in the present? Do you feel isolated and withdrawn or included and part of the world around you?

3. My Life's Road. This drawing is a visual history of your life.

4. My Family and Me. This drawing is a portrait of your family and your current relationships and family system. It shows how you view your family and your position in it.

5. This Is Me, I Am. This second self-portrait is completed after the three intermediate drawings are done. Do you see yourself as you did before drawing the other three drawings?

What did you learn about yourself in completing these drawings?

✻ ✻ ✻ ✻ ✻

Now it is time to look at ways to keep yourself safe and secure before you do the work of remembering and processing what happened to you. Chapter 2 has exercises to help.

2

Before Doing the Work: Safety, Security, and Intention

You have decided you want to work on at least one aspect of the traumas that have impacted you. You may choose to use this workbook as part of your therapy or you may want to work on the exercises in the workbook by yourself. No matter what your choice, it is important that you feel safe and secure as you work. This chapter helps you prepare for your work with PTSD—whether it is your first attempt or you are returning to the work. It consists of a number of exercises that you can use to relax, center, and ground yourself in the present, as well as to protect yourself.

First, imagine yourself as you would want to be if the traumas of your life were not impacting you. What type of person would you be? How would you approach life? What would your hopes and dreams be? What would make your life feel full? Where would you live? What type of relationship with a spouse or partner would you have? What would your relationship to your own body be? If you have any chronic illnesses at the present time, how would they be different? What would your relationship with any Higher Power be? What celebrations of your life would you want to have? How would you organize and structure your day-to-day life? Take some time to address these questions or others that seem appropriate in your journal or notebook.

If you get upset while doing this exercise, look at those descriptions as your goals. You are simply aiming to return to a pretrauma existence to the greatest possible extent.

Safety

What does it mean to be safe? One definition of safety, proposed by both McCann and Pearlman (1990) and Rosenbloom and Williams (1999), is that safety is the need to feel reasonably invulnerable to harm inflicted by oneself and others. It is also the need to feel that those you value are reasonably invulnerable to harm inflicted by themselves or others. With those definitions in mind, if you are safe, you are reasonably able to prevent yourself from being hurt, or abused, or from experiencing traumatic events. As you protect yourself, you remain present and grounded in the here and now and you are able to make good decisions.

Staying Grounded

The word *grounded* means staying present in the current time, in contrast to "spacing out" or dissociating. You may have some particular ways to remain present when things come up that remind you of trauma or when you are dealing with past experiences. Trauma survivors have made many suggestions as to how to remain grounded. Some of these include:

- using all your senses to be aware of your physical environment, and then talking to others about it

- being aware of your physical body and how you look

- being aware of your movements in space as you walk

- exercising while being aware of what you are doing

- making a plan for the day and sharing that plan with another

- challenging yourself to a contest to increase the length of time you can remain in the present

- watching television and telling yourself or others what you saw

- doing routine activities in a different way; e.g., cleaning up the house in a different order

- asking others to help you stay connected to them

- talking to yourself about the present

- planting your feet as firmly as you can on the ground in the here and now

Types of Safety

Recognizing your beliefs about safety and what you can do to change or challenge those beliefs is important if you are to protect yourself. There are different types of safety. *Physical safety* means that your body is not in danger. Maintaining it means that if a dangerous situation presents itself to you, you can recognize the danger signals, look at possible choices, act on those choices, and remove yourself from the situation if safety does not seem possible. *Mental safety* means that you are able to choose belief systems and patterns of thinking and awareness that get you where you want or need to go. *Emotional safety* means that you are able to identify how you feel in situations, recognize what your intuition tells you, and then act on these feelings and intuition, particularly when they alert you to danger. It may be important to practice feeling your feelings in order to build your awareness of them. *Spiritual safety* occurs when you learn to identify and trust in your beliefs about a Higher Power, God, or Supreme Being and then use those beliefs to protect you or to lead you to good decisions throughout your life.

Williams (1994) notes that establishing safety is the primary goal of therapy or self-protection before any work is done on memories of or emotional issues related to trauma. What cues do you have if you are physically, emotionally, mentally, or spiritually safe? Answering the following questions will help you look at your psychological need for safety (use your journal if you need more space):

Exercise: My Sense of Safety

1. How safe is your environment? Is your home safe? When Im with Dawn or in the hospital I am safe. My home, is not

2. What makes you feel safe physically when you are alone? With others? In different situations? I feel safe when Im driving. When Im with friends I feel safe

3. Are those with whom you live or interact safe? If they are, what makes the setting and those persons safe? If they are not, what makes them unsafe? NO.

4. If you are not safe in your home, what can you do about it? Save up $ and move

5. If you are not safe with or around those closest to you, what will make your situation safer? Find someone I can trust and go to them when needed.

6. How can you (and how do you) protect yourself? Humor, Anger

7. How successful are your self-protective attempts?

8. When *are* you safest? When Im @ work, w/ Dawn, or w- friends

9. When do you *feel* safest? —Same—↑

10. How can you protect yourself when you are with people you do not know? _____

_____

_____

What do your answers to these questions tell you about you and your sense of safety? _____

_____

_____

_____

* * * * *

There are times when safety is impossible to achieve unless you change your location. If you are a victim of domestic violence in any form (verbal, physical, sexual, emotional), it is of **utmost** importance that you get professional assistance to help make you safe (and to make your children safe, if you have children) so you can get out of the situation.

Exercise: Safety Assessment

As we said earlier, it is important for you to have safety if you are doing any work on trauma-related issues. Write the answers to the following questions, expanding on your answers as much as you need to.

1. Will you have a safe place in which to do the work? *yes unless I get mad with someone then I get out of control*

2. Have you set aside a specific time or day or week to do that work? _____

_____

_____

3. Will you have safe things around you when you sit down to do the exercises in this workbook? *yes*

_____

_____

4. Will you have things around you to ground you, to soothe you, to make you feel good about yourself and the work you are doing? *No*

_____

_____

5. If you are working with any therapists or helping persons at this time in your life, what makes that work safe or unsafe? *I can trust her and I know I will be safe around her.*

6. How will you protect yourself from your own strong feelings and thoughts that come up when you're doing the work, particularly if those feelings and thoughts feel harmful to you? *I keep the inside locked away and I don't talk about them.*

7. It is important for you to consider your own personal safety in your beliefs and actions. Are you personally safe to yourself? Do you have any strong or life-threatening desires to harm yourself? *sometimes sometimes if I get really depressed and angry*

8. Do you have beliefs that are not safe; e.g., I believe that I am not entitled to heal, I believe I am a bad person, I believe I am responsible for the trauma that happened to me? If so, or at any point in your work when self-harming beliefs or desires occur, stop your work and get help to prevent any harm from coming to you from yourself. You are the most important person in your life, whether you believe that or not. If you are not safe with yourself, then dealing with traumatic experiences can possibly lead you to even more unsafe behaviors.

9. What can you do to contain any harmful beliefs or actions and prevent them from taking over and hurting you? *Talking to someone when I feel they are coming on.*

10. If you were to evaluate your personal safety within yourself, how would you rate that safety:

I am safe within myself ——————————————— I am very unsafe
1   2   3   4   5   6   7   8   9   10

11. If you had trouble answering the previous question or rated yourself more toward the "I am very unsafe" side of the spectrum, here are some things you can do to help yourself, in addition to getting professional help:

- Write down three things you enjoy doing and then do them.

- Pick a positive feeling you want to have at the beginning of your day and then practice doing things to bring up that feeling.

- Make a list of your negative, unsafe thoughts and then write three thoughts to counter each of them.

- Notice when you begin to feel unsafe during a day; chart those times and what led to those feelings, then consciously do something that brings safety or self-comfort.

- When you think safe thoughts, give yourself a reward with an activity or object that is healthy.

- Do something that is positive spiritually for you.

- Find your favorite soothing music and listen to it.

- Avoid music that has themes of violence or is in a minor key.

- Use earplugs to drown out excess noise, or get a white noise machine.

- Avoid watching TV shows or movies that might trigger you.

12. Now that you have read the list of behaviors in question 11, which of them do you do regularly? _____

_____

_____

13. What are other things you can do to make yourself feel safe? _____

_____

_____

*   *   *   *   *

Creating a Safe Place

One thing that you can do is to create your own safe place. In your safe place, you may just sit and meditate or think, or you may do (or imagine doing) an activity. Generally, your safe place needs to have limited access; in other words, only you and those you totally trust or wish to protect can gain access. Your safe place needs to provide you with a sense of protection and security. It does not necessarily have to be comfortable and cozy; it can be a rocky shore along a beach or a wild landscape. What matters most is that you are safe from the dangers outside this secure location.

Before you begin the following exercises, think back over the course of your life to any and all places in which you've been safe. If you have no safe place to which you can return, think of what might make a place safe. You can find or create a safe place anywhere you choose. Would your safe place be a rocky beach or an open meadow, a castle with a moat and drawbridge or a sunny forest? As you create or remember a safe place, think of its characteristics and then add any and all items you might want to bring—weapons, furniture, equipment, items that have meaning, need protection, or make you feel safe. It is important that this place is secure for you.

Exercise: My Safe Place

If you could create a safe place in your present physical reality, and if money and time were no consideration, where would your safe place be? _____

_____

Stay in your safe place. Look around you. What do you see? Concentrate on colors and visual elements that let the feeling of safety flow in. Then concentrate on sounds or silences that belong in your safe place, feeling that they bring the feeling of safety and let it grow stronger in you. Then smell the odors of your safe place and let the good feeling flow in. Whom do you see there? Concentrate on the feelings of safety that the other brings. What do you feel in your body while imagining your safe place? Concentrate on that feeling. Then open your eyes and look around you. In the space below, write down what you have just experienced. _____

_____

_____

_____

_____

Find a single word to describe your safe place: _____

From now on, whenever you are in distress or feel the need, you can return to your good and safe place and draw strength from it (adapted from Ayalon and Flasher 1993, 73).

* * * * *

Journal Exercise: My Safe Place Collage or Drawing

Draw or collage your safe place in your journal. A collage is a group of pictures, words, and objects put on a piece of paper to represent a theme. There are no right or wrong drawings, collages, or safe places; there is only what is right for you.

* * * * *

Keeping Your Safe Space Safe

Before you begin to write more about your trauma, please take whatever time you need to reflect about your safe place and what makes or made it safe. You may take time to think about when you might have to use it. It is important for you to have a means to access your safe place quickly (Cohen, Barnes, and Rankin 1995).

If your safe place is in your home or in another physical location, it is important that you are able to keep that place private. It is **not** a place where children can come in and play or disturb your work. It is a place that has good energy. You may wish to clean that spot before you actually use it as a safe place. You may cleanse it with sage, cedar, sweetgrass, or incense. Make sure that it has nothing stressful or unsafe in it to jar you back to everyday reality (bills, paperwork, unfinished projects). You might put in something to give you white noise or perhaps include a miniature waterfall or fountain in the room. You may wish to find a book on feng shui and arrange the furniture in a way that seems to be healing. It is important that any energy you bring to this space is clean, new, and anger-free (Louden 1997). It is also important to bring things to your safe place that give you that kind of energy. Perhaps you have an object or picture that symbolizes who you want to be after you believe you are healed enough to continue on with a healthy life. Remember, when you create this safe place, it is important that you are able to see it, smell it, touch it, hear it, taste it, and feel it. It is a place where you can go whenever you choose, within seconds.

Exercise: Getting to My Safe Space

From now on, whenever you are in distress or feel the need to do so, you can use a symbol or phrase to return to your good and safe place and draw strength from it (Ayalon and Flasher 1993). You may use the space below to think of symbols that could stand for your safe place; for example, picture of a seashell (for a beach) or a small shell itself:

_____

_____

_____

_____

A phrase that I can use to get to my safe place quickly is _____

* * * * *

Getting to Your Safe Place through Visualization

When you created your safe place in your mind, you used *visualization*. Everyone uses this technique. Every time you daydream or create a fantasy in your mind, you visualize. If you choose, you may make a tape that helps you get to your safe place or to create any other pleasant visualization. This tape is private and is not to be shared with those you do not trust.

Checking In with Yourself

It is important that you learn how to notice how you feel in your body and mind and how you react when you remember, work on, or deal with the traumatic experiences that have happened to you. It may take practice for you to focus on your body and your emotions and become aware of how you are reacting. The following steps for checking in were developed by Rosenbloom and Williams (1999) to help you:

1. Stop whatever activity you might be doing.

2. Sit quietly for a short period of time.

3. Turn your attention inward and ask your body how it feels.

4. Notice if you feel any tension anywhere in your body (e.g., in your shoulders, stomach, jaw, or back).

5. Notice if you are holding your breath.

6. Notice if you are doing any behaviors that suggest tension (e.g., biting your nails, or picking at your skin).

7. Now notice any emotions you feel, if you are able to recognize them (are you fearful, sad, angry, lonely?).

8. Notice if you have racing thoughts or if you are able to stay focused.

9. If you've noticed any of the reactions listed above, take some time to use the deep breathing or relaxation techniques described in the next section.

Relaxation and Breathing Techniques

When you want to work in this workbook on specific areas that are problematic to you, you may want to use relaxation and breathing techniques either before you do the work, during the work, or after you have completed various exercises. But why do them? If you practice relaxation for several weeks, according to Benson (1984), you will have:

- reduced symptoms of anxiety

- fewer headaches and high blood pressure readings

- less insomnia

- a way to prevent hyperventilation

- a way to gain more control over panic attacks

- a way to reduce stress levels

- a way to feel more at peace

- more creativity

Schiraldi (2000) notes that there are important general guidelines for you to follow when you want to use relaxation techniques. It is important that you:

- practice the technique or techniques you choose regularly—at least daily

- concentrate as best you can while doing the techniques, trying to focus on the particular muscle groups and specific exercises

- combine relaxation with exercise

- trust in the power of the techniques to bring you some peace

- go to your safe place if you feel anxious while trying the technique

Before doing any relaxation techniques, it is important to have four basic elements present (Benson 1975). They are:

1. A quiet environment that has as few distractions as possible. Even background noise can be a distraction. It is also important that you will not be interrupted.

2. A mental device that is a constant, e.g., a single-syllable word or sound, repeated silently or in a low, gentle tone. The repetition frees your thoughts and is your single focus. Benson suggests using the syllable "one" because it is a simple, neutral word.

3. A passive attitude to help you rest and relax without forcing your response, preventing your relaxed response from occurring. Disregard any distracting thoughts that enter your mind.

4. A comfortable position that is as restful as possible. This reduces muscular effort. You may support your head and arms. You may remove your shoes and prop your feet up several inches, if you choose. You may also loosen tight-fitting clothes.

Exercise: Deep Breathing

This first exercise is adapted from Davis, Eshelman, and McKay (1995, 27).

1. Lie down on a blanket or rug on the floor. Bend your knees up toward you and move your feet until they are about eight inches apart, with your toes turned slightly outward. Keep your spine as straight as possible.

2. Scan your entire body and identify any places that hold tension.

3. Put one hand on your abdomen and one on your chest.

4. Inhale slowly through your nose into your abdomen so that it pushes your hand up; your chest should move only a little bit. Hold your breath while you count to five.

5. Smile slightly and then exhale through your mouth, taking as long as possible. Make a shushing sound as you exhale.

6. Repeat this at least five times, perhaps eventually increasing the amount of time you spend deep-breathing to five to ten minutes.

7. When you've finished the exercise, again scan your entire body to see if any tension remains.

8. Once you are familiar with the technique, you can also use it while you are sitting or standing, whenever you feel tenseness in your body.

* * * * *

Progressive Relaxation

You might also want to learn to relax by tensing and relaxing various muscle groups in your body. This is done using a technique called *progressive relaxation*. This technique helps you tense and then relax your four major muscle groups:

1. hands, forearms, biceps

2. head, face, throat, shoulders

3. chest, stomach, lower back

4. buttocks, thighs, calves, feet

You may practice this technique while you are lying down or sitting in a chair. The goal is to tense each muscle group for five to seven seconds and then relax that muscle group for twenty to thirty seconds, repeating the whole procedure at least twice. If the muscle group is still tense after you've done the procedure twice, you can repeat it for that group alone up to five times. You may also talk to yourself as you tense and relax, telling yourself anything that has to do with letting go of tension. There are numerous relaxation tapes you can buy that have this procedure, or you can read the following exercise into a tape recorder and play it back.

Another way to use progressive relaxation is to hold the tension in each of your muscle groups for about five seconds and then release the tension slowly while you say silently, "relax and let go." Then, take a deep breath and, as you breathe out slowly, silently say, "relax and let go" again.

Exercise: Basic Progressive Relaxation Sequence

This sequence takes you from your head through your neck, shoulders, arms and hands, chest, back, stomach, hips, legs, and feet.

If you do make a tape of this exercise or the one that follows, allow enough time for each exercise (five to seven seconds to tense, twenty to thirty seconds to relax) on the tape so you do not rush yourself. Also, put in two repetitions for each exercise.

- Wrinkle your forehead.

- Squint your eyes tightly.

- Open your mouth wide.

- Push your tongue against the roof of your mouth.

- Clench your jaw tightly.

- Push your head back into a pillow.

- Bring your head forward to touch your chest.

- Roll your head to your right shoulder.

- Roll your head to your left shoulder.

- Shrug your shoulders up as if to touch your ears.

- Shrug your right shoulder up as if to touch your ear.

- Shrug your left shoulder up as if to touch your ear.

- Hold your arms out and make a fist with each hand.

- One side at a time, push your hands down into the surface where you are practicing.

- One side at a time, make a fist, bend your arm at the elbow, and tighten up your arm while holding the fist.

- Take a deep breath and hold.

- Tighten your chest muscles.

- Arch your back.

- Tighten your stomach area.

- Push your stomach area out.

- Pull your stomach area in.

- Tighten your hips.

- Push the heels of your feet into the surface where you are practicing.

- Tighten your leg muscles below the knee.

- Curl your toes under as if to touch the bottoms of your feet.

- Bring your toes up as if to touch your knees.

* * * * *

Exercise: Quick Relaxation

Another quick way to relax is with whole muscle groups, tensing them for five to seven seconds and then relaxing them. This exercise is also adapted from Davis, Eshelman, and McKay (1995, 35–38).

1. Curl both fists and tighten your biceps and forearms as if you were a weight lifter posing, then relax.

2. Wrinkle your forehead and, at the same time, press your head as far back as is possible and roll it in a complete circle clockwise. Then reverse the roll. Then wrinkle up the muscles of your face in a frown, with squinted eyes, pursed lips, tongue pressed on the roof of your mouth, and shoulders scrunched up. Then relax.

3. Arch your back and take a deep breath into your chest. Hold it for five seconds and then relax. Take another deep breath, pressing out your stomach. Hold it for five seconds and then relax.

4. Pull your feet and toes back toward your face, tightening your shins. Then curl your toes and tighten your calves, thighs, and buttocks at the same time. Relax.

Successful deep muscle relaxation is a matter of practice. You may talk to yourself as you try to relax and tell yourself to let go or relax deeper in order to achieve a more complete relaxation. If you have muscle weakness or a muscular condition such as fibromyalgia, these exercises may not be for you. Check with your physician first.

* * * * *

Another Relaxation Technique

This technique is best used when you have time to try to relax as fully as you possibly can. It makes a good script to record on tape.

First, find a comfortable position and close your eyes. For the next few moments, concentrate on your breathing; use deep breathing. Try to see and feel your lungs, sensing how they feel as you breath in (pause), trying to make them completely expanded (pause), and then exhaling and sensing how they feel as you release your breath. There is no right or wrong way to breathe. What is important is that you try to relax and not worry about any of the things happening in your everyday life.

Continue to concentrate on your breathing and your lungs, picturing them as you inhale, imagining them filling with strengthening oxygen, and picturing them exhaling as you relax. Now, in your mind's eye, see or hear the message that says "relax" all over, in every bone, muscle, and nerve, tissue, feeling sensations of melting into relaxation.

Next, bring your attention to your left foot and ankle and, as you inhale, gently flex your foot. As you exhale, release and relax your foot. Now bring your attention to your right foot and ankle and, as you inhale, gently flex your foot. As you exhale, release and relax your foot. Let all the cares of the day drain out through your feet. Any noise you hear will only deepen your relaxation.

Now feel the muscles of your left calf. Inhale, contracting the muscles of your left calf and exhale, letting the calf relax. Now feel the muscles of your right calf. Inhale, contracting those muscles, and exhale, letting them completely relax. Of course, adjust your breathing rhythm to what is most comfortable for you, remembering to inhale relaxation, peace, and self-love and to exhale tension, the pressures of the day, and the impacts of trauma on you. Relaxing in this way is a learning process. It is a way to learn to be at ease, to be at peace with yourself, to be at peace with your world, and to relax.

Now bring your attention to the muscles of your left thigh. Inhale and contract these muscles, then exhale and feel relaxation pour in. Next, bring your attention to the muscles of your right thigh. Inhale and contract them, then exhale, feeling release through both your legs. Now shift your focus to your buttocks, inhaling and contracting the muscles. Then exhale and let your bottom relax.

Next, shift your focus to your stomach, inhaling and contracting your stomach muscles. Then exhale, letting your stomach muscles relax, relax, relax. Now bring your attention to your chest and inhale, feeling your chest fill with oxygen and power. As you exhale, release any tightness that may be there as you release all the tensions that are bothering you. Try to feel the feeling of relaxation as a conscious process in your mind and body.

Now bring your attention to your hands. As you inhale, close both of your hands tightly, making fists. As you exhale, release the fists. As you do so, consciously try to let go of everything onto which you are grasping, and to relax. You may open your palms as you relax to receive warmth and vitalizing energy from the world around you. You may also bring your palms, cupped, closer and closer together until you feel the energy that is between them. As you do this exercise, allow the sense of relaxation and energy to move upward through your hands into your forearms, elbows, and shoulders.

Next, focus your attention on your shoulders. As you inhale, contract your shoulders. Hold them for a few seconds in this position and then, as you exhale, feel the tension they have held release outward from them. Feel the point between your shoulders and the base of your neck. Allow warm energy to melt away any built-up tension and pressure that has been stuck there. Now feel the warm energy move up through your neck, allowing your neck to release and support your head as your neck completely relaxes.

Finally, turn your attention to the muscles of your face. Gently tense the muscles of your chin, your mouth, your eyes, your cheeks, and your forehead. Then let your entire face loosen and relax. Enjoy the relaxation you feel through your entire body for a few moments. If any part of your body is not completely relaxed, turn your attention to it. Inhale, and let the last bits of tension melt out of that part of your body. If your attention drifts, or if you feel drowsy, it is perfectly all right as long as you are safe, comfortable, and relaxed (adapted from Rosenbloom and Williams 1999, 28–30).

Trying Meditation for Relaxation

Some persons use meditation to relax and to calm themselves as they seek heightened concentration and awareness. If you are new at meditating, thoughts may come in to distract you as you try to calm and quiet your mind. If this happens, you may try to use some imagery to focus your awareness before doing the meditation. If you are able to create clear mental images of the following scenes or things, you might then be able to direct your focus to relaxing. Try to create a clear mental image, right now, of:

- the face of your best friend
- a turkey waiting to be carved
- your bedroom in your present home
- a glass of cold lemonade
- a field of wildflowers
- the aroma of cooking spaghetti sauce
- riding in a race car at a racetrack
- your bare feet on a sandy beach
- the touch of velvet on your skin
- a cat meowing

Use one of these images to focus your attention and then focus on meditating. If worries keep on entering, allow them to wander through your focus, noting them and allowing them to continue on without concentrating on them. It is also important to know how to deep-breathe and relax before you try to meditate. If this doesn't work, you may repeat a word or syllable (such as "one" or "om") over and over again, as Benson (1975) suggested. Try this at first for five to ten minutes, increasing it to fifteen minutes if you can.

When to Take a Break from Doing Work in This Workbook

If you have one or more of the following signs, it is important for you to take a break from the work in this book. This is **not** a book to do from start to finish as quickly as possible. Choose to do only the work that applies to you. You may use techniques from only one or two chapters or sections, or you may find that many of the chapters have techniques and exercises that will be helpful to you. If any exercises feel overwhelming to you and these signs come up as you are working on them, put the book away and do something else. These signs are adapted from Rosenbloom and Williams (1999). Put the work away:

- if you begin to feel that you are not present in your body or are not aware of your surroundings, or if you begin to lose your sense of time (these are symptoms of dissociation)

- if you begin to have flashbacks, or have more frequent or more intense flashbacks, of your traumatic experiences

- if unmanageable feelings begin to flood you

- if you experience anger, rage, irritability, depression, fear, anxiety, sadness, or other feelings that seem to be out of control or that seem to have no recognizable source

- if you begin to injure yourself, or to injure yourself more seriously or more frequently

- if you engage in addictive, compulsive behaviors, including abuse of alcohol, drugs, eating, sex, or working

- if you begin to develop anorexia nervosa (you stop eating) or bulimia (you eat a great deal and then make yourself throw up)

- if you become completely numb and are unable to feel emotion

- if you become unaware of emotion

- if you begin to isolate yourself and avoid others

- if you have a dramatic change in any normal life pattern

If any of these signs appear, take care of yourself before you continue with your work. Should the reactions you are having become too intense, you may find that you need a few days or weeks away. Also, if you feel overwhelmed by your work and need support and guidance, seek the help of a qualified traumatologist, preferably one certified by ATSS, or the Association of Traumatic Stress Specialists.

You may also decide to use any of the following strategies for self-care while you are taking that break:

- For physical self-care, you may decide to eat regular meals that are healthy and balanced, exercise, wrap yourself tightly in a blanket, sit in your favorite chair, get regular preventive medical care, get a massage, play sports, get rest and sleep, take a warm bath or shower, recycle, do housework or yard work, pound on a pillow, rip up a phone book, take a vacation.

- For psychological self-care, you may decide you need or want to decrease your everyday stress, meditate, journal, listen to soothing tapes, find a certified trauma therapist, commit to doing something you want to do, read something frivolous, or say "no" to others' requests.

- For emotional self-care, you may decide you need or want to spend time with family members you love *and* like, reconnect with persons you love, watch your favorite movies or TV shows, listen to your favorite music, laugh or cry, play, or fight for a cause.

- For spiritual self-care, you may decide you need or want to go to or join a church or other spiritual group, read a spiritually oriented book, spend time in nature, spend time being thankful for who you are and what you have, pray, or do something to help better the world or the lives of animals or nature.

- For professional/workplace self-care, you may want or need to take your assigned breaks during your workday, see if you can use flextime on your job, try to finish assignments when (or even before) they are due, set limits, try to develop a good relationship with other workers or your boss, try to find something in your work that is rewarding to you, or balance other aspects of your life with your work (adapted from Pearlman and Saakvitne 1995).

Exercise: My Safety Net

As you work through your traumatic experiences and symptoms using this workbook, it is also important to have connections with others available when and if you need them. It is important to find others who care about you. If you don't have family members who can help you, you may build connections with others through work, church, support groups (e.g., A.A., A.C.O.A.), or social organizations. You may list the phone numbers of these support persons below. However, if none of them is available when you are in crisis, remember you **are** able to stay safe even when they cannot be reached. At the end of this list, you may add ways to stay safe if no one is available.

The phone numbers I need to know include:

1. My best friend Kevin 643 7897
2. The local crisis line _____
3. My partner or spouse _____
4. My therapist(s) Dawn _____
5. My doctor(s) _____
6. The family member to whom I am closest _____
7. My neighbor _____
8. The local hospital _____
9. My child(ren) _____
10. If none of these persons is available and I feel unsafe, I can do the following things to remain safe until someone is available: _____

* * * * *

Working through the following pages may make you feel more vulnerable and in need of support from others. If you feel overwhelmed at any point, remember to use the relaxation and breathing strategies included in this chapter. You have many positive techniques you can to use to comfort yourself as you work through the exercises in this book. Now you are ready to begin your hard work. As you begin, keep the following passage from the German playwright Goethe in mind:

> Until one is committed, there is hesitancy ... the moment one definitely commits oneself, then Providence moves too. All sorts of things occur to help one that would never otherwise have occurred.... Begin it now.

3

Identifying and Writing about What Has Happened to You

Before you work on the symptoms that are bothering you, it is important to make sure that you are aware of where your symptoms come from—in other words, what you've experienced—without overwhelming or retraumatizing yourself. Remember, at any point during this chapter or other chapters, you can refer back to the exercises in chapter 2 to help calm yourself.

Also, you may look at the work you are doing and rate yourself and the amount of distress you are feeling at that particular time by using a subjective units of distress, or SUDS, scale. Higher SUDS levels indicate a greater need to relax, ground, or take a break.

Creating Your Own SUDS Scale

The *SUDS scale* is one way to communicate to yourself or others how much distress you are experiencing. The scale has 11 points, from 0 to 10, from least to most distress. It is important that you assign your own measures to this scale. Sometimes, it may seem as if your distress is beyond a 10. This scale is adapted from the work of Smyth (1999).

0	I am completely relaxed, with no distress. I may be deep in sleep.
1	I am very relaxed. I may be awake but dozing off.
2	I am awake but feel no tension.
3	I feel a little bit of tension; it keeps my attention from wandering.
4	I am feeling some mild distress, apprehension, fear, or anxiety, and body tension.
5	My distress is somewhat unpleasant but I can still tolerate it. (I am looking at a spiderweb with a huge spider in it, but it is several feet away and the spider can't jump that distance.)

6   I am feeling moderate distress and unpleasant feelings. I have some worry and apprehension.

7   My body tension now is substantial and unpleasant, though I can still tolerate it and can think clearly.

8   I am feeling a great deal of distress with high levels of fear, anxiety, worry. I can't tolerate this level of distress for very long.

9   The distress is so great that it is impacting my thinking. I just can't think straight.

10   I am in extreme distress. I am totally filled with panic and I have extreme tension throughout my body. This is the worst possible fear and anxiety I could ever imagine. It is so great that I just can't think at all.

You may use this SUDS scale at any point in time as you do the work in this book. You may decide on which SUDS rating means you should take a break from the work and return to the exercises in chapter 2 to calm you. You may also decide that getting stuck at a certain SUDS level means that you need to stop doing the work in the workbook for a period of time and consult with a therapist. At this point in time, what is your SUDS level? _____

Why did you choose this level? _____

_____

_____

More about Memory and Remembering

In this chapter, we will ask you to identify what happened to you through a trauma inventory; later, you will be asked to draw a trauma time line. Both exercises ask you to remember what happened to you. But what if you can't remember? What if you have only a vague inkling that something happened to you? How sure are you that the traumatic events happened to you? Some traumatic events are easily documented (through records, newspaper articles, etc.). Others may never be fully known. Where did you place yourself on the healing continuum that was given in chapter 2? You might complete this exercise in your notebook or journal for each and every traumatic event that happened to you, if you believe you need to.

Constructing a Trauma Inventory

Before you begin work on any of the symptoms that may be haunting you, it is important for you to have a sense of what you've experienced (both positively and negatively) in your life. Without going into great detail, use the list provided on the next two pages to identify which traumas you've experienced and the age or ages at which you experienced them. You may also write a very brief statement about any of the traumas you've experienced. The types of traumas you experience can impact the reactions you have about those events.

Event	Age(s)	Description
surviving a natural disaster (tornado, hurricane)		
surviving a fire		
witnessing a natural death		
witnessing a violent death		
being in an automobile accident		
being in a plane crash		
surviving an assault or mugging		
surviving a robbery or burglary		
having a murder in my family		
being exposed to war		
being a combat soldier		
being a refugee		
experiencing physical violence as a child		
experiencing neglect as a child		
being sexually abused as a child		
being emotionally abused as a child		
experiencing physical violence as an adult		
being raped by someone I knew		
being raped by a stranger		
being raped by more than one person at a time		
surviving cult abuse		
having some sort of involvement in pornography		
having some sort of involvement in snuff films		
experiencing a job-related trauma		
having a traumatic move		
surviving torture		
surviving a holocaust or genocide		
other		

As you think about all the traumatic experiences you have had, remember that you survived them and that you used many positive character traits to do so (Cohen, Barnes, and Rankin 1995). The following exercise refers to some of those traits.

Exercise: My Positive Traits

Refer to the traumatic events you experienced and identify which positive traits you used during those events. In which traumatic experiences did you use them?

How and when did you show determination? _____

_____

How and when did you show your will to continue to struggle and to eventually succeed?

_____

How and when did your faith help you, particularly faith in yourself and your support system? _____

_____

How and when did you show courage? _____

_____

How and when did you take personal responsibility for meeting your needs (including your need for safety) during your traumatic experiences? _____

_____

How and when did you exhibit your personal creativity? _____

_____

How and when did you show your resilience? _____

_____

How and when did you use your intuition? _____

_____

How and when were you able to maintain any optimism? _____

_____

How and when were you able to use any physical strength? _____

_____

What did completing this exercise tell you about your strengths? _____

_____

_____

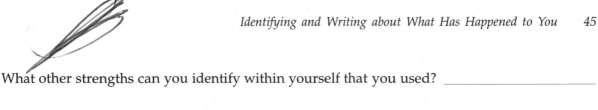

What other strengths can you identify within yourself that you used? _____

_____

* * * * *

Do You Have PTSD?

Do you believe that you have post-traumatic stress disorder, or has anyone ever diagnosed you with PTSD? The following exercise will help you determine whether it's likely you have PTSD (Davidson 1996).

_____

Exercise: My Symptoms

First, identify each trauma you are using as your reference points for the PTSD. (Use the list earlier in this chapter.) If you have more than one, photocopy these pages and do this exercise once for each trauma.

For each symptom listed, ask yourself how often in the last week the symptom troubled you and how severe your distress was. Then, in the two boxes beside each question, write a number from 0 to 4 to indicate the frequency and severity of the symptom.

Frequency:
0 = not at all   1 = once only   2 = 2–3 times   3 = 4–6 times   4 = every day

Severity:
0 = not at all distressing   1 = minimally distressing   2 = moderately distressing
3 = markedly distressing   4 = extremely distressing

Frequency	Severity	Symptom
_____	_____	1. painful images, memories, or thoughts of the event
_____	_____	2. distressing dreams of the event
_____	_____	3. feelings event was recurring, or that you were reliving it
_____	_____	4. being upset by something that reminded you of the event
_____	_____	5. being physically upset by reminders of the event (including sweating, trembling, racing heart, shortness of breath, nausea, diarrhea)
_____	_____	6. avoiding any thoughts or feelings about the event
_____	_____	7. avoiding doing things or going into situations that remind you of the event
_____	_____	8. inability to recall important parts of the event
_____	_____	9. difficulty enjoying things
_____	_____	10. feeling distant or cut off from other people
_____	_____	11. inability to have sad or loving feelings

_____   _____   12. difficulty imagining having a long life span and fulfilling your goals

_____   _____   13. trouble falling asleep or staying asleep

_____   _____   14. irritability or outbursts of anger

_____   _____   15. difficulty concentrating

_____   _____   16. feeling on edge, being easily distracted, or needing to stay on guard

_____   _____   17. being jumpy or easily startled

Add together all the numbers from both the frequency and severity columns. The higher your score, the more likely you are to have PTSD.

My score is: _____

Remember, only a qualified therapist or doctor can actually diagnose you with PTSD. For the actual diagnosis, you need one or more intrusive symptoms (the first five questions), three or move avoidance symptoms (the next seven questions), and two or more body arousal symptoms (the final five questions).

* * * * *

Creating a Trauma Time Line

One way to record your trauma history is to draw a trauma time line. Take a roll of white paper and, beginning at the end of the roll, mark spaces for each of the years of your life on a horizontal line. This line can be a foot or many feet long. You may want to start the beginning of your life a few inches from the end of the roll so you can record any events that happened prior to its beginning. Did your mother have any serious prebirth events that could have impacted you (was she battered, did she fall, was she in an accident, was there a significant death during her pregnancy, was she confined to bed, etc.)?

Put any significant events that happened to you throughout your life above the horizontal line. These can be positive or neutral events (e.g., starting school, moving to a new home, a first date), as well as traumatic events (e.g., illness, injury, abuse). Below the line, record events that happened to others who are important to you; these should be events that impacted you as an observer or witness but did not directly happen to you (deaths, births, etc.). You may use photos, magazine pictures, personal items, or drawings of yourself and others, placing them above or below the line to symbolize events, persons, and places.

If you wish, you can extend your time line into the future beyond your present age and put in some of your future intentions. This time line has been called "the Torah of trauma" by some individuals. You may find that constructing a time line is too retraumatizing to do alone; seek professional help if you need to. Also, take your time. Do a year or a few years at a time and then take a break. Take time to relax, regroup, and unwind.

What did completing a trauma time line tell you about yourself or what happened to you?

_____

_____

_____

Healing by Writing

Another way to deal with your history of trauma is to write about what happened to you. Pennebaker (1997) says that writing about upsetting experiences is beneficial to health and well-being. You might decide to write every once in a while about your traumatic experiences using a personal journal or you might contract with yourself to follow Pennebaker and Campbell's writing plan (2000). If you want to spend more time (and feel emotionally ready) to take an in-depth look at one or more of your traumatic experiences, Pennebaker suggests you use a four-day time period to write about them. During those four days, write for twenty minutes each day. Your only rule is to write continuously for the entire time. If you run out of things to say, just repeat what you've already written. Don't worry about grammar, spelling, or sentence structure.

The following exercise guides you through this four-day plan. You may do this exercise now, or return to it later. You may feel sad or depressed when you finish this daily writing assignment. If so, remember that your reactions are completely normal. Most people say that these feelings go away an hour or so after you finish. Or you can use any of the exercises in chapter 2 to relax or calm you. Note: If you have experienced extreme, massive amounts of trauma, this exercise may be too retraumatizing.

If you use this technique, remember to write about the most traumatic, upsetting experiences of your life. In your writing, really let go and explore your deepest thoughts and emotions. You can write about the same traumatic experience on all four days or about a different experience each day. In addition to writing about your traumatic experiences, you can use this technique to write about major conflicts or problems that you have experienced or are experiencing now (including those that have resulted from the traumatic events). It is critical that you really delve into yourself and into the significant experiences or conflicts that you've not discussed in great detail with others. You might also tie your personal experiences of trauma to other parts of your life as you write. How are they related to your childhood, your parents, those you love, who you are, or who you want to be?

Writing is an act of release, taking all the stuff of trauma that has bound you up and controlled you and releasing it to the universe. Writing may help you reduce your inhibitions about disclosing what happened to you and may encourage changes in the way you view your traumas. As you write, you may begin with only a few incoherent sentences and end up with a rather coherent story. Before you begin to write, however, you might want to review your list of traumatic experiences. It may help you to realize that your own traumatic life experiences may or may not be considered traumatic by others.

Journal Exercise: My Traumatic Experiences

Over four days, write about a traumatic experience in your notebook or journal. Write for twenty minutes each day without stopping. At the end of each day's writing, take some time to reflect on the meaning of what you've written, how you feel as you finish, and what you've learned. Some people have found it easier to write first thing in the morning. Then they have the rest of the day to calm down, become involved in everyday activities, or go to work. Waiting to write until evening or right before bed can lead to nightmares and increased sleep problems. When you are done, do the following exercise in the workbook.

* * * * *

Exercise: Learning from My Traumatic Experiences

I have written about my traumatic experiences for four days. This exercise has taught me the following things about that trauma, about myself, and about my world: _____

_____

_____

_____

_____

_____

_____

* * * * *

Using Metaphors to Describe Trauma

There is no one way to tell your story (Meichenbaum 2000). Sometimes everyday words do not seem adequate to describe what happened to you. In these instances, you may want to use metaphors to describe the impact of trauma on you. A *metaphor* is a descriptive way to explain trauma through a phrase that does not give a direct message. "I am a sack of dirty laundry" is a metaphor for how someone feels, perhaps after being date raped. If you choose to write a metaphorical story about your traumatic experiences, you might want to include the following:

1. a hero or heroine as a main character (you)

2. a symbol to describe the event or person that caused you to be hurt or victimized

3. something that stands for resiliency and healing

4. symbols that stand for your ideas about safety and security

5. symbols that indicate your mastery of the problem

6. a messenger that conveys a solution to any problems

7. symbols of your culture (the Star of David, ethnic clothing, etc.)

Time to Heal

Now that you have identified your traumatic experiences, it is time to begin to work on any symptoms of PTSD or complex PTSD that you are having. Remember, this is not a start-to-finish workbook. It does not ask you to expose yourself to all the gory details of any traumas that you may have had. Choose the symptoms that bother you most and then pick and choose among the healing strategies and exercises given for each of them. Each chapter from now until the end of the book treats one symptom category: first, the three major criteria for the diagnosis of PTSD, and then the seven symptom categories of complex PTSD or DESNOS. Always remember to take breaks from the work whenever you believe or feel you need to do so. Healing takes time; allow yourself that time.

4

Helping Yourself When You Reexperience a Trauma

Reexperiencing or intrusive reactions (those listed under the second criterion of the definition of PTSD given in chapter 1) are among the three major types of reactions in post-traumatic stress disorder (the other two are avoidance and physical symptoms). This chapter gives you ways to help you with intrusive symptoms. These techniques can be used when:

- memories or thoughts of the trauma suddenly pop into your mind

- you dream about the trauma over and over

- new aspects of the trauma come to you through nightmares or thoughts

- you feel as if the traumatic event is happening again

- you react to triggers such as a smell, sound, date, or any stimulus associated with your original traumatic experience that push you back into the trauma through a *flashback* (a momentary reliving of a past event in the present) or an *abreaction* (a full-blown reliving of the trauma in real time)

- you get really, really nervous or uncomfortable in a situation that reminds you of the trauma or is similar to the trauma

Building Dual Awareness

Before you work on trauma-related dreams, nightmares, memories, flashbacks, or other aspects of the trauma, it is very important for you to accept and reassure yourself that your trauma is **not** occurring in the present time. Having *dual awareness* helps you look at and work on the trauma while you are secure in the knowledge that you are really in the present environment. The following exercise gives you a tool to help you look at the trauma from the perspective of your observing self (now) and your experiencing self (then). You may do this exercise before you delve into your traumatic memories. It shows you the degree to which you have a capacity for dual awareness. This exercise was developed by Rothschild (2000, 130).

Exercise: My Capacity for Dual Awareness

Remember a recent mildly distressing event—something that made you feel slightly anxious or embarrassed. As you remember the event, what do you notice in your body? What happens in your muscles? What happens in your gut? How does your breathing change? Does your heart rate increase or decrease? Do you become warmer or colder? If there is a change in your body temperature, is it uniform (the same everywhere in your body) or does it vary?

_____

_____

_____

Now bring your awareness back into the room where you are. Notice the color of the walls, the texture of the floor. What is the temperature of this room? What do you smell here? Does your breathing change as your focus of awareness changes? _____

_____

_____

Now try to keep this awareness of your present surroundings while you remember the slightly distressing event. Is it possible for you to maintain a physical awareness of where you are as you remember that event?

End this exercise by refocusing your awareness on your current surroundings.

* * * * *

Matsakis (1998, 102–103) notes that hyperarousal (overexcitation) of the adrenal gland, which pumps out adrenaline, leads to the intrusive symptoms of post-traumatic stress disorder. She lists the consequences of this hyperarousal as:

1. constant or frequent irritability leading to outbursts of anger

2. sleep problems of all types, ranging from nightmares to difficulty going to sleep to difficulty staying asleep

3. increased sensitivity to noise, pain, touch, temperature, or other stimuli

4. increased heart rate or blood pressure

5. agitated movement, tremors when at rest, gastric distress, incontinence

6. hypervigilance (constant watchfulness because of feelings of vulnerability)

7. immediate responsiveness to situations without taking time to think things through

8. lack of self-control leading to self-shaming

9. inability to assess situations accurately

10. concentration difficulties

11. focusing difficulties after exposure to a traumatic trigger (problems with seeing the whole picture rather than focusing only on one aspect of a situation)

12. difficulties in problem solving because it is hard to maintain attention to nontraumatic aspects of the situation

13. a higher baseline level of arousal (it is easier and quicker to become aroused)

14. difficulties in calming down and soothing yourself

15. feeling "crazy" when you can't identify the trigger that led to your hyperarousal

16. memory difficulties, particularly short-term memory difficulties

17. increased use of substances

Dealing with Your Flashbacks

A flashback is a memory of the past that intrudes into the present and makes the past seem as if it is actually occurring in the here and now. Matsakis defines a flashback as a "sudden, vivid recollection of the traumatic event accompanied by a strong emotion" (1994a, 33). A flashback can occur as a slight "blip" in time or it can be a memory of an entire experience, occurring in real time just as it did in the past. This type of flashback is called an *abreaction*. Generally, the occurrence of a flashback cannot be predicted. Generally, flashbacks refer to visual and/or auditory parts of the trauma, but they can also refer to body memories (such as pain), emotions (intense anger that comes out of nowhere), and behaviors (acting in certain ways when a trigger comes up). Whenever a flashback happens, it feels as if the trauma is occurring all over again. You do not black out, dissociate, or lose consciousness during a flashback, but you do leave the present time temporarily. Rothschild says that memories "pounce into the present unbidden in the form of flashbacks" that can "reinforce terror and feelings of helplessness" (2000, 131). A flashback that occurs during sleep can be a nightmare or even a vivid dream. Meichenbaum (1994) notes that flashbacks also can appear as intrusive thoughts or reexperiences, or as intense feelings.

During a flashback, your traumas get replayed with great intensity; in many cases, unless you know how, you may not even be able to separate your flashback from present reality, reinforcing the impact of that trauma on you. Even young children can have flashbacks; however, they tend to act them out rather than express them in words. Sometimes children may act out upon others what was done to them; e.g., a nine-year-old boy who sexually acts out toward a younger sibling may be having a flashback, rather than just acting as an offender.

Ruth, thirty, suddenly feels her uncle's body on her as she is taking a shower, and recognizes his touch. The uncle molested her twenty-five years before. Margaret, thirty-five, lives in an apartment with two other persons. Their upstairs neighbors play music until late at night. When Margaret and her roommates complain to the management, the male renters upstairs retaliate by banging on the ceiling at all hours of the night and by scratching up Margaret's car and the cars of her roommates. Margaret is a date rape survivor, and these neighbors' behavior has led to flashbacks of her own attacks twenty years before. She is hypervigilant as she prepares for a potential attack.

Sometimes it is very difficult to make sense of flashbacks, particularly when there are not explicit events to use as reference points for them. Flashbacks may involve explicit memories of entire scenes of traumatic events or just parts of the events. Usually a flashback also includes some emotional and sensory aspect of the traumatic event. This means that your entire nervous system is involved when you have a flashback; your nervous system becomes hyperaroused when you are exposed to trauma triggers.

Sometimes, flashbacks occur as part of a memory that you thought had been worked through. When this happens, you might ask yourself the following questions:

- What is the flashback trying to tell me?

- Do I have more to see?

- Do I have more to feel?

- Do I have more to hear?

- Do I have more to learn or accept about what happened to me?

- Am I able to grab onto only this piece of the memory without getting lost?

Through some of the techniques in this workbook, you can learn to deal with flashbacks in different ways.

Exercise: Beginning to Deal with a Flashback

Think of a flashback you have had in the past two weeks.

Describe the flashback and what you experienced. _____

_____

Have you had a similar flashback in the past? If so, when and under what conditions? _____

_____

How did the flashback smell, feel, or sound? Who was involved? _____

_____

How did the actual traumatic experience smell, feel, or sound? Who was involved? _____

_____

How are the flashback and the past traumatic situation different or the same? _____

_____

What actions can you take to feel better as the flashback occurs? _____

_____

How can you ground yourself to stay in the present when flashbacks occur? _____

_____

How did you feel as you did this exercise? You can use it for any flashback you have. _____

_____

* * * * *

The VCR Technique

Another way to deal with flashbacks is to put the memories that repeat in a shortened form on a "VCR tape" in your mind. Then you can play the memory in small sections using the on and off controls. You can even fast-forward or rewind. These actions give you a sense of choice and control about remembering. You can also add something else to the beginning or end of the memory, to frame it—perhaps an alternative solution to what happened, or an image of your safe place.

Exercise: Using the VCR Technique

1. Before you work on a traumatic flashback with this technique, try it with a positive memory of an event that you've experienced.

The event that I am going to use is: _____

_____

When I fast-forward through this event, I (saw, felt, heard, smelled, experienced, etc.) _____

_____

When I rewind this event, I _____

_____

When I frame this event with other pictures, I _____

_____

If I were to use positive images to frame my flashback, I would use these: _____

_____

2. If you don't feel immediately comfortable with this technique, practice it more, until you are comfortable. Then try it with a traumatic flashback.

The flashback that I am going to use is: _____

_____

When I fast-forward this event, I _____

_____

When I rewind this event, I _____

_____

When I frame the event with other pictures, I _____

_____

How comfortable was this technique to use with a flashback? Was it more or less comfortable than when you used it with a positive memory? _____

_____

* * * * *

Getting Outside Your Head

One important way to deal with a flashback is to get it outside of your head into the world around you. You can do that by writing about it, talking about it, drawing it, collaging it, or otherwise representing it someplace other than in your mind.

The next few pages will give you guidance about dealing with your flashbacks. If you are currently in therapy and find doing these activities to be too powerful, wait until you are in a therapy session to complete them. If you have a supportive person who is willing to listen to you talk about your flashbacks, then work on this section of the book in close contact with that person. Working on flashbacks can be very powerful and it is important that you take care of yourself while doing so.

Journal Exercise: Defusing Flashbacks

Dolan has developed a four-step approach to help defuse flashbacks (1991, 107). To use it, answer the following questions in your journal:

1. In what situation(s) have you felt the same way before?

2. How are the current situation and the past situation similar? Is there a similar setting, time of year, sound, or other aspect? If there is a person involved, how is that person similar to one who was involved in your trauma(s) in the past?

3. How is the current situation different from the past situation? What is different about your current life circumstances, support systems, or environment? How are the persons around you different from those involved in your traumatic experiences?

4. What actions can you take (if any) to feel better now, particularly if you feel unsafe in your flashback? If your flashback is merely an old memory that does not cause you to be unsafe, you may merely need to give yourself a positive message that you **can** survive or work through it or do something different. However, if you truly are unsafe, it is important to be aware of the real danger and protect yourself.

* * * * *

The Rewind Technique

David Muss, a British psychiatrist, has developed the following technique to allow you to get rid of your unwanted, involuntary memories of the traumatic event and the emotional distress that they bring (1991). When you try this technique, do so in a safe setting; you may wish to work on it first with a therapist.

1. Find a time when you can be safe and undisturbed.

2. Find a comfortable place and sit there quietly for fifteen minutes before beginning the rewind.

3. Begin to relax, using the techniques you learned in chapter 2. Keep your eyes closed, and tense and relax each muscle group of your body, beginning with your feet.

4. Feel the calmness that comes over you as you relax. You might also think of a pleasant place or your safe place while you do this relaxing.

5. Now allow yourself to float out of yourself so you can watch yourself sitting in your comfortable place. Choose a memory in which you felt somewhat sick or frightened, e.g., just

before going down the largest drop on a roller coaster. Thinking of this memory will make you feel somewhat uncomfortable. Now look at that same scene from outside the roller coaster. Float above yourself and watch yourself. Hopefully, you do not feel as bad now.

6. Now you need to experience two films. Imagine that you are sitting in the center of a totally empty movie theater with the screen in front of you and the projection room behind you. Now float out of your body and go to the projection room. See yourself sitting in the theater, watching the film. From the projection room, you can see the whole theater as well as yourself.

7. Watch the first film. The first film replays the traumatic event as you experienced it or as you remember it in your dreams, flashbacks, or nightmares. You will see yourself on the screen. It is as if someone took a video of you during the trauma and that video is now playing. When you start the film, begin it at the point just prior to the traumatic event, seeing yourself as you were before it occurred. Remember, you are sitting in the movie theater to watch the film, but you are also in the projection room watching yourself in the theater as you watch the film. Play the film at its normal speed. Stop the film when you realized you were going to survive or when your memory begins to fade.

8. The second film is the rewind. You will not watch the rewind, but you will experience it on the screen, seeing it as if it were happening to you now, with all of its sounds, smells, feels, tastes, and touch sensations. You are actually in the film, reexperiencing the event. However, you see and experience it all happening backwards, from after the traumatic event until before the event happened. This reexperiencing takes practice and must be done rapidly. Remembering a trauma of about one minute would mean having a rewind of about ten to fifteen seconds.

You may find rewinding hard to do initially. However, keep practicing until it feels right. You may find it painful to go through the first film. After you learn this process, every time you begin to remember the trauma, you can use the rewind to scramble the sequence of events and to take you quickly back to the starting point—the good image. You will be left with the prevent memory after the rewind. As time goes by, your rewind process will happen faster and faster. It is very important to include all the frightening, awful details of the trauma in your movie. Also, as one memory gets resolved by rewind, others may appear to take its place, memories that have been hidden under the surface of the first. These too can be addressed through this process.

If you try the rewind process, use this space to describe how it worked for you.

_____

_____

_____

Other Ways to Deal with Flashbacks

You may use any of the following techniques to help you put a flashback out of your awareness and return to the present. Some of them are designed to be quick, while others take time. Do not worry if many or most of them do not work for you. Try them out and choose those that work best.

- repeatedly blink your eyes hard
- change the position of your body

- use deep breathing (from chapter 2)
- use imagery to go to your safe place in your mind
- go to your actual safe place
- move vigorously around your environment
- name objects in your environment out loud
- hold onto a safe object
- listen to a soothing tape, e.g., one a therapist made for you if you are in counseling
- clap your hands
- stamp your feet on the floor
- wash your face with cold water
- say positive statements (affirmations) about yourself
- spray the memory with a bottle of (imaginary) cleanser until it goes away
- project the flashback onto a dry erase board and then erase it; do the back and forth movements of the eraser with your hand
- draw the flashback on paper, then do something with the paper (shred it, burn it, bury it)
- put the flashback into some type of vault or container (real, on paper, or symbolically, in your mind)

Containment and Traumatic Memories

Containment means using your mind to focus attention on something other than a traumatic memory, flashback, or thought. It is possible to contain those reminders of the trauma and remain in the present, in spite of having strong feelings. Learning containment techniques can help you tolerate those feelings without taking negative action against yourself or others. Containment is based on choice rather than automatic response; it helps you store overwhelming, unsafe memories until you are ready to process them. However, containment does not involve indefinite avoidance or denial. In fact, learning how to contain memories means that using numbing and dissociation to deal with trauma is less necessary.

The following containment techniques were developed by a Dissociative Identity Disorders support group at Dominion Hospital in Falls Church, Virginia. The group noted these ways to contain traumatic intrusions (flashbacks, memory fragments, thoughts):

1. Plan ahead for potentially distressing times when you have some advance warning of them.

2. Allow yourself to cry to get out emotion.

3. Record your thoughts and feelings on paper or tape.

4. Perform a monotonous activity to distract yourself: play solitaire, do a puzzle.

5. Ground yourself in the present time by reminding yourself that you are in the here and now (use dual awareness). Grounding might include grasping a favorite object and focusing attention on that contact as a way to stay in touch with reality; using your body's contact with the furniture or floor to remind you of your present location—stomp your feet or push your body into a chair; or using your body's own physical properties by clapping your hands, or touching your tongue to the roof of your mouth.

6. Put the memories into a real or imagined container outside yourself, and then close the box until a more appropriate time.

7. Count to yourself; use your watch or pulse as ways to count.

8. Get involved in an activity that involves some type of motion (such as walking or exercising).

9. Use art materials to express your emotions or represent the memory.

10. Go to a potentially traumatizing event with your camera, and take photographs as a way to hide behind the camera and avoid some triggers.

Using Dual Awareness to Treat Flashbacks

The following flashback-halting protocol is based on the principles of dual awareness we mentioned earlier in this chapter. It is designed to reconcile the experiencing self with the observing self and generally will stop a traumatic flashback quickly, according to Rothschild (2000, 132). Practice this technique on "old" flashbacks (those you have had, processed, and perhaps put to rest) so that you can learn it well. And then use it later when you have a flashback that includes new memories or previously unknown traumatic events or material.

Exercise: Practicing Dual Awareness

The flashback I am using is _____

_____

Say to yourself (preferably aloud) the following sentences, filling in the blanks:

Right now I am feeling _____ (fill in the name of your current emotion, usually fear) and I am sensing in my body _____ (describe your current bodily sensations—name at least three), _____ _____ because I am remembering _____ (identify the trauma by name only without details) _____ _____ .

At the same time, I am looking around where I am now in _____ , (the current year), here _____ (name the place where you are). I can see _____ (describe some of the things that you see right now, in this place), and so I know _____ (identify the trauma again by name only) is not happening anymore.

How did this technique work for you? What was it like to do it? _____

_____

_____

---

* * * * *

Changing Negative Thoughts to Positive

An additional technique you can use when you have a flashback is to change the negative thoughts that occur after the flashback (e.g., I'm a failure for having this flashback; I really couldn't protect myself) into more positive thoughts. This is done through self-dialogue. Say to yourself, if you are afraid after a flashback, "This is now, not then; I did everything I could do (to protect myself) during the (traumatic event). I survived then and I will survive now."

Exercise: My Preferred Flashback Technique

What have you learned about your flashbacks and how to control or deal with them through doing these exercises? _____

_____

_____

Which exercise(s) helped you most? _____

_____

* * * * *

Nightmares and Dreams of the Trauma

You may have recurrent dreams that have some aspects of the trauma. Perhaps these dreams do not scare you, or they may be nightmares that wake you and leave you feeling fearful and panicked. Sometimes dreams about traumatic events can actually give you information about what happened to you.

A woman once had dreams about a face without a body. This face appeared in her dream on many, many occasions. The face was very dark complexioned and had a mustache and scars of pimples on the cheeks. She had no idea if the face actually belonged to a person; she knew no one that fit its shape and appearance. After years of therapy, the woman was ready to confront her older brother about the sexual abuse he perpetrated on her. She sat him down and spoke firmly what she had practiced over and over in the therapist's office—how he had harmed her and disrupted her life. The brother began to cry. He said that he had hoped she had not remembered what he had done to her when she was under eight years of age. He begged her forgiveness and then said that he needed to "come clean and tell her about the rest of the stuff." The woman was baffled by his comment. "What do you mean?" she asked her brother. He began to tell her of taking her into an attic above a deserted store with a group of his friends. One of his friends, a dark complexioned teen with a mustache and scars from acne, raped her. Her memory of the rape only occurred in her dreams, only in the face of the rapist.

The flashback-healing protocol based on dual awareness (see "Exercise: Practicing Dual Awareness" above) can be adapted to use with nightmares that may be traumatic flashbacks. You may use it as a ritual before sleep to prepare for any nightmares that may occur, or you may keep it beside your bed to use when you need it.

Exercise: Dealing with Nightmares

Say these things to yourself, preferably aloud, before you go to bed. Or, if you awake with a nightmare, be sure to try to ground yourself before you do any work on what you dreamed (see technique 5 in the section "Containment and Traumatic Memories" above for quick grounding ideas).

I am going to awaken in the night feeling _____ ,
(insert the name of the anticipated emotion, usually fear) and I will be sensing in my body

_____ , _____ ,

_____ , _____

(describe your anticipated bodily sensations; name at least three) because I will be remembering _____ (identify the trauma by name only—no details). At
the same time, I will look around where I am now in _____ (the
current year), here _____ , (name the place where you will be). I will see
_____ (describe some of the things that you see right
now, in this place), and so I will know _____ (identify the
trauma again by name only) is not happening anymore.

✳ ✳ ✳ ✳ ✳

Baker and Salston (1993) discuss ways to deal with dreams through dream preparation. In dream preparation, you follow a cognitive (thinking) procedure before you go to sleep, recognizing that you may dream a distressing dream during sleep. When the dream occurs, you write it down, talk it through, and rewrite its ending, as a means to take control of the dream. Then you do relaxation exercises and go back to sleep. Baker and Salston also suggest that you might write out your nightmares in detail and then rewrite the ending as a way to take additional power and control. The following exercise is adapted from Baker.

Exercise: Nightmare Form 1

Describe your trauma-related nightmare in the space below (if you need more space, use your journal). Describe it in as much detail as possible, including the scene, any associated feelings, and as many sensory items as you can possibly remember (smells, sensations on your skin, sounds, sights, tastes). If you have more than one nightmare about the trauma, photocopy this page and use a different sheet for each (adapted from Baker, in Baker and Salston 1993).

_____

_____

_____

_____

_____

_____

Is your nightmare an exact reenactment of the traumatic event? Yes / No (circle the appropriate answer)

Now think of ways to change the nightmare's ending: _____

_____

_____

What new information does the nightmare give you that you can use to build an understanding of what happened to you? _____

_____

_____

How has the nightmare helped you or helped you to respond differently to your trauma?

_____

_____

_____

* * * * *

Triggers: Reminders of Trauma across the Senses

A trigger is a piece of an event that intrudes into the present and reminds you of what happened in your past. When you react to a trigger of a traumatic event, your adrenal glands get aroused and memories of the traumatic event get activated, as do emotions associated with the event. These reactions may occur even when you do not recall the exact traumatic event—the physiological reactions can get resurrected by themselves (Matsakis 1994a). Triggers may exist for nontraumatic events, as well; for example, smelling brownies cooking may trigger pleasant memories of childhood. However, traumatic triggers are often unpleasant or frightening. They may lead to a flashback or to feelings of anxiety, panic, fear, anger, rage, confusion, shakiness, or numbness, or to a sense of spacing out or dissociation. They can retraumatize you.

It can be helpful to develop a list of triggers that lead to flashbacks or to the unpleasant feelings associated with trauma. Once you have identified your triggers and are aware of them, you will be more able to bring them under control, and even choose not to react to them. In your journal, you may write about, draw, collage, or otherwise represent triggers of your traumatic event(s). In the next few pages you will also be asked to write down your reactions to those triggers when you experience them. It is important to keep some type of record of when the flashback occurred after exposure to the trigger, and of where you were, what you were doing, who was with you, and what exactly happened. Once you have identified your triggers (or at least have begun to keep a trigger list), you can then learn how to avoid or defuse them in less time. It is also important that you identify ways that you got past the triggered flashbacks or feelings if they occurred previously. Identifying any small sign of returning to the present can help you control triggered reactions.

Journal Exercise: My Trigger List

This exercise has three parts: the list, your past reaction to your triggers, and you ideas for future responses.

1. In your notebook or journal, write about or list your triggers using the following topics.

   - triggers associated with what I saw

   - triggers associated with what I heard

   - triggers associated with what I smelled

   - triggers associated with what I touched or with what touched me

   - triggers associated with what I tasted

   - triggers associated with certain places

   - triggers associated with certain persons. (If a person is a trigger, try to determine what specific behavior, characteristics, or attitudes of the person trigger you. Then look at the specific aspects of the trauma that are triggered by this person, and at how the person relates to the traumatic event(s). Triggers might relate to the age of a particular person, e.g., the person may now be at the age with which you associate the traumatic event.

   - triggers associated with nature or time (e.g., weather, seasons, time of day)

2. In the next eight pages of your journal, write down your various reactions to triggers you have experienced. How do your more recent reactions compare to the reactions you have had in the past? What good things happened in those reactions? Did you experience any positive emotions or have any pleasant memories? What bad things happened? How likely do you believe it is that you will experience the trigger again? Use the following format, writing one topic at the top of each page:

   The positive and negative ways I have reacted to triggers associated with what I saw [heard, smelled, touched, tasted during] in the [the places, persons, or aspects of nature or time associated with] traumatic events are:

3. Now think of ways you might deal with each of these triggers in the future to take power away from them. Write a response for each of the eight trigger areas on a separate page in your journal or notebook.

* * * * *

Managing Trigger Events

When you learn to take more control over your triggers, the trauma loses some of its power and control over you. In controlling your triggers, it is important to plan ahead and find ways to deal with them before they occur. It is also important to identify persons who might help you deal with the triggers. Power (1992a) lists ways to manage triggers that may help you plan your own strategies and techniques. They include:

- relaxation exercises

- breathing exercises

- appropriate medication

- contact with supportive others

- establishing manageable lists of priorities

- avoiding extra stress

- structuring your life to avoid contact with certain specific triggers

As Matsakis noted, "the goal is to manage the trigger event, not . . . have no negative feelings or sensations about it" (1994b, 147). As you plan ways to deal with the specific triggers you named, it might be best to start by working on triggers that you believe are easiest to manage or control. Some triggers, such as seeing your perpetrator face-to-face, may take months or years to learn to overcome, if you are ever able to manage them. As you plan your strategies, think of your history with each particular trigger, the symptoms that the trigger evokes, the specific fears associated with the trigger, and the coping mechanisms you will use.

Remember, it is your choice how you deal with each and every trigger you have listed in your journal. You can never avoid everything that triggers you. Thus, as Meichenbaum notes, it is important to control your own inner experience rather than try to avoid everything that triggers your automatic responses (1994). You can disarm a trigger when you understand how the past is not the present.

Trigger work can be very stressful. It always involves some type of processing of the feelings associated with the trauma so you can know they can no longer hurt you. You may always turn to some of the self-soothing exercises in chapter 2 should you begin to feel overwhelmed. You may also use these calming exercises when you are aware that a trigger is about to happen. The following exercise is designed to help you with a specific trigger that you have chosen from the previous pages. If you want to deal with more than one trigger, photocopy this exercise and use one copy for each trigger. If some triggers are too difficult to face alone, do not do this exercise, or do it only in the presence of your therapist or in a group situation designed to work on trauma. Please remember, too, that you cannot get rid of the power of a trigger over night. It takes time to substitute new behaviors for old ones.

The Trigger Mapping Ladder

There are many ways to represent triggers. One of these, the trigger mapping ladder, was developed by one of the authors of this book as she worked with a group of persons diagnosed with dissociative identity disorder (formerly called multiple personality disorder). The ladder is a diagram showing that trigger events lead to an escalation of tension, which causes many different systems in a person to react and may lead to retraumatization. Thoughts and feelings, physical cues and actions can either heat up or cool down triggers. Cooling down the trigger response involves taking away its power. It helps you make the connection between your triggers and your responses, look at your thoughts and feelings, calm yourself, and find meaning in the entire process.

This process can help you bring control into your life by separating the past from the present and changing the way you react to your trigger(s). Approach each rung of the ladder slowly and calmly, and take small steps up and down it. Some images and symbols of your triggers can lead you to more information about your traumatic experiences, serving as clues to what happened to you and why you react as you do.

Exercise: Dealing with My Trigger

If you want to deal with more than one trigger, photocopy this exercise and use one copy for each trigger.

1. When you distract yourself from the power and influence of the trigger, that trigger eventually will have little or no power over your life in the present. I choose to distract myself from _____ (name the trigger) by _____

_____

Some other ways I may distract myself (examples might include listening to, singing, or whistling you favorite song as soon as the trigger starts; covering your ears or using earplugs; talking to yourself about what is real or not real, or about the present): _____

_____

_____

2. I choose to practice staying present in the now when I experience this trigger by grounding or using other techniques I have learned.

For example, I may ignore _____ (name the trigger).

I may also _____ .

Or, I may name five, then four, then three, then two, then one thing(s) I see, hear, or smell around me: _____

_____

_____

3. Now, after you have tried one or more of these ways to gain control of a trigger, write about that experience and how it felt:

I was _____ when _____ (name the trigger) occurred.

When I began to have a reaction to _____ (name the trigger), I chose to (distract myself, ignore it, stay present) by _____ .

When _____ (name the trigger) began to fade in its power, I felt _____ and then I (describe what you did) _____

_____

* * * * *

The Trigger Mapping Ladder

Going up the left side of the ladder are four phrases. Starting at the bottom, next to where it says "Trigger Event," write in the name of an internal or external trigger—a sight, sound, smell, time of year, thought, or other event or thing. Above the event or thing, write in what types of reactions you have as you become aware of your reaction to the trigger. What in your body gets tense? What emotions surface? Moving up one step to the space marked "Escalation of tension," write in how you react. You may not have a response for each one of these sections, but write in as many as you can. Once the trigger has led to your reaction, what is that reaction? Do you have a full-blown flashback? Do you feel uneasy? Do you break into a cold sweat or begin to cry? Do you feel as if you are retraumatized?

On the right side of the ladder, going from top to bottom, are a series of phrases describing behaviors that may help you deescalate the trigger. What might you do for each of them? What thoughts and feelings might help you to take away the trigger's power? One might be "I am in the present; the trigger is from my past and it is not happening now." Another response might be "I need to take five deep cleansing breaths." Again, you may not have a response to each phrase but put in whatever you can that might help you lessen the trigger's hold on you.

Here's an example of how the ladder might work for a particular situation. Let's say you are a survivor of sexual abuse. You have to go to family function, your father's birthday party, and know that your grandfather, who abused you, will be present. As you think about the party, you notice that you begin to have escalating tension both in your body and in your thoughts and feelings. How is your body reacting—where does the tension begin? At first, your shoulders get tight and your palms begin to sweat. Then you get a pounding headache and you begin to remember a specific abusive encounter that leads to pain in your lower abdomen. At the same time, you have thoughts of wanting to escape, wanting to avoid going to the party. You feel frightened and may even begin to experience a panic attack. You may even hear some of your grandfather's words in your mind and your thoughts about him swim quickly.

What can you do? How can you combat all these feelings and physical symptoms? On the right side of the ladder are spaces for you to de-escalate. You may say to yourself, "This is now, that was then; I am an adult now and can protect myself; he is a little old man." You may also recognize that the physical cues you are having reflect back to the early abuse. As you process what is going on, you might begin to look at what you can do to combat both the physical reactions and the feelings. You might set up a strategy to keep out of direct contact with him. You may ask your husband/partner to run interference. You may decide to approach him and warn him to leave you alone. You may even think of ways to avoid the party. Then you can begin to self-soothe. You may take deep breaths, go for a walk, listen to music, or write out a script to say to your abuser. As you calm, think of things that can bring you back to the here and now. When you feel calmer, look at the process and how you have helped yourself. Realize that this process is difficult and may take time (and practice) to work. Trying to do the process is the first step to overcoming major reactions to triggers!

Using Activities and Anchors to Reduce Triggers

Another way to gain some control over your traumatic triggers, dreams, nightmares, and intrusive thoughts is to participate in activities that can give you a break from reexperiencing your trauma. Helpful activities, according to Rothschild (2000), are those that need your concentration and attention so that the intrusions of trauma don't take over. It is easy for intrusive thoughts to wander in while you're watching a movie on the VCR. However, they do not come in as easily if you are doing something that demands attention and body awareness. For example, you may iron clothes, keeping enough awareness of what you are doing that you don't burn them or yourself.

Another way to help yourself is to use an *anchor*. Rothschild describes an anchor as "a concrete, observable resource," or one that is outside your own mind (2000, 91). That resource may be a beloved person or pet, a place (e.g., your home), an object, or an activity. The resource helps you feel relief and well-being in your body; thinking about it can serve as a braking tool for a trigger or intrusive thought without changing reality. Your safe place, which you described previously, is another anchor that can provide protection for you.

What are some activities you could use to control your intrusive thought? _____

_____

_____

What are your own personal anchors? _____

_____

Exposing Yourself Safely to Your Past Traumas

You may have noticed that we have not asked you to describe your traumatic memories in great detail. Such exposure is more of a task for therapy. We do not want to retraumatize you by overwhelming you with memories. The closest we have come to directly exposing you to the trauma has been asking you to write about what happened to you. Putting your traumatic experiences into a story with a beginning, middle, and end helps diffuse the strong emotions associated with the traumas (Meichenbaum 1994).

Direct exposure therapy, where you look at your traumatic memories in detail, needs to be done under the guidance of a professional in a course of anywhere from nine to fourteen sessions of sixty to ninety minutes each. Direct exposure therapy takes you back into your traumatic experience and asks you to tell:

- when the traumatic event happened

- how long it lasted

- the entire story, from the start of the incident to after it was over

- everything of which you are aware about the setting and the event

- about any earlier incident(s) similar to the one you are describing

- your interpretation of the impact the event has on you at the present moment

All of the description is done in the present tense and in great detail. Direct exposure therapy needs a great deal of preparation in order for you, as the client, to endure the process without experiencing overwhelming anxiety, suicidal thoughts, or intense fear. The motto behind doing this work is "no pain, no gain." However, the extent of pain that can be caused by exposure therapy or overexposure to the traumatic event is too great to include it as part of the work in this workbook. This description of exposure therapy is included here merely as information about another way to process what has happened to you.

Trigger Mapping

| Connection Between → Trigger and Response | Accessing → Thoughts and Feelings | Use of Self- → Soothing | Calming → Down | Returning to a calm state |

Cooling Down

Outside (physical cues and actions)

Inside (thoughts and feelings)

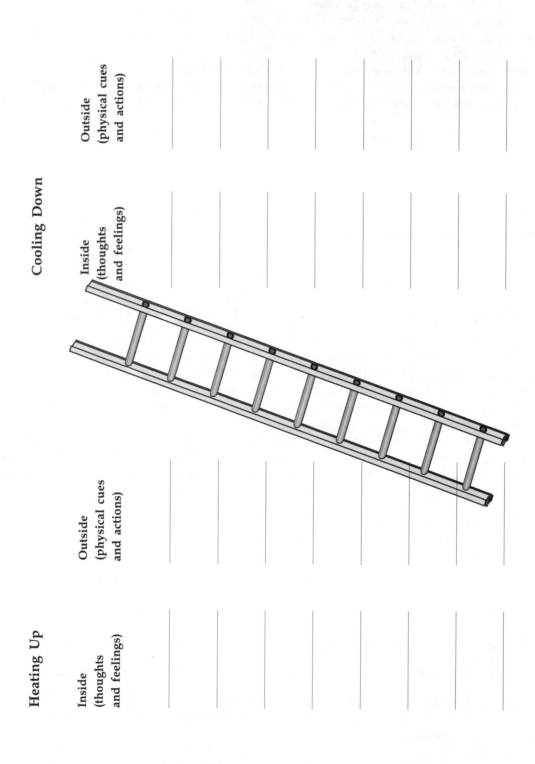

Heating Up

Inside (thoughts and feelings)

Outside (physical cues and actions)

Trigger Event → Escalation of → Reactions in many → Possible
Tension   or all systems   Retraumatizatio

The Flower Diagram

If you want to take a part of a memory or an entire memory and look at it in more detail, you might use the flower diagram below as your guide. When analyzing any memory using the flower diagram, you have six separate sections to examine: sensory information; beliefs; body reactions; emotions; wants; and actions. Try not to allow yourself to reexperience it as you write in your answers; try to imagine you are looking at it on a TV or movie screen.

Exercise: My Flower Diagram

At the center of the diagram, write in the memory that you wish to examine. In the first petal of the flower, write in any sensory experiences that come to mind when you think about the memory. What smells, sights, sounds, or touch sensations come to mind? In the next petal, write in your thoughts and beliefs about the trauma. What messages were told to you before, during, and after that trauma that you have incorporated into your own mind (your introjects)? What conclusions have you reached about the trauma (for example, I believe it was my fault; I believe I can never be safe; I believe that I caused the event to happen; I believe that I was not to blame for anything that happened)? In the next petal, record how your body reacted during the traumatic event. Did you freeze, run away, cry, or numb yourself, for example? In the fourth petal, write down any emotions that you can remember having. Were you terrified? Embarrassed? Shocked? In the fifth petal, write down any "wants" you had during the trauma. Did you want to dissociate? Did you want to just go away, or did you want to attack the perpetrator? Finally, in the last petal, record any actions you took. Did you choose to escape through dissociation? Did you fight back? Did you participate in some way? If you do not have total recall or even partial recall of any of the sections, you may have some degree of what is called traumatic amnesia, or forgetting. Just write in what you do remember. If you need more space, you may use additional pages in your notebook to record the information. Remember, try to keep a distance from the memory and the traumatic event as you complete this exercise.

Exercise: What I Learned from This Chapter

In this chapter, you have learned some ways to deal with the intrusive, reexperiencing aspects of PTSD. These are only some of the many different techniques available. Hopefully, through practice and effort, they will work (at least to some degree) for you. Remember, you can refer back to the exercises in this chapter whenever you need to do so.

What have you learned about yourself through the work you have done in this chapter?

_____

_____

How did the techniques provided in chapter 2 help you calm yourself if you needed to do so?

_____

_____

* * * * *

The diagram is adapted from Miller, Wackman, Nunnally, and Miller (1989).

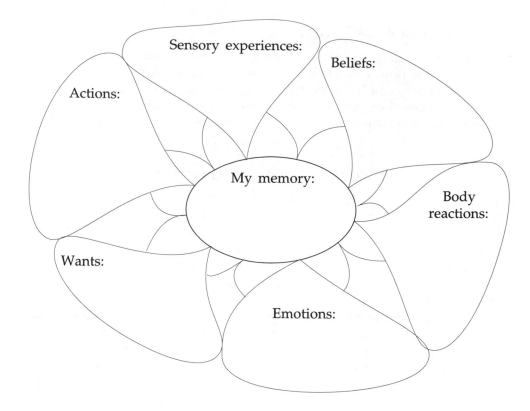

Avoiding Avoidance

There are other ways to cope with traumatic events. One way is to try to avoid or deny what happened to you. Some denial is natural but, at times, avoiding the impact on you of your traumatic events can be detrimental to you. The next chapter looks at some ways you can lessen your avoidance.

5

Coping with Trauma with Less Avoidance and Denial

It is not unusual to want to avoid remembering or reexperiencing the traumatic event(s) that happened to you. Why on earth would you want to put yourself through it all again? Why would you want to desensitize yourself (learn to deal with all your triggers, thoughts, memories)? If you were in a hurricane at the beach and lost your home, why would you ever want to live by the ocean again? If you were on a plane that almost crashed, or that did crash, why would you ever even dream of traveling anywhere other than by car or train? If you were hurt in a certain neighborhood, why would you ever even think of going there again, even if your relatives live there or it is near your place of work?

If you refer back to the description of PTSD found in chapter 1 of this workbook, you will see the list of avoidance-related behaviors and traits listed under the third criterion of the diagnosis. Which of them do you use to survive? Do you avoid places, persons, or situations that remind you of your trauma? Do you isolate yourself from others? Do you try to keep your emotions under control to the degree that you don't let yourself feel? Have you lost interest in social activities or intimacy? Do you depend on the use of substances or addictive behaviors to numb yourself out? Have you desexualized yourself? Do you instantaneously suppress things that in any way remind you of your traumatic experiences or of the feelings that you had during or after them?

Exercise: How I Avoid Traumatic Reminders

If you answered yes to any of the questions above, you may want to take a few minutes and use space provided to describe which behaviors you do and how you do them.

Do you feel unconnected with any part of yourself? If so, what part(s)? _____

_____

_____

Do you find that you have little or no recall of some aspects of the trauma(s)? Which aspects?

_____

_____

Do you have a future vision for yourself, or do you believe that your life in the future will be short? _____

_____

* * * * *

The Practical Function of Avoidance

Your affirmative (yes) answers to any of the questions in the preceding exercise mean that you do have symptoms of avoidance surrounding what happened to you. It often takes a great deal of energy to avoid dealing with any traumatic memories, triggers, nightmares, or other reminders of traumatic events you may experience. You may take major steps to avoid places, people, or events that remind you of what happened to you. You may tell yourself over and over, "I'm fine; it didn't bother me at all" while at the same time, on the inside, you know that you are still feeling all the impacts of the trauma. You may also worry about or focus on other things to try to occupy your mind so you don't think about the traumatic events. Pennebaker, who designed the writing exercise about trauma in chapter 3, found that people who try to suppress their intrusive thoughts, images, dreams, and memories end up having more threatening and more frequent intrusions that go beyond the actual trauma and involve thoughts of aggression, death, illness, failure, and other dreadful events (2000).

Perhaps you do not have the words to express what happened to you. Perhaps there *are* no words that can express your horror. Some avoidance of traumatic reminders or memories is healthy. But how do you know when avoidance is healthy and when it is not? If avoidance protects you from being traumatized further, then it is healthy. If you need to do something that is very important to you, and consciousness of the trauma would cause you to have so much pain that you could not do what you needed to do, then some degree of avoidance is healthy.

For example, George is giving a speech for his English class. He has been assigned the topic of family violence. His wife is a very verbally and physically abusive person and he is working in therapy on controlling his angry reactions to her tirades. If he allows himself to feel all the pain he associates with this topic when he does his class presentation, he will be retraumatized. He chooses to numb out his emotions, gives his speech, gets an "A," and then talks about it with his therapist. He ends up crying because his classmates could not understand how a male could be the recipient of violence.

Dennis is nineteen. He was molested by his stepfather, as was his sister. His stepfather was a minister and, when his sister revealed her abuse, he was defrocked. He shares his abuse history with his mother and fears that something terrible will happen to him because he has told. Two days after he tells, his sister is killed in a car crash. Her stepfather gets special permission from the bishop to preach at her funeral. Dennis is a pallbearer and must be there. He uses his ability to dissociate to get him through the funeral and deal with his abusive stepfather's eulogy.

Numbing and Dissociation

Matsakis notes that many trauma survivors do all they can to avoid being in triggering situations or relationships in order to avoid being hyperaroused (1998, 103–104). Instead, they numb and shut down at least partially or they dissociate. Dissociation is a way to protect yourself from perceived threat and the bad emotions that are associated with what happened to you. Dissociation is described in detail in chapter 9. Please turn to that chapter if you experience dissociation and do the exercises found there. Among the consequences of numbing are:

1. blunted emotional and physical pain, pleasure, and responsiveness; loss of interest in the world and things that previously brought pleasure to you

2. inability to discriminate between pain and pleasure (when you do not feel emotions, it is easier for you to be revictimized)

3. poor memory; clouded thinking

4. lack of emotional responsiveness leading to feelings of shame and the belief that one is shameful

5. increased need for stimulants and stimulation in order to feel alive; tendency to take risks of all kinds to create excitement and counteract the dead feeling inside you

6. self-mutilating as a way to feel alive

7. episodes of panic and rage

8. retreating from life

9. letting your emotional and physical reactions guide you

10. feeling detached from others

11. being unable to experience life because you feel empty inside

12. having no interest in sex; having sexual dysfunction

13. having no energy; feeling apathetic (not caring) and lethargic (being tired all the time)

14. experiencing mental sluggishness

Do any of these happen to you? Use the following exercise to explore when and where they do. The exercise lists a number of ways to numb yourself so that you do not feel or do not face the traumatic events that happened to you. If you use any of them, consider seeking support and help from others, such as professional trauma therapists, supportive family members, understanding friends, and fellow survivors. This exercise can then be something you share with supportive others, particularly a therapist.

Exercise: How I Numb

Put a check mark by every one of the ways you numb.

I numb myself by:

_____ self-mutilating to the extent that I cause real harm to myself

_____ separating myself from my body

_____ becoming out of touch with my surroundings

_____ staring off into space blankly for more than a minute

_____ becoming an observer of my present situation rather than a participant in that situation

_____ escaping into fantasy or daydreaming

_____ using magical thinking excessively (thinking you can control with your thoughts events unrelated to you)

_____ being unable to concentrate

_____ being unaware of potential dangers in my environment

_____ participating in high-risk activities or play (list which ones)

_____ falling asleep even when I'm around others

_____ exhibiting compulsive behaviors, including workaholism

_____ compulsively or addictively using drugs or alcohol

_____ acting much younger than I am

_____ seeing shadowy black figures or ghostlike figures, particularly when I am falling asleep or just waking

_____ being confused much of the time

_____ acting like a robot; being on autopilot

_____ feeling as if I am watching myself from outside my body

_____ rocking back and forth to soothe myself

Describe when, where, why, and how you use these ways to numb. _____

_____

_____

_____

What do your answers tell you about yourself and how you avoid your traumatic experiences or memories of your traumas? _____

_____

_____

_____

* * * * *

If you find that you checked several of the items in the preceding exercise, it is important that you focus more on personal self-care and safety than on exploring the memories of your traumatic events at this time. If you find that you are frequently numbing out, dissociating, or avoiding, you may want to ask yourself regularly, "Where am I now (in reality)?" rather than "Where did I go?" This will help you return to the present time and remind yourself where you are in the physical world. It is also important for you to identify the triggers that lead you to numbing, as well as the functions the numbing serves.

The triggers that cause me to numb out include: _____

_____

Numbing helps me to: _____

_____

Working to Reduce Numbing

As you process your traumatic events, as you began to do in chapter 4, you will see that numbing will become less necessary. If you numb because you are afraid of feeling the emotions associated with what happened to you, then it is important that you begin to allow yourself to feel in little doses. If you are extremely anxious, you may want to take medication to help reduce that anxiety.

There are ways you can reduce your attempts to avoid and numb; much of this information is found in later chapters of the book. First, allow yourself to look at what happened to you without going into the whole memory. You may use Pennebaker's writing technique in chapter 3 to help you. You may also want to develop an outline or short version of your trauma as a beginning, using the following exercise. If you are a victim of long-lasting traumatic events, please skip this exercise and turn to the later chapters that deal with disorders of extreme stress. You have had too many bad things happen to you to look at them one by one.

Exercise: An Outline of My Trauma

Before the trauma, I felt _____

Then, suddenly, _____ (name the trauma) happened.

During _____ (name the trauma) I (did or was)

_____

I also felt _____

_____

I was able to control _____

_____

I was unable to control _____

_____

When _____ (name the trauma) stopped, I was

_____

_____

* * * * *

Sometimes numbing out is necessary as a way to protect yourself from being absolutely overwhelmed by all of the bad things that happened to you. If you feel helpless in the face of your memories and therefore want to avoid them, use the following exercise to think of ways that you can take some control over your life in other areas.

Exercise: Areas Where I Have Control

I have control over my life:

_____ at work (if so, how and when?): _____

_____

_____ at home (if so, how and when?): _____

_____

_____ with children (if so, how and when?): _____

_____

_____ with pets (if so, how and when?): _____

_____

_____ at play (if so, how and when?): _____

_____

_____ when doing my spiritual practices (if so, how and when?): _____

_____

* * * * *

Keeping Safe While Facing Your Fears

If you do not feel safe enough to work on any of your memories, please turn back to chapter 2 and work on modifying and challenging your present beliefs about safety. If you need to look at your beliefs about trust, please turn to chapter 13 which looks at how to build positive relationships.

If you are going to face your traumas at all, it is important that you learn to look at yourself in a realistic way and learn how to respond to threats in an accurate, realistic manner. What are your fears? What do you believe will happen if you begin to look at your traumas? Do you believe that someone will come and get you if you tell? Do you believe that someone will still punish you if you talk about what happened? Do you believe that there are persons out there who still have control over your life and who can hurt you if you deal with your traumas?

Annette was abused by her father beginning at age four. She continued to be molested until she was eighteen years of age and married. She told her mother about her abuse when she was twelve and her mother beat her. Annette finally confronted her father about the abuse in a therapy session with her therapist present. She had made a tape of what she remembered and had played it over and over with her therapist. They had talked about her memories, worked on what she would say, and practiced her confrontation. Her mother came with her father to the session. Her father admitted what he had done and Annette taped his response. Still, she continued to fear his retaliation and what the confrontation would mean. She got suicidal and ended up in a hospital. She has now taken the tape to the police and the police want to prosecute her father. Still, she fears what he will do to her and that she will lose any contact with her mother and siblings because she told.

Tolerating Your Fears

Learning to deal with what happened to you means learning to tolerate painful emotions without needing to hurt yourself or trying to numb them out. Some of the emotions that get associated with trauma are grief, guilt, shame, and fear. They are described in more detail in chapter 7. There are exercises in that chapter that can help you deal with these emotions. Probably the hardest emotion to deal with is trigger-based fear. Again, identifying your triggers and then working on ways to take away their power is a very important way to give you control. If you have not done them already, go back to chapter 4 and use the exercise "Journal Exercise: My Trigger List" to identify your triggers.

Exercise: My Most Frightening Triggers

Now, list the five triggers which cause you the most fear or pain, beginning with the worst.

1. _____

2. _____

3. _____

4. _____

5. _____

* * * * *

In the next exercise, you will choose three things you can do for each of these triggers to help you gain control of them. For example, if you are triggered by the smell of a particular cologne that your abuser wore, you might:

a. Go to a perfume store and smell different colognes; include the one you fear as one of those you put on a tester strip. Take the strip and rip it up or stomp on it after you are done.

b. Buy a bottle of the cologne and smash it.

c. Take the cologne and spray it on something you really like to change your association with the cologne.

Exercise: Controlling My Most Frightening Triggers

Choose three actions to help you control each of your 5 triggers:

Trigger 1: _____

a. _____

b. _____

c. _____

Trigger 2: _____

a. _____

b. _____

c. _____

Trigger 3: _____

a. _____

b. _____

c. _____

Trigger 4: _____

a. _____

b. _____

c. _____

Trigger 5: _____

a. _____

b. _____

c. _____

Now that you have listed what you can do, choose one or two triggers to work on, beginning at the bottom of your list with trigger 5—the least terrible trigger. Do what you have said would work.

Write what happened when you did the three things: _____

_____

_____

What has this exercise taught you about your triggers and the power they can have over you? _____

_____

✳ ✳ ✳ ✳ ✳

Another way to deal with triggers is to learn new activities that you will enjoy, and combine some part of a trigger in the activity, making the trigger become something positive. These techniques take time. Do not expect a trigger to lose its power overnight.

If looking at your triggers is painful, you might find ways to look at your fears indirectly, including writing (letters, journals, poetry), doing art projects (drawing, collaging, photo journaling), dancing or participating in other types of creative movement, playing or listening to music, and constructing (objects, structures, rituals). What activities might you do to help you express your traumatic experiences indirectly? _____

_____

_____

Other Ways to Reduce Numbing

Trauma experts, such as Wilson (Wilson, Friedman, and Lindy 2001) and Courtois (1988), gives us other ways to deal with numbing:

1. Lessen your efforts to try to avoid memories of the trauma.

2. Increase your contact with others; join some type of social organization.

3. Lessen your use of self-medication of any kind.

4. Work on your belief systems (perhaps using a workbook such as *Life After Trauma: A Workbook for Healing* by Rosenbloom and Williams).

5. Learn to appraise the threat in situations using your head, not your emotions.

6. Look at the losses trauma has caused you and develop a plan to work through them.

7. Work on identifying triggers that cause you to "numb out."

8. Learn to stay more present in your safe place.

9. Use the grounding techniques you have learned to separate the past trauma from the present.

10. Learn to pace yourself and how you deal with your trauma; set up a certain time period during a day or week to work on your traumas; journal or do a trauma-inspired craft.

11. Develop a flowers diagram about a part of the trauma that bothers you most and that you most want to avoid (use the flower diagram exercise at the end of chapter 4, or make a copy in your journal or notebook).

Exercise: What I Learned from This Chapter

How have the exercises in this chapter helped you face more of what happened to you?

_____

_____

_____

_____

_____

6

The Physical Side of PTSD

Trauma overstimulates your autonomic nervous system. This overstimulation means your arousal levels are chronically high, which can have serious impacts on your body. These can include having difficulty falling or staying asleep; feeling irritable or having outbursts of anger; having concentration and memory problems; being hypervigilant; being startled easily; and feeling that you have no reserve of energy to help you heal. If you find it is too difficult for you to protect yourself, your body may begin to shut down through illness or even through dissociation. Some survivors of trauma seem to express the trauma through immune system–related illnesses such as chronic fatigue, fibromyalgia, irritable bowel syndrome, headaches, and severe tension. Identifying triggers, as you have in the previous two chapters, can help you control your body—these triggers can lead to hypervigilance and jumpiness as well as to fear and terror.

The body of a trauma survivor—your body—needs soothing and care. This chapter helps you look at and deal with some of the physiological symptoms of the increased arousal involved in PTSD. Doing the exercises provided can help you calm down or reconnect with and get a measure of control over some of your body's reactions. The end goal of these exercises is to help you normalize how your body reacts so that you can return to some level of calm and order, or *homeostasis*.

If you have symptoms of any type of physical disease or if your physical symptoms have persisted for longer than a few days or weeks, seek medical care from a physician who understands the impact of trauma.

Techniques for Sleeping

Many survivors of trauma have trouble falling asleep or staying asleep. In fact, Matsakis says that "sleeping problems are perhaps the most persistent of PTSD symptoms" (1994a, 167). To be sure, getting to sleep and staying asleep can be a challenge even if you don't suffer from PTSD.

It is possible for anyone to sleep better by improving their sleeping environment: by removing triggers from that environment, creating an atmosphere conducive to sleep, and using good sleep practices. As a trauma survivor, it is important that you prepare yourself for sleep. One way is to avoid seeing, hearing, and thinking about traumatic things before going to bed. If you watch television or videos late at night, choose things that are light and free from the triggers of your traumas. For example, if you've survived a natural disaster, don't choose something with sirens or fire or devastation. Think about positive things in your life as you go to bed. Put on soothing music or a tape of waves, sounds, a gentle rain, or other soothing sounds. You may also want to try a different sleep schedule. If you are a "night" person, wait until midnight to go to bed and then get up at seven or eight if possible, if you need that much sleep. Try to avoid using over-the-counter or nonprescribed drugs or substances to numb yourself into sleeping. However, you may turn to a cup of warm milk or some turkey (both of which contain L-tryptophan, a soothing amino acid) to help you relax. Or you may take melatonin, if your doctor agrees that it does not interfere with any medications you take.

If you were traumatized during sleep or in a bedroom, it is very important for you to identify any parts of that bedroom or of sleep that might trigger you. Develop a trigger list for sleep or for the room (see the exercise "Journal Exercise: My Trigger List" in chapter 4). For example, if your room now happens to be the same color that the room you were traumatized in was, you may paint it a different color. If your furniture is arranged in a similar fashion, you may change that arrangement. Begin to change things that are possible to change.

If your partner is not a safe sleeper, you may want to talk with him or her about alternatives, including using twin beds or agreeing on ways to wake up your partner when there are triggers.

Kelly liked to sleep on a mat in the corner of her bedroom. She couldn't understand why, in the middle of the night, she would leave her queen-size bed and end up on the floor on this mat. As she began to work on her past traumas, she realized that she had been molested on a queen-size bed as a child. She began to work on ways to make her bed and bedroom safe: she got rid of the queen-size bed and bought a twin bed, which she put against a wall. She then slept with her back to that wall to protect herself.

Researchers have worked out many ways that might improve your chances of a good sleep. The following list is adapted from Matsakis (1994a) and from the Metropolitan Washington Council of Governments (2001). If there are things that have worked for you in the past and have made your sleeping easier, try them again. If there are things that have not worked, even if others suggest them, don't try them.

1. Physically exercise sometime during the day, but not right before bed.

2. Listen to relaxing music.

3. Listen to a relaxation tape.

4. Practice relaxation techniques before going to bed.

5. Pray.

6. Medicate with prescribed medications.

7. Talk to others if the others can soothe you or calm you before you go to bed; don't argue.

8. Write or talk into a tape about your day, but not about your traumatic experiences.

9. Eat something light and avoid caffeine.

10. Try not to drink anything in the two hours before going to bed, so you don't have to get up to go to the bathroom.

11. Do a boring task.

12. Read a very boring book.

13. Get up at a set time, no matter what time you fall asleep.

14. Sleep in the same place; don't bed-hop or place hop (the bed is for sleeping, not the living room couch).

15. Set the thermostat at a comfortable, cool temperature.

16. Use a night-light if necessary.

17. Take a walk in the late afternoon or early evening to tire yourself out and raise your body temperature. Falling temperatures (after you stop your walk) sometimes make you sleepy.

18. If you find you have trouble falling asleep because you worry a lot, schedule a "worry time" during the day and use up that time at least two hours before you plan to go to bed.

19. Keep a record of the number of hours you sleep each day and how you feel after you have slept so that you can look for sleep patterns.

20. Check with your doctor to see if any medications you are taking get in the way of sleep.

21. Use a white noise machine or wear earplugs (if it is safe not to hear) to drown out noises that might get in the way of sleeping (e.g., the music from a noisy neighbor or street traffic noises).

22. Take a warm bath about four hours before bedtime; as your body cools down after your bath, you may find it easier to fall asleep.

23. Follow a set bedtime routine, such as the following:

    - choose a regular bedtime that works for your needs, and then go to bed at this time for at least one week

    - about two hours before that bedtime, use the ability you have to contain, numb, or avoid traumatic reminders to put away any issues about trauma recovery

    - do something relaxing

    - begin to get ready for bed at least an hour before your actual bedtime by doing your personal care routines (get your clothes out for the morning, brush your teeth)

    - check out your room and make sure it is safe and comfortable: check your closets, windows, and doors; put away anything that might trigger nightmares, flashbacks, or intrusive thoughts (pictures, drawings, belongings)

    - gather anything you want to have in bed with you (special cover, stuffed animal, pets)

    - continue to contain any thoughts and feelings that might trouble you

    - use a relaxation technique of some kind to help you get to sleep

    - lie down and give yourself permission to sleep

    - if you use music or a tape turn it on

    - close your eyes and go for it

Exercise: My Bedtime Plan

Use the space below to design your own bedtime plan. Be specific as to what you will do.

1. _____

2. _____

3. _____

4. _____

5. _____

6. _____

Try this plan for ten nights. After ten nights, come back to this page of your workbook and write down what happened to your sleep patterns. Did you sleep better? _____

_____

_____

_____

* * * * *

Another Sleep Routine

Baker and Salston (1993) suggest that you try the following sleep routine, which integrates several of the suggestions already made.

Before you try this strategy for the first time, come up with ten things you hate to do around your home. These things might be cleaning and defrosting a freezer, cleaning the toilet, dusting a room, balancing a checkbook, or similar things.

Two hours before going to bed, start preparing yourself. Tell yourself, "I am now going to get ready to go to bed and go to sleep." Take a warm bath or shower and get into your sleeping clothes. If you do not wear clothes to bed, get into a bathrobe until you are ready to turn out the light. Stop all liquid intake, with the exception of warm milk or a few sips of water. Now do a relaxing activity. Read a long historical novel, knit, listen to soft music. Don't watch TV or a video and don't watch the news.

Once you go to bed and turn out the light to go to sleep, you have thirty minutes maximum to get to sleep. You may choose to do a relaxation exercise during those thirty minutes if you find you do not fall asleep right away. If you are not asleep in thirty minutes, you have to get up and do the first thing on your list.

If you fall asleep and then wake up at some point during the night and can't seem to fall back asleep, you have fifteen minutes to get back to sleep. If you aren't asleep in fifteen minutes, you must do the first thing on the list and then go to bed. If you already did the first thing on the list earlier that night and then fell asleep, you are to do the second thing on the list, then go back to bed. Again, you have fifteen minutes to go to sleep. Continue doing the things on your list until you go to sleep and stay asleep.

Each night you can't sleep, begin again at the top of the list. Even if you have cleaned your refrigerator every night for five nights, on the sixth night you are to clean it again as if it were filthy. If this technique does not help you sleep soundly within four weeks, see your doctor and get some medication to help you sleep.

Exercise: My Ten Things to Do When I Can't Sleep

Now make your list. Remember, these are the ten things that you hate to do the most. They must be things to do inside your home that will not wake up others who are sleeping. Also, you must be able to complete them within about thirty minutes. If a chore will take longer than twenty to thirty minutes, break it down into parts. The one you hate the most should be number 1; you'll always start with this one when you can't sleep.

1. _____

2. _____

3. _____

4. _____

5. _____

6. _____

7. _____

8. _____

9. _____

10. _____

* * * * *

Good Sleep Hygiene

Saindon (2001) has suggested numerous self-help tips that include some of the previously listed sleep hints. She notes that sleep problems are a common symptom for those recovering from traumatic events and that many usual methods for falling asleep may no longer work after the occurrence of a trauma. Instead, thoughts of reenactment, rescue, or renewal, nightmares, and sleep terrors may interfere with the sleep cycle. To practice "good sleep hygiene," she recommends:

1. No reading or watching TV in bed. Reading and watching TV are waking activities. Use your bed only for sleeping. (If you can't sleep after being in bed for thirty minutes, use the routine suggested above.)

2. Go to bed when you are sleepy or tired, not when it is your habit to go to bed. Don't nap during the day.

3. Wind down during the second half of the evening before bedtime. Don't get involved in anxiety-provoking activities or thoughts ninety minutes before bed, and don't exercise within three hours of bedtime.

4. Do at least five repetitions of deep breathing exercises before you go to bed.

5. Try to relax your muscles, beginning with your toes and ending with the top of your head.

6. Keep your room cool, not warm.

7. Counting sheep is stimulating; don't do it when you are lying in bed.

8. Don't use alcohol, drink coffee, or smoke cigarettes two to three hours before bedtime.

9. Add a positive, desired ending to any repetitive nightmares or bad dreams you realize you are having. Think of the dream before you go to sleep and add the new ending, in case it comes up again.

10. Write about your hopes and dreams every night before you go bed to free up your mind.

11. Listen to calming music or a self-hypnosis tape.

Body Sensations and Body Awareness

Developing body awareness possibly can help you lessen, and even eliminate, some trauma symptoms, restoring you to a more normal level of functioning. Body sensations may remind you of your prior traumas. If you are going to work with your own bodily sensations when they are triggered by trauma, it is important that you develop awareness of your body's sensations and what those sensations communicate to you. Does your body tell you when it is hungry, tired, and sad or when it is satiated, rested, and happy? How does it do so? If you cannot feel your body sensations, try the following exercise.

Exercise: My Body Sensations

Draw an outline of a gingerbread person below on the right side of the page. On that drawing, using the following colors to identify where your body feels:

Anger (red)

Sadness (blue)

Fear (black)

Calmness (pink)

Pain (orange)

Happiness or joy (yellow)

What does completing this exercise tell you about your body? What do you see in your drawing? Where do you carry your emotions? Any idea why? _____

_____

_____

* * * * *

Developing Body Awareness

Rothschild suggests the following exercise to develop basic body awareness (2000, 101–102).

1. Do not move. Notice the position in which you are sitting. See what sensations you notice through your whole body.

2. Are you comfortable as you continue to be immobile?

3. How do you know if you are comfortable or not? What bodily sensations indicate that you are comfortable or not?

4. Do you want to change your position? Notice the impulse but don't move.

5. Notice the source of your impulse to move. What part of your body would you move first? Don't move. Instead, follow the impulse to move back to any discomfort that might be driving it. From where does that discomfort come?

6. Now change position. What changes occur in your body, including your breathing and your state of alertness?

7. If you have no desire to change your position, you may be comfortable. Look for a signal that suggests you are comfortable. How is your body positioning itself? Is it relaxed, warm?

8. Now change your position, even if you are still comfortable. If you are sitting, get up and move to another chair, or stand. Hold your new position for two minutes and then ask yourself again if you are or aren't comfortable and what bodily sensations answer that question. Do you feel tense, relaxed, warm, cold, numb, aching, or able to breathe deeply? Are you more alert and awake in this new position?

9. Try a third position. Evaluate it the same way. What is the temperature of your hands and feet? Do you notice how you breathe? Do you feel numb in any areas of you body—in your throat? Your back? Below your waist? Many times when trauma has occurred in the body, a normal reaction is for part of it to numb out. You might also ask yourself to notice, without looking, the position of various parts of your body at the present time.

After you have tried this exercise, are you more aware of your body? Why would you say you are more aware?

_____

_____

Trauma and Hyperarousal

Normal body reactions to traumatic events include fear-based reactions, such as shock, and *shutdown* (the total numbing that comes from extreme stress). If your body played a central part in the way you responded to a traumatic event when it occurred, then it is essential for your body to be included in the healing process (van der Kolk 1997). Trauma is often experienced in the body as physiological arousal. You may become addicted to getting a similar state of arousal, and do things to get that feeling. Some of the things you may do to get your body to respond can be very risky, if not potentially dangerous and life-threatening. This is called being addicted to trauma or being an adrenaline junkie.

If you are not aware of which sensations are safe and which are dangerous, you may perceive them all negatively. Your body sensations are supposed to tell you when you are hungry, full, tired, alert, cold, warm, comfortable, uncomfortable, scared, or calmed. Rothschild concludes that "life would be very dangerous if . . . sensations and emotions could not be perceived" (2000, 104). Having an awareness of body sensations can also anchor you in the present. It is more difficult to stay lost in your past if you are aware of your body sensations in the present. Learning to recognize hyperarousal as a part of body awareness is a skill that is acquired through practice (Rothschild 2000).

Exercise: My Body and My Trauma

If your body or a body part could speak about how it was treated during the trauma or traumas, what would it say? _____

_____

How was your body a battleground during the trauma? (It may not have been one; if that is the case, you don't have to answer this question.) _____

_____

Are you alienated from your body in any way? Do you see any or all of your body as toxic, ugly, or powerless? _____

_____

How is who you are on the outside different from who you are on the inside of your body?

_____

_____

Right now, is your body:

____ relaxed, with deep, easy breathing, slow heart rate, and normal skin tone

____ slightly aroused, with quickening breathing or heart rate, skin color that is normal or paling or graying, and slightly moist skin

____ moderately aroused, with rapid heartbeat and respiration, and paling skin

____ hyperaroused, with accelerated heart rate and respiration, pale or grayish skin, and cold sweats

____ endangering hyperarousal, with all of your body systems on alert

Does the way your body reacts change when your past trauma is triggered? If so, how?

_____

_____

What other body reactions might you have in reaction to your past trauma? Do you have

_____ headaches

_____ worry lines carved into your forehead

_____ tics and involuntary movements

_____ red splotches when you are stressed or talk about trauma

_____ hives that come and go

_____ sores that arise in places where you were hurt

_____ physical reminders that appear out of the blue (e.g., rope marks around your wrists or welts on your back that appear and disappear

_____ aching legs

_____ genital/reproductive problems that can't be explained by doctors

_____ stomach problems

_____ too-frequent trips to the bathroom

What do any items you checked say about your traumas? _____

_____

_____

* * * * *

The Importance of Body Awareness

Again, building awareness—of all kinds—is the first step to controlling trauma-based reactions. Developing body awareness will help you establish a positive relationship with your body. Body awareness can help you discharge stored up emotion and to reconnect to numbed parts of your body by identifying why they are numb or unable to feel or why they react as they do. Body awareness helps you feel your emotions and then self-soothe. Getting in touch with your body can help you retrieve memories, ground yourself in the present, problem-solve about physical reactions that cannot be otherwise explained, and limit your use of body-related dissociation. If you have access and the financial resources to do so, you may wish to try massage and other types of body work, such as Reiki or cranio sacral therapy, to help you get in touch with dissociated body sensations and feelings. Use of these healing strategies may help you learn that some forms of touch are not associated with abuse. If you are in therapy, you may suggest that your therapist do a session together with your bodyworker, as the touch from massage or the closeness to touch from Reiki might uncover previously buried memories and emotions.

Anger and Rage

Irritability and outbursts of anger are other symptoms of increased arousal that face many trauma survivors. Anger and rage are often by-products of trauma; in other words, persons who have experienced traumatic events often focus their emotions onto other people, events, or circumstances. When a traumatic event has knocked your socks off and there is no explanation that makes sense as to why the event happened, your anger may erupt, overshadowing your emotions of fear, grief, sadness, shame, or guilt. Your anger may be directed at the perpetrator of the traumatic event, if you know that individual. If the perpetrator is a person who was supposed to protect, love, and honor you, your anger may become rage. Your anger may be directed at those who seem to have survived a similar event undamaged. Your anger may be directed at "the system" for its continued hurts as you have to deal with law enforcement, the criminal justice system, attorneys, insurance companies, and even therapists. Your anger may erupt at the normal events of life that frustrate you, rather than at its true sources. Your anger may also erupt toward yourself and your own body, particularly if you blame yourself for what happened to you or to the others who were impacted by the event. On the positive side, your anger may also motivate you to make changes in yourself or to work for a cause. As Cohen, Barnes, and Rankin note, anger can become a "typical response to the injustice of traumatization" (1995, 58).

There are many different levels and types of anger. However, trauma survivors often lump all of them together in one big pot. When anger is trauma-based, there may be many reasons for feeling angry. Matsakis (1994a) says that you may be angry at:

- people you blame for what happened to you, as individuals, groups, or organizations
- your own symptoms that keep sneaking up on you and smacking you in the face
- your physical limitations or disabilities that were caused by the traumatic events
- the behaviors you have used to try to avoid the traumas, including addictions to substances, gambling, spending, work, or other things
- the lack of understanding of those around you
- your inability to get financial compensation for what happened from insurance companies, your perpetrator, or responsible institutions or organizations
- society for subsequently traumatizing you, e.g., through a legal system that doesn't seem able to punish those responsible
- yourself for not acting to protect yourself or to prevent the trauma from happening

Do any of these reasons for anger apply to you? _____

_____

_____

Expressing Anger

You may be angry about what happened to you, your life, or those you love. You may want to lash out at someone, something, somewhere, somehow. Perhaps you have a specific perpetrator in mind as the target of your rage or anger. Or you may wish it were possible to lash out at nature itself for sending the tornado that destroyed your home. When it is impossible to focus anger on whomever or whatever deserves it, you may turn that anger onto others, including those you love. If any of the statements in the following is true, you may be using inappropriate ways of expressing anger.

Exercise: How I Express Anger

Check any items that apply to you.

_____ 1. I am the authority and force my opinion on others, even if means my showing anger to do so.

_____ 2. I time my angry attacks well. I strike out when the other person is vulnerable, tired, involved in something, or has her or his guard down.

_____ 3. I have a way of arguing that is unbeatable. I either monopolize the conversation, ignore the feelings of the other person, refuse to listen to the other person, or talk so much that the other person gives up.

_____ 4. I never forget a sin or slight against me and let my anger build and build until I explode.

_____ 5. When I am angry, I shout, scream, throw things, hit, or become violent.

_____ 6. I don't get mad; I get even by getting revenge.

_____ 7. I walk out or refuse to talk after I have become angry. Then the other person has no chance to participate, discuss, or fight back.

_____ 8. I use sarcasm or say things that are hurtful to others when I am angry.

_____ 9. I play people against one another.

_____ 10. I play a martyr role; I put guilt on others.

_____ 11. I never accept an apology; I hold a grudge for years, if necessary.

_____ 12. I throw everything into a fight, including the kitchen sink; I bring up everything that has ever made me angry, even from years in the past.

_____ 13. I secretly gather ammunition for my next fight. I go through e-mail messages, wallets, or pockets, or listen in on phone conversations so I can use that information later against the other person.

_____ 14. I refuse to talk about my anger; talking would be a waste of time.

_____ 15. When I think bad thoughts, I make bad things happen.

_____ 16. I say things when angry that are hurtful and irreversible.

_____ 17. If I get angry with _____ , she or he will get angry back and will be aggressive toward me. I know this will happen but I do it anyway.

_____ 18. If I share the reasons for my anger with _____ , it will devastate him or her to know the truth.

_____ 19. If I allow myself to be angry, I will reveal who and what I really am and will be even more vulnerable.

_____ 20. My anger is ugly; if I express it, others will think negatively of me.

_____ 21. I must avoid making others angry at me or at other persons or things at all costs.

_____ 22. I must avoid showing my own anger at all costs.

_____ 23. If others are angry at me, I must fix it or fix them to make everything right.

* * * * *

The more statements you checked in the preceding exercise, the more unhealthy is your way of expressing anger, and the more you need to work on learning different ways to express it. Before looking at some of the ways to get anger out in a healthier manner, let's look at what anger is.

Anger: A Signal Emotion

Anger is a *signal emotion*; it warns you of a threat to your well-being or of actual danger. Your anger is real. However, what you do with your anger involves making choices. If you make inappropriate choices when you express your anger, that anger can lead to self-harm, depression, feelings of helplessness, risk-taking, and explosive outbursts. Expression of anger exists on a continuum and ranges from annoyance and irritation to fury and rage. When anger is associated with trauma, angry outbursts can be out of proportion to what provokes them. These outbursts can be quick and explosive, and can bring about physical symptoms including high blood pressure, headaches, and body aches and pains. There are times when anger becomes rage; rage is anger accompanied by helplessness, it occurs when you believe you have no control over a situation, person, or event. When you have experienced a trauma, anger often becomes the central emotion that you feel. Angry thoughts about revenge may consume you. According to Enright and Fitzgibbons (2000), your anger is more destructive if you focus it on another person or people; it is intense, even in the short term; it leads to a learned pattern of annoyance, irritation, or frustration with others who are not the source of your anger; it is extremely passive; it is extremely hostile; or it is developmentally appropriate for someone much younger than your actual age (e.g., you act like a two-year-old and have a temper tantrum).

In reality, anger can be helpful to you:

- Your anger is natural and a part of you.

- Your anger is a signal about what is happening around you.

- Your anger helps you know yourself better.

- Your anger tells you to protect yourself.

- Your anger tells you to make necessary change(s).

- The reasons for your anger can be shared with those who matter to you.

Exercise: How Anger Has Helped Me and Hurt Me

Think of any ways anger has helped you. What are they, and when did the situations in which anger helped occur?

My anger has helped me deal with what happened to me by:

1. _____

2. _____

3. _____

Now, think of ways anger has caused you problems.

The ways that my anger hurt me (and those around me) are:

1. _____

2. _____

3. _____

What do your answers tell you about how you may want or need to change the way your anger helps and hurts you? _____

_____

_____

Resolving Anger

Working out trauma-related anger is not easy. As Schiraldi (2000) notes, to resolve anger, you must do the following:

1. Reexperience and express enough anger to get in touch with your feelings.

2. Develop an understanding of yourself and what happened in order to figure out why you really are angry.

3. Do what you need to do to give a sense of closure and finality to the situation.

4. Try to bring the trauma to completion by looking for justice, confronting someone or something, or getting an apology. Sometimes these things are not possible. Your perpetrator may be dead or unwilling to apologize. The legal system may not give you justice.

5. Take responsibility for the anger you have and choose how to express it.

6. Put that anger into words or pictures that describe the feelings behind it. If you write about your anger, describe what triggered its occurrence, what body sensations happened, and who was involved. This is a safer way to get out the anger without hurting yourself or others.

7. Generally, anger is the way you express fear or hurt. It is important to identify what lies beyond your anger. Whom do you believe hurt you? Is there an appropriate target for your anger? If so who or what is that target?

8. Look at the unhealed hurt lying behind your anger—this hurt, according to Schiraldi (2000), is generally from your past. Be sure to self-soothe before you look at the hurt.

9. Put your anger outside of yourself. Don't turn it against yourself or use it to think badly about yourself. Let those who hurt you know why you are angry, without criticizing or attacking them. Listen to what they have to say about what happened.

10. Learn how to protect yourself in other ways, so it feels safe for you to let go of anger.

It's important to remember that you choose to get angry and to react as you do. When you get very angry and lose control, you can become powerless. Therefore, it helps to learn what you can do to express your anger rather than lose control.

Exercise: Alternative Expressions of Anger

The alternatives I can use when I am angry include:

1. _____

2. _____

3. _____

4. _____

5. _____

* * * * *

If you had trouble thinking about alternatives in this exercise, suggestions in the following pages may help you. You might express your anger about what happened to you in words, pictures, or actions. You may use space in your journal to write about your anger or draw a picture of your anger. You may also take one or more pictures from a magazine that symbolize your anger, decide how and why the pictures are representative, and glue those pictures in your journal or notebook. You may also say the following statements, or something similar, to yourself:

> When I am very angry, I can do things to take care of myself, just as I have done in other situations. When I am very angry and want to defend myself with excuses, I need to remember that I can just listen; ask questions; check to see if I understand what is being said to me by repeating back what I have heard and then asking if I have heard correctly; and look for some point of agreement. (Schiraldi 2000, 132)

Other things you can do when you have to deal with anger might be to go to a gym and work out, take a long walk, or change anger into something that is functional and helpful. If you were to change your anger, you might look at its physical signs (is your jaw tight? are your fists clenched?), its cognitive signs (are you suspicious? do you jump to conclusions? is all your thinking black and white?), and its behavioral signs (do you take on a fighting stance and puff yourself up, or give people dirty looks?).

Exercise: My Anger Signs

Which of these signs do you have and how could you change them? _____

_____

_____

Other things I could change about my anger include:

1. _____

2. _____

3. _____

4. _____

5. _____

What do your answers say about you and the way you deal with anger? _____

_____

_____

* * * * *

Relaxing to Control Anger

One way to deal with anger is to do relaxing breathing. Breathe in slowly through your nose, hold that breath for five seconds, and then breathe out very slowly through your mouth. If you repeat this five times, you will have a chance to calm yourself and defuse your anger.

Sometimes, it is good to turn to your relaxation exercises before anger takes over. It can help to have a relaxing place or scene already in mind prior to when you need it. This scene is generally not your safe place because you do not want to introduce anger and rage into it. McKay and Rogers note that you can create a scene for yourself, as shown in the following exercise (2000, 31).

Exercise: My Relaxing Scene

1. Where and when does your scene occur (choose the time and place)? _____

_____

2. What do you see in that scene? _____

_____

3. What do you hear? _____

_____

4. What do you feel on your skin? What can you touch or are you touching? _____

_____

5. What do you smell? What do you taste? _____

_____

_____

6. What feelings are you having (e.g., peacefulness, joy, calmness)? _____

_____

7. What else would you add to your relaxing scene? _____

_____

8. Now, think of a positive trigger word or phrase that you can use to jet-propel yourself to your scene, should you need it. My word or phrase is _____ .

---

* * * * *

Anger and Self-Care

As you know, taking control of anger is difficult, because anger can be a very disabling emotion. To get anger under control, it is important for you to change your irrational thinking and the negative messages you say to yourself. For example, do you say that you deserve to be treated badly because you are such a bad person and have done so many horrible things? Do you believe you should be punished by others or that you deserve their angry outbursts? Becoming aware of these thoughts and messages is a first step toward changing them. You must also realize that another person does not cause the angry feelings you have. It is your decision how you react to a person that leads to your expressions of anger. What anger-producing self-messages do you have?

Exercise: My Anger-Producing Messages

1. _____

2. _____

3. _____

Now identify your personal sequence for expressing your anger-producing self-messages. Here is a possible sequence; you may not need to fill in all the blanks, but consider each carefully

1. I say to myself: _____

2. Then I think: _____

3. Then I put the blame on: _____

4. Then I make this judgment on whatever or whomever I have put blame: _____

_____

5. Then I act out my anger by: _____

6. To release my anger, I usually:

　　• _____

　　• _____

　　• _____

What does this exercise tell you about the messages that you say to yourself? _____

_____

You have the ability to change each message to a positive one. Take any of the negative messages you say to yourself that you have listed previously and see how you might change it:

1. _____

2. _____

* * * * *

Exercise: A Situation That Caused Me to Feel Angry

Now, keeping all of the information about anger you have read and the exercises you have done in mind, you may apply it to a specific situation.

1. The situation that really upset me and caused me to feel anger was _____

_____

_____

2. Write a few sentences that describe you in the situation. You may refer back to the suggestions of Enright and Fitzgibbons (2000) in the section "Anger: A Signal Emotion" or those adapted from the work of Matsakis (1994a) in the section "Anger and Rage" earlier in this chapter. _____

_____

_____

3. Now try to think of that situation in a different way. McKay and Rogers (2000) suggest that you answer the following questions (if you need more space, write in your journal):

   - What were my needs in this situation? _____
   - How was I trying to get them met? _____
   - What were my fears? _____
   - What was my level of stress? _____
   - What traumatic events were influencing me? _____
   - What nontraumatic events were influencing me? _____
   - What did I not know at the time that would have helped the situation? _____
   - What skills did I use to react? _____
   - What skills did I lack? _____
   - What emotional limitations impacted me at that time? _____
   - What physical limitations influenced me? _____
   - What values and beliefs influenced how I behaved? _____
   - What rewards or sources of pleasure did I hope to get? _____
   - What resources did I have to help me? _____
   - What other resources did I need? _____
   - What would these questions lead you to say or write about the situation overall?

_____

_____

4. Now think about some alternative ways to deal with the situation that could help you resolve the anger without resorting to an outburst. Which of the following might work for you?

_____ Leave the situation so you can cool down and not act impulsively or aggressively.

_____ Take time to be alone because it is hard to be angry if you are alone and don't have a target for your anger.

_____ Exercise your anger away. If you can't do something physical, do some isometric exercising. Put your hands against a wall and push very hard until you are exhausted.

_____ Yell and scream by yourself until you are worn out.

_____ Hit a pillow, pound or tear a phone book, throw bottles into a recycling bin.

* * * * *

Exercise: A Situation Where I Expressed Anger Inappropriately

Think of a time when you were being hurt and had angry thoughts and emotions that you may have expressed inappropriately. Describe that situation and your emotions below.

1. The situation in which I was harmed and victimized was: _____

2. I believed that _____ (name someone who hurt you) harmed me deliberately because: _____

3. I believe that _____ (the person who hurt you) should have done something different. This could have been to: _____

4. I got angry because: _____

5. I expressed anger this way: _____

6. Perhaps I could not have done things differently because: _____

7. However, if there was something I could have done to express anger appropriately, I could have: _____

What has this exercise and the one before it said about you and your anger? _____

_____

_____

* * * * *

Distractibility and Trouble Paying Attention

If traumatic images, thoughts, dreams, flashbacks, and other intrusions are constantly in your head, or if you are using energy to keep them out of your head, you may find that you have difficulty concentrating or paying attention. If you seem to have excess energy and are always on the go, you may get labeled as attention deficit/hyperactivity disordered when you really are just trying to avoid dealing with, thinking about, or reexperiencing your traumas. If either of these statements are true about you, you may use some of the following techniques to increase your ability to concentrate:

• You may do relaxation visualization exercises.

- You may make lists of what you need to do.

- You may make lists of what you need to remember.

- You may read several paragraphs in a book and then summarize what you have read in writing.

- You may practice thought stopping if you have intrusive thoughts getting in the way of thinking.

Thought Stopping

If you have intrusive thoughts, you may try to stop them by yelling "**stop**" either out loud or in your mind, as you visualize the word *stop* on a stop sign or in flashing lights, whenever a thought begins to come in. Another way is to get a good supply of thick rubber bands and put one on your wrist. Leave it on, even when you go to bed. Every time a painful image or thought pops into your mind, consciously decide if you want to think about the image or thought. If you decide that it is something you want to think and that you will not become overwhelmed or unable to concentrate on other things, keep it in your mind. However, if you don't want to think the thought or see the image, then snap the rubber band on your wrist, hurting yourself.

At the same time that you snap the rubber band, allow yourself only three minutes to look at the thought or image. If, after three minutes, you are still thinking the thought or seeing the image, snap the rubber band again and give yourself another three minutes. Continue this process until the thought or image weakens. It is important that you use this technique each and every time you have an intrusive image or thought that you don't want. If you use it only every once in a while, the number of involuntary intrusions may actually increase (Baker and Salston 1993).

Hypervigilance, Superawareness of Danger, and Startling Easily

During the traumatic events that happened to you, were you very aware of what was going on around you? In the present time, are you very observant or overaware? Are you always on edge? Being overaware or hypervigilant may be one of the symptoms of PTSD you are experiencing. Meichenbaum has listed metaphors that might help you identify these feelings (1994, 112). Do you ever feel as if or believe:

1. You are a time bomb about to explode.
2. You are a volcano about to erupt.
3. You have a short fuse.
4. You are at your breaking point.
5. You are ready to snap.
6. You are walking on eggshells.
7. You are coming apart at the seams.
8. You are over the edge.
9. You are about to have a meltdown.
10. You are in attack mode.
11. You are on alert.
12. You are ready for a fight.
13. You are ready to flee.

Do any of these describe you or do you have other terms that describe you? _____

If you find that these or other images of you indicate that you are extremely watchful and hypervigilant, you may use the following techniques to calm down:

- Do whatever you need to do in the house to feel safe; check the locks on the doors, make sure windows are shut, etc.

- Use a paradox when you are checking safety—checking doors and windows five times is not enough; make yourself check them ten times.

- Ground yourself in the reality of your present environment—become aware of whether or not it really is safe or if you truly are in danger.

Self-Harm

Self-harm does not mean only hurting your body or doing things to your body that bring you pain. There are many ways that you can harm yourself and sabotage yourself as a trauma survivor. Using the writings of Zampelli (2000), you may choose to complete the following checklist to see exactly what self-defeating behaviors you use. Once you have completed the list, go back and identify the ten behaviors you use the most, then write where and when you use them. Then go back again to those ten behaviors and ask yourself what this behavior says about you (Rosenbloom and Williams 1999).

Exercise: My Self-Defeating Behaviors

Check all that apply to you.

_____ I waste time.

_____ I avoid working toward a goal I have set by doing meaningless things.

_____ I get physically ill when I have something pressing to do.

_____ I change the subject when I am uncomfortable.

_____ I use a "geographical cure" when I am uncomfortable rather than face a situation (that is, I physically go someplace else).

_____ I refuse to look people in the eye when I talk to them.

_____ I avoid emotional intimacy.

_____ I communicate indirectly.

_____ I do something distracting during a conversation (bite my nails, play with jewelry).

_____ I overeat.

_____ I use substances to excess.

_____ I use alcohol to excess.

_____ I am a shopaholic.

_____ I lie to cover up, impress others, and get out of a problem.

_____ I smoke.

_____ I am disorganized.

_____ I am generally late to appointments.

_____ I put myself in risky situations.

_____ I miss important meetings and appointments.

_____ I do not make important phone calls.

_____ I don't write things down.

_____ I have excessive debt.

_____ I forget important things on a regular basis.

_____ I overspend without getting into debt.

_____ I remain in a harmful situation even though it is self-destructive.

_____ I go along with what others want, even when it is bad for me.

_____ I don't try to change myself.

_____ I ask for help from the wrong people.

_____ I take on more than I can handle.

_____ I believe I am special and unique.

_____ I believe things have to be perfect around me.

_____ I am impatient and "want it now."

Now rank your top self-defeating behaviors and describe the situations where you do them:

1. _____

I use this behavior when I: _____

2. _____

I use this behavior when I: _____

3. _____

I use this behavior when I: _____

4. _____

I use this behavior when I: _____

5. _____

I use this behavior when I: _____

6. _____

I use this behavior when I: _____

Now, taking those top six, use the following strategy for each (you may do the first one here; do the next five in your journal or notebook).

Write the behavior: _____

Ask yourself the following questions: _____

1. What does that behavior say about me? _____

_____

2. Now what does *that* say about me? _____

_____

3. And what does *that* say about me? _____

_____

The answer to the third question gives you your core belief—the deep belief that under-lies the behavior.

* * * * *

Dealing with Fear

Fear is another very common trauma-based emotion that can greatly impact the body. It is quite possible that you were very afraid during and after the traumatic event or events occurred. If you have been a victim of lifelong trauma, you may not even know what it is like to live without fear. How many times a day or week do you feel jumpy or nervous? Do you shake, tremble, or hide? How often do you look around in a state of panic, waiting for the other shoe to drop? Do your muscles tense up and ache? Do you get bouts of diarrhea, stom-ach pain, or headaches when any reminder of the trauma intrudes? Do you find that you cry, whimper, or become speechless if you believe you are about to be retraumatized? If you answered "yes" to yourself as you read this paragraph, it is likely that you are experiencing trauma-related fear.

Some of the fear and terror that you had during your trauma was normal. If you were in danger of being hurt or even killed, it's no wonder you were afraid. However, that traumatic situation is in the past—unless you are still being hurt or are in danger of being hurt again. If this is the case, it is more important for you to try to get out of that situation and to protect yourself than do work in a workbook that might cause you more pain.

Panic Attacks

If you had a panic attack during the trauma or if you experience panic attacks now, there are books and other materials available to help you. This workbook is not designed to repeat what those books say, but it is important that you recognize that panic reactions occur sud-denly and involve feelings of fear and terror, doom and danger (Meichenbaum 1994). You may use your ability to dissociate and avoid to limit your susceptibility to panic attacks and fear responses. Panic attacks include body reactions and sensations, feelings of fear and anxi-ety, thoughts (expecting a panic attack to occur, predicting it will occur), and behaviors (avoidance, hyperventilation).

When you were being traumatized, your body recognized danger and responded by fleeing, freezing, or fighting. However, after the trauma, if you continue to be hypervigilant and hypersensitive to such a great degree that you respond with panic when there is no objec-tive sign of danger, you may end up relating to the world as if it is a constant war zone. You may even diagnose yourself with a serious medical condition (e.g., a heart attack or nervous breakdown) when you are feeling anxious and panicked. You may start to hyperventilate and have tingling sensations in your hands and feet. You may tremble or even faint.

A panic attack is not a sign of imminent death. Panic attacks do not just come out of the blue without any trigger, even though they seem to do so to many persons. If you begin to recognize what is truly dangerous to you, or if you reduce your inaccurate perception of danger and control your thoughts about danger, your panic attacks will begin to decrease.

How can you control your panic attacks and master the fear of arousal that they cause? Meichenbaum lists six steps (1994, 43):

1. Recognize when you have the physical sensations that indicate a panic attack is coming—face your symptoms (Weekes 1986).

2. Note how you misinterpret body signs that something serious is wrong.

3. Catch yourself beginning to hyperventilate and control your breathing; accept your symptoms.

4. Interrupt the panic attack and identify the trigger that began it and the feelings that accompany it (helplessness, hopelessness, sadness, loss); begin to try to relax.

5. Use various coping strategies, such as changing what you are doing, grounding yourself, doing something fun, or calling someone. Realize that your panic attack will subside naturally within about five to ten minutes and that you are not dying.

6. Take charge of your behavior and, when you have interrupted the panic attack, take credit for what you have done.

Other means of controlling, limiting, or recovering from a panic attack include using the skills you learned in chapter 2 to relax, float, breathe gently, and decrease your arousal. If you fight and overtense, the attack will last longer. It also helps to recognize the memories that led to the attack so that you can work on them (perhaps using techniques from chapter 4). Let your body readjust itself chemically. Get good sleep (perhaps using the exercises at the beginning of this chapter), eat properly, and exercise well. Also, list your strengths and the sources of your resilience (you may use the final chapter of this workbook to do so).

Journal Exercise: Picturing Your Fear

Another way to gain some control over your fear and panic is to draw a picture or construct a collage of your fear. You may draw that picture or create that collage in your journal or notebook.

* * * * *

Using Affirmations

An *affirmation* is a positive thought you repeat to yourself over and over in order to combat, challenge, or even change negative thoughts and a negative self-image. They make statements in the present tense that represent what you want to bring into your life or how you want to see yourself (Zampelli 2000). Affirmations are a form of positive self-talk that can state how you really want to see yourself and your body. Thus you are the best person to create your own affirmations. Although others may say positive statements to you about your body, if you do not buy into those statements, you will have a hard time believing them and won't say similar statements to yourself.

An affirmation begins in a personal way with the word *I* ("I weigh the right amount for my frame") or the word *my* ("My ability to finish a job is excellent") In addition, affirmations occur in now time, not in future time. An affirmation is "I do a good job," not "I will do a good job." Affirmations can also be statements designed to counteract your trauma-related fears ("I am able to walk to work alone"; "I can drive my car by myself after the accident").

Affirmations are stated in your own personal language, which fits you and your personal style of relating to the world. If you do not believe the affirmation you create is totally true, then write it with a conditional word or words that imply positive movement: "I am becoming more able to be a capable person" or "I am constantly trying to do my best." The most effective affirmations are realistic and include hope, and may even be based on faith.

Affirmations do not take the place of hard work. However, they are one way to change your beliefs about yourself and your way of dealing with the world ("I can relate to others without getting angry"; "I can do _____ without being afraid") and lead to the ability to change any self-harming behaviors that are based on those beliefs. Affirmations are not meant to help you avoid your emotions or to control events or others. If your affirmations are to work, you need to repeat them over and over and over to yourself until you actually begin to believe them. When you believe them, you will begin to see your world from a different perspective.

Begin by writing several of your affirmations down in this workbook, five times each, to start getting them into your mind. If you find that you have trouble saying an affirmation to yourself at least twenty times a day, then take some notebook paper and write the affirmation at the top of the page. Before you go to bed, fill that entire page with the affirmation, saying it out loud each time you write it. You may also rewrite it numerous times before you begin your day in the morning.

Writing affirmations uses more than one of your body's means of expression: it involves eye/hand coordination to write, language to say the affirmation out loud and put it on paper, and thought to start the entire process. Writing helps an affirmation to become a habit of thought, a new self-message that you have incorporated into yourself and made a part of your belief system.

If you do not want to write the affirmation over and over again, you may choose to write the affirmation down once and then say it to yourself over and over again. Repeating the affirmation over and over will also help you eventually believe it and feel as if it belongs to you. Repetition also will help you accept that the affirmation is a more acceptable way to describe yourself. It is particularly helpful if you have positive, action-oriented affirmations available to say to yourself when you are in a state of crisis, to help you to get through the situation, e.g., "I am able to do what is best for me" or "I am able to be assertive in this situation."

Exercise: My Affirmations

The affirmations I have chosen to use are: _____

_____

_____

_____

Now write each one five times in the space below (if you need more room, use a page in your journal or notebook):

1. _____

_____

_____

_____

2. _____

_____

_____

_____

_____

3. _____

_____

_____

_____

_____

4. _____

_____

_____

_____

_____

5. _____

_____

_____

_____

_____

* * * * *

What has this chapter taught you about yourself and your physically based reactions to trauma? (For more information on this subject, look at chapter 10.)

You have now looked at all the various symptom clusters or criteria that make up the PTSD diagnosis, including symptoms of intrusion (thoughts, memories, dreams, nightmares), avoidance and numbing, and body responses. Yet these symptoms do not include some very important associated symptoms that go along with the disorder. The next chapter looks at several of them, including guilt, shame, and loss.

7

Dealing with Associated Symptoms of PTSD: Guilt, Survivor Guilt, Shame, and Loss

While symptoms such as guilt, shame and loss are not part of the criteria for a diagnosis of PTSD, they are commonly felt by many survivors. If you experience guilt, survivor guilt, shame, or feelings of loss, then this chapter may help you.

Guilt

If you feel at all responsible for the traumatic event or events you have experienced, there is a good possibility that you have some feelings of guilt. Guilt occurs when you feel bad about your behavior: what you did or did not do before, during, and after the traumatic event. Guilt can be a positive emotion if you really were responsible for what occurred. For example, if you were driving drunk, lost control of your car, and killed someone, you are guilty and have good reason to feel guilty. If you were using illegal drugs and provided those drugs to someone else, and that person went into cardiac arrest, you are guilty. If you perpetrated violence against another person in any circumstances other than self-defense, you have every reason to feel guilt.

Exercise: My Feelings of Guilt

Do you feel any deserved guilt about the trauma or traumas that happened to you or in which you participated? List what you did and why you deserve to feel the guilt. I feel guilty because:

1. _____

2. _____

3. _____

4. _____

5. _____

Now look at the circumstances of the trauma. What did you or did you not do to cause the trauma or traumas to happen? Think of yourself as a reporter looking at the event and writing a factual story. Answer the following questions (adapted from Figley 1989):

What happened? _____

_____

Why did it happen? _____

_____

Why did it happen to me? _____

_____

Why did I act the way I did during the event or events? _____

_____

Why have I acted as I have since the event or events occurred? How have I changed? _____

_____

_____

If the event or events happened again, how would I act? Would I want to do anything differently? Would I be able to do anything differently? _____

_____

_____

What did this exercise teach you about your actions? _____

_____

* * * * *

Now it is time to look at the actual level of responsibility you had for the event. You may have a distorted sense of your responsibility. For example, Susan was a victim of sexual abuse when she was six years of age. She blames herself for what happened. In fact, her perpetrator was a coach, thirty-five years old, left in charge of her while her single-parent mother was away on a business trip. What degree of responsibility did that coach have for the abuse? _____ percent. What percentage of responsibility did her mother have? _____ percent. And Susan? _____ percent. In this situation, does anyone else (society, for example) have any responsibility? How much?

The technique that follows helps determine the percentage of responsibility that you have for the trauma or traumas you experienced; it was developed by Scurfield (1994).

Exercise: My Responsibility

1. Reviewing what you wrote in the previous exercise, what are the central details of the traumatic event or events as you remember it or them? Use the first person ("I") to answer this question. _____

   _____

   _____

2. Now, what percentage of the responsibility, at this point in time, do you believe you have (had) for the event? I am _____ percent responsible for what happened. Are you sure this is your percentage of responsibility? (answer yes or no) Could it be more or less? Examine your responsibility in detail, including both irrational and rational statements, factual statements, and your feelings (Matsakis 1994a). (You may need to use extra paper.) You may use these questions as prompts: Do you believe that the event and its consequences were the result of your innocent mistake? Your inability to make a decision that was appropriate? Your competence or incompetence? Your abilities and knowledge, or your stupidity? Your thoughtfulness or thoughtlessness? Your carefulness or carelessness? Your impulsivity or immaturity? Your lack of skill? Your lack of morality and, thus, your sin? Your lack of character? To what degree and in what ways do you blame yourself for the occurrence of the traumatic event? How responsible are you for the injuries or damages to others during and after the event? _____

   _____

   _____

   _____

   _____

3. Now look back at the level of responsibility you assigned to yourself originally. It was _____ percent. Could you now convince someone that you truly are _____ percent responsible, based on what you have just written? How would you now revise your percentage of responsibility? _____

   _____

4. Now think about anyone else who was involved in the trauma. What was each person's role? Assign a percentage of responsibility to each person involved? _____

   _____

5. If others have some degree of responsibility, what happens to the responsibility you have assigned to yourself? Look again at what you did or did not do during the trauma or traumas and what you could and could not have done, and decide your level of responsibility. My total responsibility is _____ percent, because: _____

In what ways do you still feel responsible? (For example, if you did not tell, why not? Were you threatened? Were you ever taught to tell?) _____

_____

6. If there is any part of the event or events for which you still feel responsible, might you consider that you have already been punished enough by your own beliefs or actions? How much more must you suffer? Self-forgiveness may be a very long process for you, depending on your actual responsibility for what happened. Still, it is important that you ask yourself exactly what it would take for you to be able to forgive yourself for any involvement and responsibility you had. Take the space below to write your answers to some or all of these questions: What would you need to do to be able to forgive yourself? If you have not done this act or these actions, what is stopping you? Do you need to get more information about the event before you can forgive yourself? Is there something missing in your explanation of what happened that might lead to your forgiveness? If you are unable to forgive yourself, are you at least able to accept who you are and what you did? _____

_____

_____

_____

_____

7. If you still believe you need to pay for your responsibility in the traumatic event or events, think of non–self-destructive ways that might occur. _____

_____

_____

_____

* * * * *

To summarize the preceding exercise, the steps are to:

1. Verbalize what happened using "I," the first person.

2. Ask yourself, "What percentage am I responsible for? Am I sure? Is it possible my responsibility is more or less than that?"

3. Convince yourself and others that you are and deserve to be _____ percent responsible.

4. Challenge that level of responsibility by looking at who else is responsible, and then state anyone else's percentage of responsibility.

5. Recalculate any responsibility to make a total of 100 percent while looking at what you did and did not do.

6. Describe the level of suffering you have had for the percentage of responsibility you gave yourself and decide if that suffering is or is not enough, and if it fits or does not fit with your actual percentage of responsibility (Schiraldi 2000).

7. Figure out ways for payback if that is appropriate, and then commit to moving on with life.

Journal Exercise: What I Learned from Responsibility Exercise

What did this exercise teach you about the trauma or traumas that happened? About yourself? About your responsibility? Did these learnings show you that there was any way you could have prevented what happened?

* * * * *

As Schiraldi noted, "guilt affirms morality" (2000, 182)." The successful resolution of guilt involves a series of stages of denial, processing, and resolution. When you process guilt, you assess any harm that you did and your responsibility for that harm. If you find that you are guilty to any degree, then it is appropriate for you to express how sorry you are and make appropriate amends. Many beliefs that get associated with guilt include "shoulds" and "ought to's." If these beliefs are inaccurate, it is important to challenge them by asking yourself what each of the beliefs says about you and then by looking for evidence, both pro and con, to dispute or support the belief.

If you continue to feel guilty for any part you played in the trauma, ask yourself what your guilt can do for you? Does it provide a way for you to atone (in part or totally) for what you did or the part you played? Does your guilt motivate you to change your behavior? _____

Are you still saying "If only . . ." to yourself after answering these questions? When you say "if only," you may be placing blame on yourself that you do not deserve. The guilt you feel now may be due to the messages others instilled in you at an earlier time, perhaps during the trauma itself. One way to combat guilt, particularly if the trauma happened when you were a child, is to gather photos of you at the time the trauma occurred or look at children now who are the same age you were then. Does this help you see yourself as small and helpless, perhaps in contrast to a large adult perpetrator? Recognizing that a small child can do little to defend himself or herself against an adult perpetrator will help you realize that a child is *never* responsible for any abuse perpetrated against him or her. You can also look at any real choices you had the chance to make during the traumatic situation (if you were given any), as well as evidence that shows how you made and acted on those choices.

Schiraldi suggests that you answer the following questions about your reactions during a traumatic situation in order to put them in perspective (2000, 195–196):

- Were you able to think coolly at the time of the trauma?

- Were you aware of all of your options at that time?

- Were you able to make choices?

- Were any of those choices positive or good ones?

- Was this situation familiar to you, or was it new and different?

- Did you have any way to know, for sure, which option was best?

- Did you have a clear awareness of all possible outcomes of all your options?

- Did anyone or anything take away any of your options?

- Were you missing important information that would have helped you make good choices?

- Did you have time to weigh all the options and make good choices?

- Did other things get in the way of your making your choices (fatigue, hunger, confusion, panic)?

- What outcome did you intend?

- Did you try to harm someone on purpose?

- Did you make an honest mistake that led to your harming someone?

- Did you make a reasonable decision under the circumstances, even if it wasn't the right decision?

- Did you accomplish any initial goals you had when the traumatic event began?

- What other coping strategies could you have used?

- Did you avert a worse traumatic situation?

- What else could you have done, in an ideal world, to deal with the trauma?

- If your best friend reacted the way you did, would you understand his or her actions? What would you say to that person? Could you forgive him or her?

It's important that you remember, as Schiraldi said, "Guilt can be adaptive [healthy] if it is realistic and if it leads to improvements in . . . behavior and character" (2000, 27).

Survivor Guilt

Matsakis (1999) writes about survivor guilt, the guilt that comes from the belief that your actions or nonactions during a traumatic event may have caused or could have prevented the death, injury, or mistreatment of others. Survivor guilt also occurs if you believe you should have experienced death, injury, or mistreatment yourself, but somehow escaped your fate. You may try to keep this aspect of guilt secret because you fear others would condemn you if they learned what you did or did not do.

For example, say you are a war veteran. During the war, you were leading your platoon across an open field. You told two of your men to assume certain positions as they walked beside you. Each of them was killed; you lived. Your guilt says that it should have been you who died, because one of the men switched places with you and had you been walking where he was walking, you would have been dead. Since that time, you keep seeking direct or indirect ways to kill yourself to "take his place." His ghost comes to you in nightmares, and you think that you owe him your life. Your guilt over his death has grown and grown and grown, even though in reality you are not responsible for it. Had you known that death lay in that path, you would not have sent him to walk there. You would not have walked there either. But you did not know. Naturally, you wish that things had turned out differently and that no one had died in battle. Your pain about the losses of your friends is deep, and your sadness does not go away.

If you were driving and were involved in a car wreck that was your fault and some of the friends riding with you were killed, you may experience similar guilt. You may choose to harm yourself because you do not believe you deserve to be happy or successful. However, you did not have the power to stop their deaths, no matter if you caused them to die through your acts of commission (doing something) or omission (not doing anything). Your survivor guilt may be a way to honor the dead and not forget them without grieving them or putting their deaths to rest. If you truly were responsible for the deaths, your survival guilt may be particularly strong. If you believe that you suffer from survival guilt, the following exercise may help you to identify its existence (Matsakis 1999).

Exercise: My Survivor Guilt

Fill in the blanks of any statement that applies to you.

I made it out alive from _____ when _____ did not.

I made it out less damaged or injured than _____ .

I escaped the emotional pain and distress when _____ happened.

I escaped social disgrace and humiliation when _____ happened, and _____ did not. I wish I could die to join _____ .

I should have died when _____ happened and _____ should have lived.

If _____ had lived and I had died, _____ would have had a better life or been a better person than I have had or been.

_____ is luckier than I am because she or he has no more pain or suffering and I am stuck here with all this pain.

I dream of _____ . In my dreams _____ happens.

At times, _____'s ghost haunts me.

I fantasize that I could relive _____ and change the outcome to _____ .

I have never talked about _____ and/or _____ because of my involvement, which was _____ .

I am so guilty that I believe I have lost my soul because _____ .

I wish that I had the courage to kill myself but am afraid of what will happen to me after death, because I did _____ .

I will be punished if I ever talk about _____ .

I no longer have religious faith or a sense of spirituality because _____ .

When I have periods of intense grieving about _____ , I _____ .

When I have periods of intense rage about _____ , I _____ .

I use substances because I try to numb what happened. I use _____ when _____ .

If I watch movies or documentaries about _____ or similar events, I become very depressed and emotional and I _____ .

I cannot live for myself; the reason I stay alive is for _____ .

I am living for someone who died named _____ .

I don't deserve to live. If I had my way, I would _____ .

I should have died on (date) _____ when _____ because _____ .

I believe _____ would have had a better life than I have had and/or would have had more to live for, had she or he lived.

I now sabotage my personal relationships with _____ by _____ .

I sabotage my professional relationships with _____ by _____ .

My guilt is there because I was negligent during or after the traumatic event and I _____ .

In hindsight, I know that I could have prevented what occurred by _____ .

I also know that I must deal with the fact that I participated in the following amoral actions _____ .

I feel that doing _____ has made me lose my faith.

I have tried to escape my guilt by _____ .

What did you learn about yourself through completing this exercise? _____

_____

_____

_____

If completing this exercise has triggered you or brought up new memories, list those memories here and then go back to some of the exercises in chapters 3 and 4 to work on them.

_____

_____

_____

* * * * *

Matsakis (1999) says that healing from survivor guilt does not mean that you are to forget what you did or forget those who were hurt or who died. It also does not mean that you will never have regret or guilt again. It does mean that you will look at your responsibility in the events realistically and honestly and will let go of at least some of the destructive ways you use to punish yourself. Part of healing from survivor guilt is to grieve the losses. Ways to deal with loss are found later in this chapter.

Another way to deal with survivor guilt is to find restorative experiences that are economic, vocational, political, or interpersonal and that allow you to help others or somehow atone for what happened before. Matsakis describes seven stages of healing from survivor guilt (1999, 164–165). You can refer to this seven-step process as you complete many exercises in this book:

1. remembering what happened

2. separating survivor guilt from other emotions

3. examining your role in what happened before, during, and after the trauma; looking at your errors in thinking and your irrational emotions, perhaps by using the exercise "My Responsibility," found earlier in this chapter

4. countering self-blame and irrational guilt through newly constructed statements about the self that are based on true responsibility

5. accepting guilt for what you did do

6. examining the personal consequences of your guilt to your own self-esteem, self-care, physical health, emotional health, job performance, life contributions, and life

7. making a commitment to being honest about the guilt and to taking action toward putting that guilt to positive use

Now take some time to identify a guilt-producing event that you want to describe in detail here. This activity may trigger your traumatic reactions. It may also bring new information to you. Remember to refer back to some of the exercises in chapter 2 to calm yourself when you need to do so.

Exercise: Events That Caused My Survivor Guilt

1. What event or events caused you to have survivor guilt? Describe the event or events here, and use your notebook or journal if you need more space. _____

_____

_____

_____

2. It is also very important for you to look at any beliefs or thinking errors you have that are getting in the way of your healing or at least lessening your guilt. Answering these questions about each of your chosen traumatic events can identify some of your beliefs and help you decide which (if any) of them you want to challenge.

   • Do you make wrong conclusions about your degree of responsibility for the event? Do you assume too much or too little responsibility? _____

- Do you believe you could have prevented the event from occurring? _____

  _____

- Do you come up with the wrong conclusions about why you made the decisions you did? _____

- Do you believe what you did was ethical? _____

- Do you have full information about the event to judge the decisions you made? If not, where can you get that information? _____

- Do you judge yourself against some ideal picture of what might have happened?

  _____

- Do you have good intentions to make up for what happened? What are they?

  _____

- Will you follow through on one of those intentions? Which one? _____

  _____

- Are you using only your emotions to judge yourself in relation to the event?

  _____

- Do you still believe you were totally responsible for what happened (even after completing the exercise "My Responsibility" above? _____

- Could you really have prevented the event? _____

- Did you really have the power to stop the event? _____

- Could you really have reacted differently? _____

- Do you really believe that, if you had died during the event, another person would have survived? _____

* * * * *

Another way to deal with survivor guilt is to try new ways of self-talk and new ways to think about what happened. Whenever you have an irrational thought about your guilt, try to counter it with something more positive and realistic.

Exercise: Substituting Positive Thoughts

Look at the previous exercise. Identify five irrational thoughts about your participation in and responsibility for the event:

1. _____

2. _____

3. _____

4. _____

5. _____

Now what positive thoughts might you substitute for each of these negative thoughts?

1. _____

2. _____

3. _____

4. _____

5. _____

* * * * *

Exercise: A Healing Monologue

Matsakis suggests you stand in front of a mirror and repeat the following monologue to yourself three or four times a day until you can recite it almost automatically (1999, 222).

During _____ , the following situation happened _____ . Whenever I remember what happened, I usually think _____ (put in the thinking error here), and feel guilty. When I feel guilty about _____ , I need to remind myself that I am thinking incorrectly. Instead of thinking _____ , I need to view the situation as _____ (put in the more positive, realistic thought). I also need to remember that I displayed the following strengths during the event _____ and can give myself credit for those strengths. It would be a mistake for me to concentrate only on these good things, though, because I am guilty (in reality) for _____ . However, it would also be wrong for me to concentrate only on the negative aspects of what happened.

* * * * *

Making Amends

You may also deal with your survivor guilt by making amends. One way to make amends is to create a ritual for healing. This process is described in the section "Healing Rituals" later in this workbook. Matsakis notes that making amends can lessen feelings of guilt and that "there is always something you can do to make amends, even if it is not perfect or powerful enough to change the past" (1999, 226). You might do something to work with the living (volunteer at a hospital), or for a cause that in some way deals with the trauma you experienced (Mothers Against Drunk Drivers). Perhaps you can make amends financially (donating funds to help construct a trauma center for teens).

Journal Exercise

If you were to make amends, describe in your journal or notebook how you would do it.

* * * * *

Exercise: What I Learned from Survivor Guilt Exercises

What was it like to do the exercises having to do with survivor guilt? What did you learn about yourself by doing them? About your guilt? _____

_____

_____

* * * * *

Shame

Another emotional response to traumatic events that is common to many survivors, though not a symptom of the PTSD diagnosis itself, is shame. What is shame? Shame goes beyond guilt and is more difficult to overcome. Guilt means you feel bad for what you (supposedly) did or did not do during a traumatic event. Shame means that you feel bad for what or who you actually are. It is a deep feeling that originates from feeling flawed when you believe that only perfection is acceptable. Shame sometimes results from being used in an unacceptable or degrading manner (e.g., shame over feeling physical arousal while you were being molested).

Shame is a form of self-torment that includes feelings of inadequacy, inferiority, embarrassment, and disappointment and can lead to the formation of a shame-based identity—a situation in which your entire self-concept is based on your shame. Shame does not seem to get discharged through crying or expressing anger (Rothschild 2000). Feelings of shame may lead to aggression against yourself for violating your own inner standard of acceptable behavior. If you feel shame, you feel as if you are exposed to the world as bad. When you have been violated through a traumatic event, particularly if you were a victim of childhood abuse, you may feel shame about what happened to you. Your perpetrator may have told you messages during the abuse or afterwards that now make you feel ashamed (e.g., you liked what happened to you, you chose it, etc.). You may have accepted those messages as true and as part of you rather than as messages that are false and have come from outside you. These messages, called *introjects,* are lies that you no longer need to accept as your truths. Your own truth lies in you—you can make your own choices now about who you are and what you believe.

You may feel shame if and when you are put in a situation in which you have no power to choose. Then you feel wrong, bad, or worthless, or like you don't measure up because the bad thing happened to you. Shame is a painful emotion because it involves very negative, critical judgments of yourself that lead to feelings of humiliation, inadequacy, and low self-esteem. Feelings of shame can also lead you to seek isolation and separateness. The roots of shame lie in your abuse, violation, assault, or betrayal and in your damaged, undermined, or destroyed sense of self.

Exercise: My Shameful Beliefs

Before you look at your personal shameful beliefs, first see if any of the following statements describe you. Put a check by each one that does. These statements may have originated in the messages told to you. If any of these messages came from abusers, note their source or sources after each belief.

Belief   **This belief comes from:**

_____ I cannot take risks. _____

_____ I am not allowed to be seen or heard. _____

_____ I am invisible. _____

_____ To avoid disapproval, I do things I don't want to do. _____

_____ I am not allowed to ask for what I need. _____

_____ I am inferior to others. _____

_____ I must treat myself negatively because I am bad. _____

_____ My beliefs about myself are all negative. _____

_____ I must be perfect. _____

_____ I am a disappointment to_____ .

_____ My interests, choices, and wants are not of value to others. _____

_____ If something goes wrong in my world, it is my fault. _____

_____ I constantly look for ways to prove I am to blame for _____ .

If you hold any other shameful beliefs, list them here. _____

_____

_____

Of the beliefs listed above, which are the three most powerful and shameful in your life? You do not have to come up with three: one or two such beliefs can control your life. If you have more than three, continue the list on another piece of paper.

1. _____

2. _____

3. _____

Now look at each of these beliefs and at their sources. What situation or situations led to their becoming a part of you? Who said them first? What facts lie behind them? Complete the exercise below for each of the beliefs you listed above. If you have more than three, you can complete the exercise using those beliefs on separate pieces of paper.

1. The belief: _____

The situation: _____

The speaker: _____

The facts of the situation: _____

_____

The belief I can substitute for this shaming belief: _____

2. The belief: _____

The situation: _____

The speaker: _____

The facts of the situation: _____

_____

The belief I can substitute for this shaming belief: _____

3. The belief: _____

The situation: _____

The speaker: _____

The facts of the situation: _____

_____

The belief I can substitute for this shaming belief: _____

* * * *

The primary ways to combat shame are to recognize it, identify it, name it, name or describe the events that created it, and then substitute a new belief or beliefs. According to Power, "Healing from shame is the primary journey of the wounded heart. . . . Restoration is a process; . . . begin with recognition you are separate [from the shameful event], then deal with feelings of vulnerability, woundedness, and pain" (1992b, 60).

Use the following exercise to work out some new, healing beliefs and behaviors.

Exercise: Healing from Shame

I can also choose to assert myself when I am with persons who still try to shame me by:

1. _____

2. _____

3. _____

I can create positive affirmations to combat shaming. Three I am able to use (and am willing to at least try to believe) are:

1. _____

2. _____

3. _____

If someone tries to shame me or if shameful feelings start to return, I can nurture myself by:

1. _____

2. _____

3. _____

* * * * *

Grief and Loss

Trauma frequently includes loss. You may have lost your sense of safety and security, the meaning and purpose of life, your physical health, your ability to relate with others, your identity, your self-esteem, or someone or something you love. Loss leads to grief. Grief involves stages of disbelief or shock, anger or irritability, anxiety, depression, impaired concentration, and sleep disturbance—symptoms similar to those of post-traumatic stress disorder itself (Figley, Bride, and Mazza 1997). If the trauma you experienced involved death, the first reaction you may have had to that death is shock or denial, both of which function to protect you from distress and pain. The first goal for dealing with grief is to accept the reality that the one you love is dead. The shock or denial reaction is legitimate; it generally gives way to a feeling of disorganization and a need to adjust to a world without the loved one. In other words, you begin to move on.

Journal Exercise: The Grieving Process

In order to begin working through your grief, you may want to write down everything you miss about the person who died. Use your journal, and start by completing the following sentences:

Since _____ died, I never can _____ .

We never can _____ .

You may also try to answer the following questions:

- Why me?
- How can I go on?
- What do I need?
- What does this all mean?
- Why did this have to happen?
- What can I do?
- Who am I now?

You may also draw the place of death with as many details as you remember, tell the story about the death in detail aloud or in writing, or write a letter to the dead person (Ayalon 1992).

* * * * *

The final phase of grieving involves acceptance, the establishment of an ongoing relationship with your loss and with your loved one, and the recognition that you will never be the same. It also involves transcendence beyond the death using personal spirituality and faith, as well as channeling your energy into and reaching out toward something positive, such as a new person, career, project, or mission. Finding transcendence often means changing your attitudes toward life, death, yourself, suffering, and spirit.

Sometimes, it is possible for you to create positive statements about your grief. Some examples of these statements might be:

- All emotions are natural, healthy, and necessary.

- Grief is one of my emotions and can be empowering.

- Grief can release my energy.

- It is necessary for me to feel grief, accept it, and express it to achieve resolution of what happened to me.

- Grief is a way to show how much I cared for _____ .

- Grief is a step to making changes and handling crises.

What other positive statements about grief can you make? _____

_____

As you work through your grief, it may help if you:

- Realize that no one can grieve for you, and that you have the strength to do it for yourself.

- Remember that the purpose of grieving is to help you accept the reality of your loss.

- Keep in mind that trying to numb the pain of your loss will make the grieving process longer.

- Try to keep a normal routine while you grieve.

- Get help when you need it.

- Try to avoid making any extreme life changes or important decisions after your loss(es). Wait a few months at least.

- Remind yourself that grief is painful but that you will survive (adapted from Grand 2000).

Healing Rituals

When you feel guilt, shame, or grief, you may want to create a healing ritual to help yourself or to honor the person who died. A *healing ritual* is a structured activity designed to help release grief and pain. A ritual may help you find support from those around you as you learn to relate to the trauma in a new way. According to Williamson and Williamson (1994), rituals help to fulfill needs for inner nourishment and meaning and are a way to experience both inner and outer transformation. They also are a means to enhance our spirituality and to bring about emotional healing after crisis and trauma. Rituals often spring from the symbols and images of everyday experiences. These symbols can give meaning, purpose, and energy to our lives. According to Catherall (1992) there are seven steps to a ritual. These steps are explored in the exercise that follows, which is intended to help you design your own ritual.

Exercise: My Healing Ritual

I want to do a ritual for _____ because _____

_____ .

1. Select a location to do the ritual. The location might be a grave, a mountaintop, a statue's base, or the Vietnam Veterans Memorial Wall. My location is _____

2. Select a symbolic "something" that stands for what you have suffered. What symbols might stand for your life before, during, and after the trauma? What did you lose because of the trauma—a home, innocence, your childhood, a loved one, certain possessions? My symbol is _____

3. Select any props you might want to use in your ritual. Props help to build the scene. You may want to use appropriate candles, stones, or pictures. My props include _____

4. Decide if there is anyone else you want to include in the ritual who might give you support. This might be a friend, spouse, partner, child, or therapist. My companion is _____

5. Think of what you want to say at the ritual. Do you want to give a eulogy to someone who has died? Do you want to say goodbye to someone or something? Do you have a poem, joke, anecdote, or song? For example, a memorial service was recently held at the first tee of a local golf course for a golfer who had died of cancer. It was a beautiful, warm day and those in attendance were asked to participate. Poetry, personal music, and stories were shared, and those who wanted to participated in a symbolic golf tournament in honor of him. My healing words are _____

_____ .

6. Choose a guide, leader, or assistant if you need one, and decide how that person can help you. My guide or help is _____ .
He or she will help me by _____ .

7. Decide how you will bid farewell to persons, feelings, events, or times of your life. You can use the ritual as a way to release your pain and hurt. Do you want to use the ritual to get rid of something, e.g., possessions that belonged to a perpetrator or drawings of abuse? I will be saying goodbye to _____ .

Once you have put the ritual on paper, consider whether you want to actually do it. Can you make a commitment to do the ritual? When will you do it? _____

If you like, write a bit about how completing this exercise helped you? _____

_____

_____

* * * * *

The Rituals of the Phoenix Rising

Williamson and Williamson (1994) describe the ritual of the phoenix rising as an example of a healing ritual. The phoenix was a symbol of the Egyptian sun god and was believed to live for 500 years. According to the myth, it then burned itself to ash on a pyre but did not die. Instead, it rose to live again in a state of youth. The phoenix can be a symbol of immortality and regeneration, as well as of transformation from what you are to what you want to become. You may use this ritual to shed things that are holding you back, such as survivor guilt, shame, worry, fear, lack of self-esteem, or indecision.

The ritual involves designing a personal phoenix medallion and creating your own affirmation to put on the medallion. The affirmation might say something like, "From the ashes of past traumas, I rise as a phoenix to a new freedom and sense of being." You may also choose your own personal symbols of freedom and transformation to use in this ritual. Williamson and Williamson suggest you take a black marking pen and write words that are personal symbols of freedom on the back of the medallion you have created. These words might include "faith," "self-love," "forgiveness," "patience," "praise," "strength," "truth," "spirituality," "redemption," "peace," or others.

Journal Exercise: My Phoenix Medallion

Take a few minutes to decide on your own personal words and affirmations and write them in your journal. Now, close your eyes, and think about what your medallion will look like. (You can also make a real medallion from clay or cardboard or other materials.) Draw a picture of the front and back of your medallion in your notebook or journal. Close your eyes and think some more before you write your healing words or affirmations on your medallion's back. You may draw a picture on its front as well. This medallion becomes a visual reminder of your commitment to growth. Put the medallion in a special place or carry it with you so that you can have access to it regularly. You may look at your medallion as often as you need to to remind you that you always have new opportunities to heal.

* * * * *

Regular Rituals

Rituals do not have to be onetime events. Sometimes participation in a regularly observed ritual unites you and others who have similar pasts or traumas and gives you a sense of group identification. Once a year, certain Quaker meetings are followed by a separation ritual for women who have lost a child. Women go to a designated tree and put an offering or gift on it for each child lost. The children may have died, been aborted, been miscarried, or been put up for adoption. These women share their grief and provide each other with support.

Another ritual occurred at 9:02 A.M. on April 19, 2001. At that time, in Oklahoma City, the names of each of the 168 victims of the Oklahoma City bombing were read as their empty chairs sat mournfully in the empty field that used to be the building in which they died. This ritual honored the victims and assured the survivors that their loved ones are remembered. When rituals such as these are repeated regularly, perhaps yearly, they can bring a sense of order through their familiarity and provide a safe way for the living to express their feelings both symbolically and directly.

8

Difficulty Regulating Emotion

(Complex PTSD, Category 1)

In chapter 1, we gave you a proposed description of a new diagnostic category of trauma called complex PTSD or disorders of extreme stress not otherwise specified (DESNOS). Why might a different diagnosis be necessary? As we said previously, you can be exposed to different types of traumatic events. The first type, type I exposure, means that you have experienced a single distinct traumatic event or, over the course of a lifetime, a few distinct traumatic events. Many persons experience only a few traumas in the course of a lifetime.

Judy was in a car accident when she was thirty. She was driving when a car came out of nowhere and hit her car on the passenger's side. Judy had several broken bones from the impact but her injuries were not life-threatening. Her boyfriend died when he was thrown through the windshield. He had refused to put on his seat belt. She watched as he flew out of the car and hit the pavement in front of other cars that then ran over him.

Ted was walking down a quiet street about 10 P.M. when three young teenagers approached him and demanded his money. Ted noticed that they were carrying weapons: one had a knife, another had a gun, and a third had what looked to be a sawed-off shotgun. When he saw the weapons Ted handed the boys his wallet. However, they wanted his jewelry, too. When Ted was unable to get his ring off his finger, the boy with the knife suddenly grabbed Ted's hand and cut the finger off. The boys ran. Bleeding heavily, Ted screamed for help and then collapsed. A policeman found his finger two blocks away but doctors could not reconnect it.

In both of these cases, the victims developed PTSD. However, neither Ted nor Judy had a lifelong history of trauma that suddenly roared up and needed to be treated as well. After a few months, both Ted and Judy returned to a new sense of normalcy, forever changed by what happened, but able to function. Judy now insists that every passenger in her car always wears a seat belt and Ted will never walk alone down a relatively dark city street at night again. He also has begun karate instruction and is learning to defend himself physically.

But what if Ted and Judy had had a lifetime of trauma prior to these events? What if Ted had been severely beaten by his father for the first fifteen years of his life, or if he also had witnessed the beating of his mother, brothers, and sisters while his father was drunk? What if Judy had been regularly molested by her brother between the ages of five and nine, had been physically attacked by her father, and had been told by both parents that she was never wanted and it would be better for everyone if she would just die. Do you see yourself as a Judy or Ted in the first situations (involving type I trauma, or a single, serious trauma) or in the second situations (involving type II trauma, or years of serious trauma)?

Do you feel as if you have lived in a war zone for most (or all) of your life? Do you have a hard time even thinking that you have a sense of self? Do you generally feel unsafe and untrusting, and believe that personal power is an illusion? Do you lack good self-esteem and positive intimate relationships? Are you isolated, without connections to others except perhaps in the work environment? Do you find it hard, if not impossible, to attach to others? Do you find it difficult to monitor how you act or to stop yourself before you act in an impulsive way that sometimes hurts you? If you answered "yes" to any one of these questions as you read this paragraph, you may have symptoms of complex PTSD. You may refer to chapter 1 of this workbook for a description of the seven dimensions of complex PTSD. If you want to, turn to the appendix to find a questionnaire that identifies the various symptom clusters of complex PTSD. You may complete it now. The higher the numerical response, the more likely you are to exhibit the characteristic of complex PTSD. However, there are no criteria yet that set the number of characteristics for each of the seven symptom categories that you need to have an actual diagnosis.

This and the following six chapters will examine each of those dimensions in some detail and will provide techniques and exercises to help you bring your symptoms under control. Not everyone has difficulties in all of the seven dimensions. As you read through this workbook, choose which of the seven dimensions apply to you and work on those chapters.

Trauma and Emotional Health

An emotionally healthy person is able to enjoy intimacy as well as being alone. A person who has experienced type II traumas (which lead to complex PTSD) tends to either be too dependent on others in an intimate relationship or is so terrified by any intimate connection that he or she flees from a relationship to aloneness. However, when alone, the survivor often feels an unbearable sense of abandonment and again longs for connection. So the survivor tries to connect and again becomes terrified of rejection and abuse. His or her relationships begin to take on a pattern of being too close and running away.

Does the previous paragraph describe you? Can you keep a clear sense of who you are when you are with others or with a partner or spouse? Can you self-soothe? When you feel very emotional, can you still make good decisions? Are you able to keep distance emotionally when others are overreacting; can you still make good decisions in such a case? Do your behaviors and your words match each other? Can you tolerate some pain if the pain means you will grow stronger in the end? If you have answered "no" to any or all of these questions, you might also find it helpful to look at the seven categories of complex PTSD symptoms in chapter 1, turn to the chapter that deals with each of the categories that applies to you, and practice some of the techniques found there. Even if you are not a type II trauma survivor and have answered "yes" to these questions, you may still find some of the exercises helpful.

Bloom (2000) writes that people start with a normal potential to grow. You started life with the potential to be a healthy, happy human being, within the context of certain genetic and bodily predispositions. However, if you were traumatized early in life, the effects of trauma soon interfered with your physical, psychological, social, and moral development. If you were repeatedly traumatized, you may have developed *learned helplessness* in order to endure abusive situations; that is, you learned that it was useless to try to get away. Later, even if you could have escaped, you may not have done so, or you went from one abusive situation into another (e.g., from a violent family situation to a harmful dating or marriage relationship). If you continued to have positive feelings toward an abuser, you may have also experienced what is known as *traumatic bonding* (you have a deep bond with the person who abused you).

Exposure to repeated trauma, type II trauma, may prevent you from attaching in a healthy way to others. It may cause you to be unable to control your emotional arousal. In a matter of milliseconds, you might go from being okay to being in a rage. You may also find that you do not have enough trust in others or yourself to allow yourself to develop a stable relationship. Instead, you may become aggressive toward others (either outwardly or in a more subtle, passive form), as well as toward yourself when things don't go your way.

Your capacity to regulate your own internal emotional states, your body sense, and your response to external stress helps to define who you are (Cole and Putnam 1992). If you were a victim of type II trauma, you may lack a predictable sense of yourself, have a poor sense of separateness from others, have a disturbed body image, have poor impulse control, and become suspicious and distrusting in social situations.

Does this description sound familiar to you? Are you able to be emotionally upset without hurting yourself? Are you able to be emotionally upset without becoming aggressive? Are you able to stay present when you are emotionally upset, without dissociating? Are you able to find words to identify bodily sensations that occur when you are upset? Are you able to find words to name emotional states; that is, are you able to name how you feel, and do those feelings match the situation?

Exercise: What Type II Traumas Have I Experienced?

The following lists describe type II traumas and their symptoms. Check which characteristics of Type II trauma that you have experienced:

_____ chronic, extremely invasive experiences

_____ long-standing, repeated exposure to extreme events

_____ ongoing physical abuse

_____ ongoing sexual abuse

_____ chronic neglect combined with other abusive experiences

_____ ongoing horror that never seems to end

_____ living in a world that is unpredictable and at times terrifying

_____ having persons supposed to protect me show little regard for me

How many of these did you check? What do you think this says about your earlier experiences? _____

Now, which of the following symptoms of type II trauma do you experience now?

_____ massive denial

_____ self-anesthesia in parts of my body

_____ dissociation

_____ self-hypnosis

_____ continued attachment to those who hurt me

_____ aggression turned toward myself through self-mutilation

_____ absence of feelings

_____ sense of overwhelming rage

_____ unremitting, chronic sadness

_____ loss of memory of a large part of my childhood

_____ indifference to pain

_____ lack of ability to empathize with others' feelings

_____ inability to name my emotions or recognize emotions in others

_____ uneasiness with intimacy

_____ serious emotional distancing

_____ desire to remove myself from the possibility of pain and hurt in any way possible (adapted from Kelly 1999)

* * * * *

Alterations in Your Ability to Manage Emotions and Impulses

As we have stated, there are seven categories of impact or symbols that make up what is now called complex PTSD or disorders of extreme stress, not otherwise specified (DESNOS). The first category involves alterations in your ability to manage emotions and impulses. This includes difficulties managing your expression of emotions (including anger and rage), the tendency to harm yourself through self-mutilation, problems from dangerous risk-taking, preoccupation with self-destruction or suicide, and sexual risk-taking and inappropriate sexual behavior. The goal of working through this chapter is for you to learn to modulate and control your emotion and regulate your emotion-driven responses.

Feelings generally can be associated with joy or with pain. Each feeling of pain has an opposite feeling associated with joy. For example, the opposite of fear is hope; of sadness, joy; of hate, love. Painful feelings that result from exposure to trauma frequently are denied and avoided. Many trauma survivors have a hard time keeping their feelings under control. Many times, people with complex PTSD are also not aware of the range of feelings that exists and have only limited emotional responses to most situations. Having feelings or recognizing having certain feelings may make you want to hurt yourself. Examples of feelings that may lead to self-hurt include anger, sadness, shame, emptiness, guilt, and betrayal. But if you do not know what many different feelings are like, you also cannot use them either positively or negatively.

Are you able to name the feelings you have at different times? Do you know the difference between dislike, disregard, anger, frustration, rage, and hostility, among others? Learning how to name feelings and then recognize (them both in yourself and others) are the first steps in trying to bring the feelings under control.

If you cannot find words to identify your emotions and if you are not able to know what you feel, then it is very difficult to plan how to cope with those emotions. When you name and then learn to tolerate your emotions, you gain the ability to "own" them and you become more in touch with yourself.

Exercise: Recognizing My Emotion

Which of the following emotional states do you personally know, and whi
the past two weeks? Please circle those you have felt in the past two weeks
those about which you can say that you know how they feel.

abandoned	cranky	friendly	loyal	
accepted	crazy	fulfilled	lucky	
aching	crushed	full	mad	thrilled
affectionate	curious	furious	mean	tired
alone	defeated	giving	miserable	tolerant
aloof	dejected	glad	patient	tortured
amused	delighted	grateful	peaceful	trapped in time
angry	dependent	grouchy	pleased	
annoyed	deserted	grumpy	powerless	troubled
anxious	desirable	guilty	preoccupied	trusted
apologetic	desperate	happy	proud	ugly
at peace	devastated	helpless	regretful	unappreciated
aware	different	hopeful	rejected	unaware
betrayed	disappointed	hopeless	remorseful	understood
bitter	discouraged	humiliated	responsible	unfriendly
bored	distressed	hurt	revengeful	unhappy
brave	dominated	impatient	safe	upset
calm	doomed	inadequate	screwed	useless
capable	eager	incompetent	serene	valued
caring	easygoing	innocent	shamed	victimized
cautious	ecstatic	insecure	shocked	violated
cheerful	elated	interested	shy	vulnerable
composed	embarrassed	irate	sorry	warm
confident	enraged	irked	stimulated	weary
conflicted	excited	irritated	stunned	whipped
connected	exposed	isolated	stupid	wiped out
content	foolish	jealous	sweet	withdrawn
courageous	frantic	joyful	sympathetic	wonderful
				worthwhile

These are only a small proportion of the words that are associated with feelings. Were you
able to identify and imagine or remember having most of them? What has completing this
exercise taught you about yourself? _____

_____

* * * * *

Using Feelings Appropriately

Learning to use feelings as ways to guide appropriate behavior is a second step in working on these symptoms. If your goal is to develop a self that has some personal power, it is important that you are able to experience both pleasant and unpleasant emotions without over- or underreacting and, if things really get rough, that you are able to self-soothe. The goal is for you to be able to look at possible ways to express your emotions and then make choices.

Exercise: How Do I Regulate My Emotions?

If I get very, very sad, how do I express that sadness? Do I become extremely depressed or do I cry and grieve and then go on? _____

_____

If I get very, very happy, am I able to keep that happiness contained, or do I seem to get out of control? _____

---

* * * * *

Linehan (1996) encourages the development of *mindfulness*, or the ability to observe, name, and describe your feelings and reactions without judging yourself or seeking escape or relief from them immediately, if not sooner. Sometimes the emotions that you feel are ones you associate with past traumas. For example, anytime you feel the slightest bit of fear, it may take you back to an abusive situation in which you felt terror. Learning to know when the fear is truly due to something in your present and not something from your past helps you lessen the power of the past over you. If you were abused in childhood, it is possible that you may find it very difficult to contain your emotions, regulate your aggressive acting out toward yourself and others, and feel empathy for others.

One technique for controlling an emotion (adapted from Schiraldi 1999) has the following steps:

1. Allow yourself to feel enough of a certain emotion (joy, sadness) to get in touch with it without either going out of control or detaching yourself from it.

2. Use the experience of feeling the emotion as a way to learn more about yourself. What other emotions are present as well? Do these other emotions grow from the original emotion? You can look at each of them separately.

3. Identify the source of the original emotion. Go as far back as is necessary, often to a trauma.

4. Say or do what you need to in order to get a sense of closure on the situation that led to the emotion.

5. Look for a way to find an outcome to the emotion—perhaps writing a good-bye letter to someone who has left or died, organizing a ritual (see the section "Healing Rituals" near the end of chapter 7), or doing something for someone else.

6. Move on, away from the emotion; don't allow yourself to be stuck in it. Return to the activities of daily life.

Exercise: Practice Controlling an Emotion

Can you think of a situation in which you have had an overwhelming negative emotion? Describe it here and name the initial emotion that arises from it. _____

_____

_____

Now apply the six steps just described to that emotion.

1. _____

2. _____

3. _____

4. _____

5. _____

6. _____

Was this exercise helpful? What did it teach you about that emotion? Can you think of another situation in which it might help you bring emotions under control? _____

_____

_____

If you are not able to write about your emotion, you might consider drawing that emotion or collaging it in your journal or notebook or on a separate piece of paper.

* * * * *

Expressing Emotion

What are some other ways you might learn about, deal with, and express emotion in appropriate ways? You may go back to chapter 6 and look at the ways to deal with anger that are given in that chapter. Other techniques to help you with your emotions include:

1. learning to identify cues and triggers that lead to emotions, then writing down the differences in what you feel with possibly different emotions (anger, fear, etc.)

2. rehearsing ways to deal with emotions ahead of time when you are not sure how to handle a situation (e.g., saying out loud, "I need some time to think over what it is I need to do."

3. role playing situations that involve emotion with others, including your therapist if you are in counseling

4. discussing emotions with others

5. practicing expressing emotions with those you trust and then asking for feedback

6. using relaxation techniques to combat arousal when emotions become too intense

7. monitoring your beliefs about situations: looking at what happens to those beliefs to lead to emotional reactions, and then attempting to challenge and change the beliefs so they do not lead to what Meichenbaum (1994) lists as the most damaging kinds of self-talk:

- catastrophic interpretations of events ("this is sooo awful; I just can't stand it anymore")

- demanding and coercive language involving shoulds, oughts, have to's, need to's

- overgeneralizations using *never* and *always*

- negatively labeling yourself as stupid, impossible, and so forth

- categorical thinking: calling yourself labels like asshole, shithead, S.O.B., and others

- black and white thinking—a situation is either all good or all bad with no gray in between

In chapter 11 we will discuss problem-solving techniques. You may turn to that chapter for additional ideas. It is also important that you look at exactly how you feel about feeling your feelings. In order to know how you feel, you might complete the following exercise (adapted from Miller et al. 1989).

Exercise: Feeling My Feelings

1. List any feelings that you enjoy having. _____

_____

_____

2. List any feelings that you may not enjoy having but that you at least are willing to accept having. _____

_____

_____

3. List any feelings that you find unacceptable to feel. _____

_____

_____

4. When you have the feelings you listed in question 3, what do you do with them?

_____

_____

5. List any feelings you may be embarrassed to feel. _____

_____

_____

6. If you have those feelings, what do you do with them? _____

_____

_____

7. List any feelings you may be ashamed to feel. _____

_____

_____

8. What do you do with those feelings if you have them? _____

_____

_____

* * * * *

Being Afraid to Have Feelings

Being afraid to feel and show feelings may really be related to your beliefs about your unmet basic needs for safety, trust, personal power, esteem, and intimacy (Rosenbloom and Williams 1999). You may be more afraid of being rejected, abandoned, punished, or criticized than of the specific emotion itself. What really would happen if you allowed yourself to show an emotion you feel?

For one day, try to express your emotions honestly (without hurting yourself or others). Record what happened in the space provided below.

Emotion I expressed   **What happened when I expressed it**

_____   _____

_____   _____

_____   _____

_____   _____

_____   _____

_____   _____

Expressing emotions means taking a risk. Taking that risk can be productive; it can lead to emotional development and self-improvement. This type of risk-taking is in contrast to risk-taking that is not productive and that may occur just for thrills or an adrenaline high. Nonproductive risks often involve hazardous actions that can jeopardize health, career, relationships, and other major areas of life—or life itself (Ilardo 1992). Expressing emotions honestly can bring about gratification either immediately or over time, as you become more honest with yourself and others and as you let go of emotional baggage that has collected over time. Expressing an emotion means taking a chance; however, the end result of release from being a hostage to your emotions is worth that risk.

More on Self-Harm and Self-Mutilation

Self-mutilation is a special type of self-harm. It is direct, controlled, and repetitive, it does not have the intent of suicide, it is not related to being impaired mentally or cognitively (e.g., being retarded or autistic), and it is socially unacceptable (Suyemoto and Kountz 2000). Self-mutilation generally happens when you feel a deep loss that leads to feelings of tenseness, anxiety, anger, or fear, and you express those feelings by harming your body in a very controlled manner. The most common form of self-mutilation is self-cutting. Cutting (and self-mutilation in general) is:

- a way to manage painful emotions that you can't express in words by doing something that is concrete and active

- a way to stop feeling feelings and therefore control them

- a way to prove you are alive

- a way to reenact trauma and abuse

- an addictive action that can become compulsive

- a boundary violation of your body

- an expression of self-blame

- a way to self-soothe

- a way to communicate an emotion

- an expression of self-hate

- a way to resist taking care of yourself in a positive way

- a way to maintain a stable sense of self if you are threatened with the loss of your identity

- a way to escape the pain of a perceived rejection

- a way to have physical evidence of emotional injury

- a way to distance yourself and set boundaries between yourself and others who will reject you for self-mutilating

- a way to stop, induce, or prevent dissociation (see chapter 9)

- a way to release endorphins so you do not feel pain

- a way to self-punish for doing certain behaviors or having certain thoughts or feelings that were punished in childhood by others

(Suyemoto and Kountz 2000; Alderman 1997)

As Alderman writes, "most self-inflicted violence is the result of high levels of emotional distress with few available means to cope" (2000, 7). You may use or experience self-mutilation as a way to get control over your body, challenging those around you to care enough to notice and do something. Do you see hurting yourself as a way to express your rage toward powerful others through hurting yourself? Self-mutilation of any kind can be a substitute for anger toward another as well as a desire (unconscious or conscious) to inflict pain on that person. Sometimes, the desire to hurt yourself is a way to fight depression and anxiety or a way to numb yourself out through a type of self-medication. Sometimes self-mutilation is a way to show how much you hate yourself. Eating disorders involving self-starvation and purging yourself to the point of physical pain can also be a form of self-mutilation. You also may self-mutilate as a way to reconnect your body and mind. Some people say that they are able to believe and recognize that they are real and alive if they see blood. Self-mutilating, to them, may calm their intrusive trauma-based thoughts by giving them the endorphin release that brings calming and lessens their arousal.

If you self-mutilate, complete the following exercise. Above all, it is important for you to go to a qualified therapist to get help. No self-abuse is okay; it is a way of revictimizing yourself. There are other ways for you to communicate your pain and anguish without taking it out on your own body. When you have very strong emotions of any kind, you do not have to act on them. Setting up a plan of alternative reactions to strong feelings is one way to bring self-mutilation under control.

Exercise: My Reasons for Self-Mutilating

1. List ways you self-injure here: _____

_____

_____

_____

2. Now answer the following questions about each of these behaviors (do the first behavior here in the workbook and do the others in your journal):

How does the behavior help me survive? _____

_____

How does the behavior give meaning to my trauma? _____

_____

How does the behavior give me a sense of mastery and control and power? _____

_____

How does the behavior release endorphins and make me feel better? _____

_____

How does the behavior give me revenge? _____

_____

How does the behavior reinforce my feelings of guilt, shame, and self-blame? _____

_____

How does the behavior punish me? _____

_____

How does the behavior reenact what I learned earlier in life? _____

_____

How does the behavior bring me affection, care, and emotional closeness? _____

_____

3. Check all the items that you feel apply to you in the list below.

I mutilate myself because

_____ I want to show that I own my own body.

_____ I want to express my rage at myself.

_____ I hate myself.

_____ I want to distract myself from other pain.

_____ I want to numb out my feelings.

_____ I have a message to give that I can't say directly.

_____ I am asking for help.

_____ I want to be rescued.

_____ I believe my body is a battleground.

_____ I want to cleanse myself.

_____ I want to somehow atone for my sins.

_____ I want to express my shame.

_____ I am trying to express my pain.

_____ I am taking over where my abuser left off.

_____ I am retaliating against myself for telling secrets.

_____ I am doing what my abuser brainwashed me to do, if I told.

_____ I am trying to connect my mind with my body.

_____ I am trying to make sure I am real, through bleeding.

_____ I am trying to bring my emotions under control.

_____ I am trying to prove that I am alive.

_____ I am trying to get a "high."

_____ I am trying to manage my flashbacks or memories.

_____ I am trying to release intolerable emotional tension.

_____ I am trying to buy myself time by focusing attention on physical rather than emotional pain.

_____ I need a release valve.

_____ I need to get into a "neutral zone."

4. Now take each of the reasons for self-injuring that you checked and think of five other things you might do to express that emotion or action. For example, if you checked "I want to cleanse myself" as a reason for self-mutilating, what are five other things you could do to cleanse yourself that do not involve self-mutilation? They might be to take a bubble bath, take a sauna, go to a day spa, use herbs to purify my body, or do some other form of cleansing ritual. You may think of others that might apply to you. There is space below to write your reactions to one of your reasons. You may do the others in your journal or notebook.

My reason for self-mutilating: _____

Five things I could do instead: _____

_____

_____

_____

_____

5. What did completing this exercise teach you about yourself? _____

_____

_____

_____

* * * * *

Beliefs Leading to Self-Mutilation

You may also have a belief system that allows you to mutilate yourself. These beliefs frequently are distorted and may even have come from your abusers (as introjects you have taken into your own brain and now experience as your own beliefs). These beliefs are generally black and white or all or nothing beliefs.

Exercise: My Beliefs about Self-Mutilation

Check which of the following statements you believe, if any:

_____ Self-mutilation doesn't hurt anyone but me and it really doesn't hurt me.

_____ It's my body, I can do what I want with it.

_____ It's no big deal and shouldn't upset anyone.

_____ If I don't hurt myself this way, my pain will be worse.

_____ The scars are there for a reason; they remind me of (telling, needing to be punished, my shame, etc.).

_____ No one knows about it, anyhow.

_____ I need to be punished for what I did.

_____ It just shows how bad a person I am.

_____ It keeps people away.

* * * * *

None of the statements in the preceding list is accurate or true. Each is a distorted belief. Self-mutilation is never a healthy way to express pain or hurt. If you checked any of these statements, it's important that you work with a therapist to help change these beliefs. Other things you might do with that therapist include developing an impulse control log (write what, when you felt the urge to harm yourself, you did instead), and think of ways to express your feelings that are not harmful to you. In the impulse control log, you may want to identify any triggers that led you to self-mutilate. Other techniques to control self-mutilation include:

- Try to focus your attention on something other than the need to self-mutilate, e.g., focus your attention on doing a crossword or jigsaw puzzle or some other intellectually stimulating challenge. This minimizes emotional pain.

- Make a list of alternatives to self-harm.

- Write or draw the abusive intent rather than act on it.

- Substitute physical activity to get the same adrenaline high, if that is the motivation.

- Make a collage of acceptable methods of self-expression.

- List the introjects that lead to self-harm.

- Develop a safety contract with your therapist or some other significant person and agree not to self-mutilate for a specified period of time; include rewards for following the contract and consequences if you break it.

- Develop a collage of each emotion that you find difficult to handle or express including ways to release that emotion without self-harm.

- During a period of time that you don't feel self-destructive, prepare a list of reasons why you don't want to self-mutilate. Then, when you feel the urge to hurt yourself, go back and review this list and try to add another one or two reasons to it.

- Prepare a list or photo gallery of positive accomplishments in your life. When you feel the urge to self-mutilate, look at that list or album and then tell yourself, "I've accomplished all this good in my life and don't deserve to suffer more; I'm a good person."

- Learn to identify the early warning signs that a feeling is becoming intolerable and then self-soothe or do something else. This technique involves identifying patterns of self-injury as a first step to changing those patterns. How often do you self-injure (daily, weekly, sometimes, rarely)? Then look at what you were doing, thinking, or feeling both right before the self-injury happened and right after it happened (Trautman and Connors 1994).

- Look at the backlash that happens after you harm yourself—from others and from yourself. Do you: feel crazy, hurt physically, feel shame, try to hide from others? Use memories of that backlash as reminders why you do not want to hurt yourself.

- Create a safe toolbox that includes a non-harm agreement, an impulse control log, a list of your self-harm alternatives, writing materials and art materials so you can get out your feelings and thoughts in other ways, and a life plan (Alderman 1997).

- If you must see blood on yourself, get a tube of fake blood and use it to visualize the effects of self-mutilation without actually carrying out the act.

- Use affirmations to change your beliefs about why it's okay to harm yourself (see the exercise near the end of chapter 6).

The Cutting Edge (P.O. Box 20819, Cleveland, Ohio 44120) is an excellent resource: a newsletter for those who self-injure.

Changing Your Beliefs Through Affirmations

As we discussed in chapter 6, regular use of affirmations can change your beliefs about yourself and your emotions and actions based on those beliefs. This kind of real change has six stages, and it does not happen overnight. These stages are:

1. Precontemplation (My negative beliefs about myself are right; I don't need to change them.)

2. Contemplation (Well, maybe I do need to make some changes.)

3. Preparation (I guess I can begin to focus on what I need to do and what affirmations I might write or say.)

4. Action (I will do and am doing this; I am saying or writing the affirmations on a daily basis.)

5. Maintenance (I am beginning to believe the affirmations. I don't need to say them as often and I sort of believe them; I am beginning to see things in a different way and feel better about me.)

6. Termination—the ideal end (Wow, I actually am okay and don't need to see myself so negatively. Sometimes I forget that I am okay, but I recover quickly. The affirmations really are acceptable ways to describe myself—they work even when I am in crisis. I am able to do what is best for me.)

Exercise: My Affirmations around Self-Mutilation

In the space below, write three affirmations that you want to say to yourself or write to yourself that you eventually hope to believe. Remember to put them in present tense and use the word "I."

1. _____

2. _____

3. _____

Now write each affirmation five times to begin to get familiar with it.

_____

_____

_____

_____

_____

_____

_____

_____

_____

_____

Are you willing to write or say each of these three affirmations twenty times a day for the next month? If so, fill in the blanks below:

I am willing to commit to saying or writing each of these three affirmations twenty times a day for the next thirty days. At the end of that time, I will return to this page and write how I feel about the exercise and my beliefs.

_____ (sign) _____
Your signature   Today's date

Thirty days from that date is _____ (fill in date). In the last thirty days, this exercise has:

_____

_____

_____

* * * * *

Modulation of Feelings and of Sexual Involvement

Schiraldi writes that some studies "have indicated that males and females with PTSD are more likely to experience sexual problems than those without PTSD . . . [including] sexual disinterest, aversion, dissatisfaction, performance difficulties (including painful intercourse and impaired arousal)" (2000, 318). If you were a victim of any type of sexual abuse or sexual assault, you may feel shame if you have sexual feelings, and sex can become a trigger that is associated with humiliation, danger, and the need to keep a secret.

You may have flashbacks during sexual relationships. If so, it is important that you ground yourself in the present as soon as you become aware of the flashback, perhaps by focusing on your safe place and on relaxation. It is important to stop any sexual response or activity you might be having until the flashback is done. It is also important to let your sexual partner know immediately what you are experiencing, asking him or her to reassure you and comfort you that you are in the present (Dolan 1991).

Some trauma survivors believe that they must self-injure if they have sexual feelings or arousal. Learning to substitute pleasure-oriented touch and imagery for self-injurious images and actions can be a long, hard process. Trauma may have impacted your ability to express yourself sexually to the point that you either ignore your sexual needs and wants or act out your sexual needs and wants aggressively, impulsively, or nonintimately. The next paragraph contains questions about your sexual feelings and behaviors. You can read and think about them, or write about them in your journal or notebook.

What behaviors are involved in any sexual behavior you have? Are there specific triggers that lead to your having or wanting to have a sexual encounter or relationship? When you want to be sexual, what thoughts motivate your behavior? Do you expect a negative outcome from any sexual experiences you have?

When you are sexual, how much control do you feel you have over what happens? If you feel out of control in a sexual encounter, what feelings do you have? Do you get confused, do you feel pain and shame, do you feel anger toward yourself or your sexual partner?

Then what do you do? Do you continue to have sex even though you don't enjoy it? Do you get angry toward your sexual partner? Do you try to manipulate the situation? Do you stop the sexual act itself? Do you physically leave?

If any of these things happen, then how do you feel? Do you feel vulnerable and powerless? Do you believe that your partner will no longer care for you or love you? Then what do you do? Do you seek to protect yourself through distancing from your sexual partner? Do you use substances, numb out, sleep, or isolate yourself? Do you self-injure?

Physical Boundaries

A *boundary* is any type of division or separation that you set between what is permissible or possible and what is not. You have many different types of boundaries around you and within you. One type of boundary involves physical space. It is important for you to recognize the amount of physical space that you need around you in order to feel comfortable when you are with others.

Exercise: My Physical Boundaries

Answer each of your following questions, using your journal or notebook if you need more space.

How close is too close? _____

_____

If someone comes too close, how do you feel? _____

_____

Are there situations in your life at the present time in which persons come physically too close to you? What are they? _____

What do you do when a person approaches you and you do not want to be approached? Are you able to be assertive and maintain your physical space? _____

_____

What is your definition of unwanted physical contact? _____

_____

How do you react if someone violates your boundary of physical contact? For example, how do you react if someone:

- brushes up against you

_____

- stands too close to you

_____

- touches you on your body in a nonsexual way when you do not want to be touched

_____

- tries to touch you in a sexual manner and you do not want to be touched

_____

- stares at you

_____

- hits you

_____

- talks too close to your face

_____

* * * * *

Body Language and Physical Boundaries

You can use body language (the way you position your body and the facial expressions you have) to say "stay away" or "come closer." Such body language includes:

- folding your arms across your body
- turning your body away
- turning your head away if someone is talking to you
- staring back at someone in a positive manner
- staring back at someone in a hostile manner
- looking down and avoiding eye contact
- moving closer to someone

- making eye contact
- smiling

Think about what other types of body language you might use to say "stay away" or "come closer?" _____

_____

_____

Boundaries and Healthy Sexuality

Setting a physical boundary can invite in or keep away potential sexual partners. Appropriate boundaries are an important part of healthy sexuality. Healthy sexuality can be fun, playful, and authentic; it usually exists within the boundaries of a loving, respectful, giving relationship. It is part of relationship building and maintaining because it involves shared vulnerability and control. If you want to work on normalizing your sexual feelings, you might consider following the strategies suggested by Schiraldi (2000). These include:

1. Think of your genital area as a normal part of your body; use its proper name and acknowledge its unique functions.

2. Neutralize any feelings of disgust you have toward sex. Start by considering whether you think all sex is disgusting, or just certain aspects of it.

3. Look at any feelings of shame that you have about sex and then develop positive affirmations to shift your focus toward the positive aspects of yourself and your sexual being.

4. Develop your own description of what healthy sexuality is.

5. Follow Engel's sexual paradoxes to develop a satisfying sexuality (1995):

   - The harder you try to make good sex happen, the less happens, so relax and take your time.

   - You can cure your sexual dysfunctions by not trying to cure them.

   - The way to have sex when you want to is to learn to know when you do not want to have it and then say "no."

   - The way to please your partner sexually is to learn what feels good to you.

6. Before trying to have sex, learn to touch yourself and your partner sensually.

7. Learn the differences between sex, love, affection, and attention.

8. Be prepared for the inevitable flashbacks that will occur during sex (the techniques you have learned in chapter 4 should help).

9. Develop your own personal healing sexual imagery or stories to use if you need some fantasy during sex; these stories are typically built around what would lead to your safety.

Emotional Boundaries

A second type of boundary is an *emotional boundary*. Having an emotional boundary means that you are able to set limits without worrying whether or not you might hurt or disappoint another person. Asking for what you want or deserve is another way to set an emotional boundary. Asking without worrying whether or not you will be abandoned, disliked, hurt, or attacked occurs when you have good emotional boundaries. If you have good emotional boundaries, you can refuse to be sexual without fearing that the person who wants a sexual relationship with you will be so hurt or angry that he or she will abandon, reject, or punish you. You have the right to say "no" emotionally as well as physically.

Setting and Maintaining Boundaries

Part of setting boundaries is to create a personal "bill of rights." This bill of rights can allow you to set boundaries and take risks. In one of the next exercises, you will have the opportunity to add to the rights listed below.

- I have the right to choose my own sexual partners.

- I have the right to say "no" to a request for sex.

- I have the right to keep others out of my personal space.

- I have the right to stop any sexual activity in which I am involved if and when I have a flashback.

If you say "no" in a firm manner when it is right to say no, you will be able to survive the reactions of those around you. It may feel very strange to think that you are able to say "no" to someone or something. You may find that saying "no" brings up many different emotions.

Exercise: How I Feel When I Say "No"

1. When you say "no," which (if any) of these emotions have you felt in the past? Circle those that apply to you.

I feel	scared	anxious	strong	nervous
	ashamed	guilty	angry	powerless
	relieved	empowered	rejected	abandoned
	disliked	pressured	manipulated to	change my mind

2. There are positive and negative ways to say "no." Listed below are examples of each. Which have you ever used and when? Put a check in front of each that you have used and then write a sentence or two when you have used it. When I say no (or try to say no):

_____ I become passive.

_____ I shut down.

_____ I get angry and turn that anger toward another person.

_____ I explode in rage.

_____ I escape through substances.

_____ I withdraw.

_____ I make clear statements.

_____ I make good decisions.

_____ I state what is good for me.

_____ I negotiate if that is necessary.

_____ I communicate what I want.

_____ I listen to the wants of others.

_____ I take a time out if necessary.

_____ I keep my needs and safety in mind at all times.

_____ I know I have the right to say no.

* * * * *

Exercise: My Personal Bill of Rights

If there other rights you would like to add to those given earlier, write them here. _____

_____

_____

_____

What has completing the last few exercises taught you about setting sexual boundaries? _____

_____

_____

_____

* * * * *

An Aside about Suicide

Many trauma survivors feel suicidal and have suicidal thoughts and plans. Some act out those thoughts when they are particularly stressed and triggered; some act them out on a regular basis. It is important to develop ways to cope with and control your suicidal impulses. In order to do so, if you have had these impulses, it is important that you ask yourself: What is the meaning and role of those impulses? Do the impulses and fantasies related to planning suicide lead to an adrenaline rush or a sense of calm and peace? If you have these impulses, what else might you use to bring you relief?

Learning to find ways to relieve any intolerable feelings you have through less destructive means is the first step to bringing suicidal impulses under control. Writing in the online newsletter *Survivorship,* Collings (2001) has created the following list of reasons not to kill yourself:

- Because you deserve to live.

- Because your life has value, whether or not you can see it.

- Because it was not your fault.

- Because you didn't choose to be battered and used.

- Because life itself is precious.

- Because they were and are wrong.

- Because you are connected to each and every other survivor and so your daily battle automatically gives others hope and strength.

- Because you will feel better, eventually.

- Because each time you confront despair, you get stronger.

- Because if you die today you will never again feel love for another human being . . . or see sunlight pouring through the leaves of a tree.

- Because you have already won . . . no one can take that away.

- Because the will to live is not a cruel punishment, even if it feels like that at times; it is a priceless gift.

- Because we need survivors to offer testament against this horror and despair.

- Because no one knows better than you the meaning of suffering, and agony deepens the heart.

- Because you deserve the peace that will come after this battle is won, and it will be won, but only minute by minute.

- Because I am furious that we have to suffer the pain of another's evil and filth.

- Because you, too, will one day feel fury.

- Because it is critical that you survive.

How do you relate to this list? _____

_____

_____

Exercise: What I Learned from This Chapter

What have you learned about yourself and your ability to modulate your emotions and actions from working on the exercises in this chapter?

_____

_____

_____

_____

_____

_____

_____

9

Alterations in Attention or Consciousness: Dealing with Dissociation and Traumatic Amnesia

(Complex PTSD, Category 2)

Two of the most important features of the second symptom category of complex PTSD or disorders of extreme stress, not otherwise specified (DESNOS) are dissociation and depersonalization (Rothschild 2000; Herman 1999). The other is trauma-induced amnesia. We discussed dissociation in chapter 5 as a symptom of avoidance in PTSD.

If you *dissociate*, your awareness of the world around you splits off in some way. According to Branscomb, dissociation means "the separation of things that were previously related or 'associated'" (1990, 3). Perhaps you no longer feel parts of your body during a traumatic event. Dissociation can occur at the level of physical sensation: dissociation can occur at the level of thinking: perhaps you separate out various aspects of the experience and remember only certain ones. Perhaps you get yourself into difficult situations and suddenly feel numb: this is dissociating at the emotional level. It is possible to dissociate at one or all of these levels at any point in time.

For example, say you are driving. You stop at a stop sign, look both ways, and then pull out to cross the road in front of you. Suddenly you hear and feel the impact of another car hitting you. It has come out of nowhere. Your car spins and you end up across the road turned in the opposite direction from where you began. Your first reaction is to breathe, notice where you hurt, and then look at your body and your car from the inside. You have a few bumps but basically you are all right. The car is crunched. You get out and see another car in the intersection. Your reaction is one of rage and anger; you go to the other driver and begin to yell. However, you are not aware of the motorcycle that's also in the intersection. This motorcycle was also coming across the intersection and its rider witnessed the entire accident. You have dissociated part of what you obviously saw during the accident. Rothschild writes that "amnesia of varying degrees is the most familiar kind of dissociation" (2000, 64).

Or you may dissociate your physical pain and some of your emotions. After your accident, you get out of the car and walk to the other car. You are not yet aware of the huge bruise on your leg or the significant bump on your head. The only emotion you feel is anger at the other driver; you do not yet feel relief that you are not seriously hurt or fear that the accident happened. You did not dissociate your consciousness, though, as some people might have done: you are aware that you are still in your body.

One way to look at dissociation is to use Levine's SIBAM model of dissociation (1992). SIBAM stands for *sensation, image, behavior, affect,* and *meaning,* the five elements of any experience.

- *Sensation* means your physical reactions and body (somatic memories).

- *Image* means the pictures that remain in your head.

- *Behavior* means what you did during the trauma.

- *Affect* means your emotions.

- *Meaning* means how you make sense of it all.

One or more of these elements can become dissociated during a traumatic event rather than staying intact in a whole memory. Thus, you might have a strong alarming emotion (affect) related to your father's presence. The presence of your father means "danger" to you. You react to the danger by saying to yourself that you have to get away; in other words, your behavioral goal is to escape. You may also get a headache or goosebumps when he is near. However, as you try to make sense of your feeling of danger, you may have no visual memory (or image that tells you why your father's presence spells danger). (This model does not take into account that you might merely have forgotten that aspect of the event, rather than dissociated it.) However, the model does make sense in terms of the discussion in chapter 1 of the types of memory. According to Rothschild (2000), *implicit memory* involves sensory images (visual memories, auditory memories), body sensations (pain, numbness, tingling), emotions, and automatic behaviors. Explicit memory involves facts, sequences of events, beliefs, and meaning. Do you have a sense that you dissociated to any degree during your traumatic event or events? Did you dissociate what you did (how you behaved), what you felt emotionally (your affect), what you experienced in your body, your awareness that the event was even happening (your sense of time, your knowledge of the trauma), or from your choices (your will) during the traumatic event? (You may want to write about that dissociation in your journal or notebook.)

Dissociation is a way to withstand an overwhelming event; it is a survival strategy to use during that event. The more severe your trauma (as in complex PTSD), the more naturally you dissociate to protect yourself.

How frequently do you use dissociation now? Do you daydream, have imaginary play, or go to a fantasy world to escape? Do you watch TV for hours without remembering anything you watched? Do you play computer or video games for hours on end?

Exercise: When Do I Dissociate?

List up to five situations that lead you to space out or dissociate at the present time:

1. _____

2. _____

3. _____

4. _____

5. _____

* * * * *

Traumatic Amnesia

Dolan describes *traumatic amnesia* as the "complete repression of memories associated with a traumatic event" and notes that it is "an extreme defense reaction to inescapable trauma" (1991, 141). Do you have no memories of certain periods of time in your life, particularly in childhood? You may be experiencing traumatic amnesia.

Dolan (1991) says that overcoming amnesia is important if a person is to resolve symptoms that seem to have no origin, including repetitive nightmares symbolically representing traumatic events; dreams of being chased, killed, or mutilated; eating disorders; sexual dysfunction; chronic anxiety attacks; and other symptoms of PTSD or complex PTSD. We believe, as does Dolan, that it is important to retrieve only what is absolutely necessary for healing. In some instances, no matter how hard you try, no matter how many years of therapy you have, no matter how much validation by others you receive, you may never remember all or even part of what happened to you during your "missing years."

Memory is not a video camera and your memory is not infallible. You may find that you have flashes of memories in situations that in some way resemble the traumatic events that occurred or may have occurred but that you do not remember. Perhaps if you are in a state of intense fear or rage you may have flashes or images of something that happened to you. Perhaps you may have what might be a trigger experience that suddenly allows you to make sense or have a sense of what happened to you in your past.

One way to attempt to get to what you cannot remember is to look at the possible source of a symptom, Why do you have pains in your genital area if you think of your grandfather? Why do you have problems breathing or a panic attack in your shower when you think of your uncle? Be aware, however, that just because you have certain symptoms, you are not necessarily a victim of a certain type of trauma or abuse. However, if others who know you and your family give you verifiable information that leads you to realize that you were a victim, even if you have no memory of it, you may find that you may have to live with this incomplete knowledge and missing memory.

How do you know if you are dissociating? Schiraldi (2000) provides a list of indicators of dissociation; these form the checklist below.

Exercise: How Do I Dissociate?

Please check off any of the following indicators that you have or do.
When I dissociate, I:

_____ lie very still

_____ am slow to respond to others

_____ seem to move in slow motion

_____ have flat (muted) emotions

_____ don't feel pain

_____ stare off blankly into space

_____ tune out

_____ am an observer of the present situation, not a participant

_____ have lapses in my memory

_____ feel as if I am on autopilot

_____ feel as if I am a stranger in my own world

_____ feel as if I am watching myself from outside my body

_____ feel as if I am in a fog

When do you feel the sensations or do the behaviors you checked? _____

_____

_____

* * * * *

What Do You Do about Dissociating?

The first thing to do about dissociating is to realize when you dissociate and why. Building awareness of triggers that might lead to dissociation can help you prepare yourself for the dissociative experience or can help to prevent it from occurring. Grounding techniques, such as those discussed in chapter 2, can also help you prevent dissociation or cut it short.

The following technique for dealing with dissociation comes from the field of neurolinguistic programming (NLP); it was developed by Bandler (1985):

1. If you find that you have dissociated some aspect of a traumatic event, allow yourself to put the event on a movie screen and then sit in the audience (much as was done with the rewind technique in chapter 4.

2. Now go to your safe place to anchor yourself (see chapter 2 for information and exercises about your safe place).

3. Now freeze what you saw, heard, etc. (mentally put it in a container on ice, or compartmentalize it in some other way) and move back into your body.

4. Spend time comforting both your present self and the younger self who experienced the trauma. Tell that younger you that she or he is going to be okay and that she or he was not responsible for what happened. Explain all the details of the trauma that you observed to your younger self.

5. Use grounding techniques, such as those in chapter 2, to return to the present time.

There are many other ways to deal with dissociation. One excellent resource is the Sidran Traumatic Stress Foundation (see Resources).

Exercise: What I Learned about Dissociation

What have you learned about yourself by completing the exercise on dissociation? Are there parts of what happened to you that are totally gone from any type of memory (body, emotional, or cognitive memory)? Do you dissociate frequently? Are you more able to identify the triggers for that dissociation? _____

_____

_____

_____

* * * * *

Remember, your dissociative responses to trauma were *adaptive* at the time that the traumas happened to you; that is, they were behaviors that helped you survive. They may still be adaptive at times, when you need to protect yourself. However, it is up to you to try to decide when and where that occurs and, if dissociating seems to be *maladaptive* (harming rather than helping you), it is up to you to implement some of the exercises in this workbook or find some other way to get help in bringing your typical responses under control.

10

Somatization: How Trauma Impacts Your Body

(Complex PTSD, Category 3)

The third system category of complex PTSD is *somatization*, or the ways the body remembers trauma. Survivors of long-term trauma frequently have problems with their digestive systems; they also often have chronic pain, cardiopulmonary symptoms, and sexual symptoms. Some of these may be *conversion symptoms*, where problems related to trauma and abuse attach to the parts of the body that were hurt during trauma. Body memory (also called *somatic memory*) is part of what is known as *implicit memory*. Rothschild notes that persons with PTSD suffer many "images, sensations, and behavior impulses ... disconnected from [the] context, concepts, and understanding" (2000, 42) of the trauma. These contextual cues, understandings, and concepts are parts of the *explicit memory* of the trauma (implicit and explicit memory are discussed in chapter 1).

The nervous system communicates somatic memories of trauma between the brain and all other parts of the body. When the memories of trauma are stored as sensations, similar sensations can trigger the memories, causing what is known as *state-dependent recall* of the trauma. Your body can "remember" a trauma that your conscious mind is not remembering. So you're experiencing an implicit (body) memory or trauma without the explicit (thought) memory needed to make sense of it. Various body parts may hurt or have symptoms that are in some way trauma-connected, and you have no knowledge of how those parts of the body were involved in trauma.

Emotions that are connected to trauma also may be carried in the body. Rothschild writes that "emotions, though interpreted and named by the mind, are integrally an experience of the body," and that emotions "feel different on the inside of the body" or each individual" (2000, 55). She further explains that there are many phrases in the English language to express the links between emotions and the body:

- You are a pain in the neck. (Anger gets expressed in muscular tension.)

- I am all choked up. (Sadness is often felt as a lump in the throat and tearing eyes.)

- You make me sick. (Nausea often accompanies disgust.)

- I have butterflies in my stomach. (Fear often is felt in a racing heart or in trembling hands.)

If you have turned some of your symptoms of trauma back onto your body, it is important that you allow those symptoms to speak: that you identify their origin and their relationship to what happened to you. It is also important for you to learn to develop a baseline state of calm by working on the exercises in chapter 2. Additionally, it is important that you have one good medical doctor who understands trauma and the impacts of trauma, rather than a number of different doctors who treat you for the trees without seeing the forest. Trauma can cause you to amplify and generalize your physiologic symptoms. The best course of action is to make sure that you have no serious medical condition and then look to the trauma basis of your symptoms, working on the memories from which they come. You can use the techniques in chapter 4 to do this work.

Chronic Pain

What is pain? Generally, when you have a pain in your body you immediately think that something is wrong medically, and you want to fix it. However, with survivors of ongoing, complex trauma, there may be no physical cause for the pain they feel, or the amount of pain you feel is not necessarily in direct proportion to the physical injury you have. Pain is a psychological problem as well as a medical or physical problem. Curro (1987) found that pain had four dimensions: motivational (your desire to avoid or escape from pain), cognitive (your experience with and memory of pain), affective (the feelings you associate with pain, including fear, anxiety, stress), and discriminative (your nervous system's response to what causes the pain and its onset, duration, intensity, quality, and location).

What do you do if you have chronic pain that is not based in a medical condition? How do you get relief when the tendency of the medical community is not to prescribe enough pain medication to control the pain stimulus? One way to work with pain is to use what are known as cognitive behavior techniques or cognitive behavior therapy (CBT). The adherents of cognitive behaviorism say that your thoughts influence your feelings and behavior, and your feelings and behavior influence your thoughts. If patterns of thinking and behaving are destructive or maladaptive, they can be challenged and changed. CBT teaches persons with pain to question and challenge those thoughts, feelings, behaviors, and reactions and also use relaxation, imagery, and distraction (Grant 1997).

Researchers who have learned about trauma have helped us see that mind and body are one. Emotional learning occurs with a part of the brain called the amygdala; another part, called the hippocampus, is responsible for thoughts associated with those emotions (LeDoux 1997). These two parts of the brain are also involved in processing information after a trauma. The hippocampus is able to "remember" the facts of the situation and the context of the trauma. Van der Kolk (1996) has found that beliefs and cognition give meaning to the affect (emotion) that a trauma brings. Thoughts activate the amygdala and trigger emotions.

So what does this all mean to you? The emotions or emotional memories of a trauma get incompletely processed and then are constantly getting reactivated through triggers. Chronic pain is part of this conditioned emotional learning and "is a kind of recurring 'trauma,' since the traumatic event consists of recurring pain attacks or constant physical discomfort" (Grant

1997, 36). Trauma and its associated pain get associated with emotions and the cognitive appraisal (that is, the judgment or perception) of pain. Over time, the true pain that occurred with the trauma becomes a psychological response as well.

If pain doesn't get better over time, and if it gets more and more associated with emotions such as anxiety or fear, you may eventually have less awareness of your body and bodily sensations. You may even begin to dissociate chronic pain. Over time, dissociation maintains your traumatic stress reaction Eventually, you may be told to "learn to live with your pain" or "try to manage it" because no one can find a cure or way to stop it through pills or medical treatments.

So what does that mean for you, the trauma survivor with pain? If you have endured serious trauma, your emotional responses are the major source of information for your thoughts and the meanings you attach to things. Your thoughts *appraise* (look at, value, question) your emotional responses. If you are to change your emotional responses, it is important to look at your emotions and to work on challenging and changing the meanings associated with those emotions. If you are to understand the sources of your pain, you need to go back and process your traumatic experiences (as in chapter 4) and reconnect with as much information about your traumas as is possible.

Relaxation strategies (chapter 2) may help you reduce the intensity of your pain because they reduce emotional tension (Gatchel and Turk 1996). Exposure to and desensitization of parts of your traumatic experiences or your triggers can also help lessen suffering and tension (Grant 1997). As Grant has written, "chronic pain can be a somatization of unresolved trauma, and treatment of the trauma can lead to significant reduction in physical symptoms" (1997, 63).

Eye Movement Desensitization and Reprocessing (EMDR)

One way to work on pain is through eye movement desensitization and reprocessing (EMDR), a technique developed by Shapiro (1995). She observed that certain eye movements are able to reduce the intensity of disturbing thoughts that have not otherwise been dislodged or released. When information in the brain is associated with trauma or chronic pain and gets frozen in time along with its associated emotions and memories, EMDR seems to change the way the information is processed. After EMDR, pain sensations and the way a person experiences and perceives pain get changed. It is a technique that must be done in the context of a therapeutic relationship. The five tasks of pain management using EMDR are:

1. check that your pain is being adequately managed

2. check your medical diagnosis to see if it is correct and if you accept it

3. identify and prioritize targets for EMDR

4. do relaxation exercises and change pain sensations through desensitization

5. develop resources for psychological pain management through EMDR

If you are interested in working on your pain using EMDR, contact the Eye Movement Desensitization and Reprocessing Institute (see Resources).

Exercise: My Pain

Do you have any pain that cannot be diagnosed medically? _____

_____

_____

_____

_____

Have you ever looked at the sources for that pain outside your actual physical body? What was the result? _____

_____

_____

_____

_____

What I have learned about myself from completing the exercises in this chapter is: _____

_____

_____

_____

_____

11

How Trauma Impacts the Way You View Yourself

(Complex PTSD, Category 4)

As we said earlier, repeated instances of overwhelming trauma can impact all parts of yourself: the way you see yourself (your identity), your body image (and body sensations), your internalized images of others, your values, and your sense of purpose and meaning. Loss of your sense of you, as a person, as a self, may lead you to believe that you are not really a person. Instead, you view yourself as some type of worthless piece of garbage, or as evil. If your traumas began very early and were quite severe, you may have developed a fragmentation of yourself called dissociative identity disorder (previously called MPD or multiple personality disorder). This permanent damage to your sense of self can never be totally overcome. However, it can be modified. We have discussed ways to modify and deal with feelings of guilt and shame in chapter 8. It may help you to refer to that chapter and its exercises as you work through this chapter.

The traumatic experiences you had may have led you to believe that nobody can ever possibly understand what you went through and what happened to you. Not only can others not understand the traumas themselves, but they cannot understand why you react as you do and why you think so poorly about yourself. McKay and Rogers (2000) discuss how triggers that bring back various aspects of the trauma (emotions, thoughts, memories, etc.) can lead to negative perceptions of yourself in relation to others. When you perceive that you have been harmed and victimized deliberately and intentionally, as well as that you were totally helpless and powerless to do anything about what happened to you, you can develop feelings of helplessness.

Exercise: My Feelings of Helplessness

Which of these thoughts do you have? Check those that apply to you:

____ People ignore my needs.

____ No one understands me.

_____ When they look at me, people don't really see me.

_____ People expect too much from me.

_____ People take advantage of me and use me.

_____ People want to control me.

_____ People are always yelling at me for things I didn't do.

_____ People don't do what I want them to do.

_____ People manipulate me.

_____ People bully me and are mean to me.

_____ People say cruel things to me.

_____ People have no respect for me.

_____ People don't treat me fairly.

_____ People don't hear what I say.

_____ People don't care about me.

_____ People don't help me when I need help.

_____ People reject me.

_____ People don't value me.

_____ People take me for granted.

_____ People think I am stupid.

_____ People see me as unattractive.

How many of these statements did you check? _____

What do the ones you checked say about you? _____

_____

_____

When the statement you checked says "people," go back and write down beside the belief the names of those people; for example, who takes you for granted or bullies you?

What did you learn about the persons who hurt, abuse, or disregard you? _____

_____

_____

_____

Are there few or many such people? _____

Do other persons see this abuse and disregard for you? _____

---

* * * * *

Where Beliefs about the
Self Come From

In many instances, your beliefs have been gathered from others and are introjects, as we stated earlier in this workbook. You have a choice to accept or deny those beliefs. In this chapter we will give you strategies to challenge them.

Your *schemas* are your beliefs and expectations about yourself, others, and your world. Schemas guide and organize how you process information and how you understand your life's experience. Your schemas become your basic rules of life; if they are based on distorted information, they can lead to distorted ways to view yourself, others, and the world. Your strongest schemas are those that have been the most powerfully reinforced. You may develop new schemas to serve old functions; you may also try to apply old schemas to new situations.

Five basic psychological needs motivate behavior, according to McCann and Pearlmann (1990). We have previously discussed the basic need for safety. The other needs are trust, power, esteem, and intimacy. It is your *ego resources* that allow you to meet your psychological needs. Your ego resources are your intelligence, your sense of humor, your will power, your ability to look inside yourself (introspect), your awareness of and ability to set boundaries, and your ability to make self-protective judgments. Adequate ego resources allow you to keep yourself stable as an individual. They help you tolerate and regulate your emotions (as we discussed in chapter 8), moderate self-hate, and be alone without being lonely.

Trauma disrupts your psychological experience of the world. It distorts your schemas about safety, trust, power, esteem, and intimacy. You develop new schemas that the world is dangerous and that you are powerless. Your beliefs may become negative and disrupt your identity, your emotional life, and your ability to meet your psychological needs. Sometimes these schemas can keep you chronically anxious and hypervigilant. Continuously seeing the world as dangerous and threatening will lead to feelings of fear, anxiety, and panic. If your trauma history prevents you from trusting, you will be suspicious and guarded, and your life will involve feelings of abandonment, disappointment, reluctance to ask for help and support, self-doubt, disappointment, betrayal, and bitterness. You will be led to make bad judgments about others and will put yourself in difficult, risky positions, and you may avoid close relationships.

A basic need of life, according to McCann and Pearlmann (1990) and Rosenbloom and Williams (1999), is to have power and influence over what happens to you and over what happens to others. However, a life of traumatic experiences can lead you to believe that you are helpless to control forces outside yourself. The list of statements you checked in the preceding exercise indicates those beliefs and feelings of weakness, helplessness, and powerlessness. You may believe that you must try to dominate others to avoid being dominated yourself, or give way to others' demands rather than face the world assertively with personal power.

Journal Exercise: My Beliefs about Power and Control

If you are interested in exploring your own beliefs about power and control, you might ask yourself the following questions, and answer them in your journal or notebook.

1. What does personal power mean to me?

2. In what situations in my life right now do I have to share power with others? Who are those others?

3. In my past, when was I forced to give up my personal power?

4. When do I try to control others?

5. Where is my locus (place) of control—is it inside me or outside of me?

6. Over what aspects of my life do I have control?

7. Do I get into power struggles? With whom? How do they get resolved?

8. How do I react to maladaptive expressions of power in others—threats, manipulations, suicide gestures, etc.?

9. Where does my own sense of power come from? Is it from my job? My size? My gender? My culture? My accomplishments?

10. When my power is threatened, do I try to dominate another person or am I appropriately assertive?

11. What are my fantasies about power?

12. Do I see myself as an independent person? Where? When?

13. Can I rely on myself or must I always rely on others?

* * * * *

Exercise: Identifying My Core Beliefs

The answers you give to the questions in the preceding exercise are the first step toward identifying your beliefs about power. Now, choose one of your answers and ask yourself the following questions:

1. What does that belief say about me? _____

_____

2. Now what does *that* statement say about me? _____

_____

3. And what does *that* statement say about me? _____

_____

* * * * *

This third question gives you your core belief—the deep belief that underlies the others. If you want to challenge or dispute that belief, you have several options:

1. You may look for evidence or proof that your belief is valid.

2. You may find others and debate your belief with them.

3. You may try to use imagery and visualization to change certain aspects of the belief.

4. You may also ask yourself the following challenging questions about that belief (partially adapted from Resick 1994).

   - What is the evidence for and against the belief?

   - Is the belief a habit or a fact?

   - Is my interpretation of the situation accurate or not part of reality?

   - Am I thinking in black and white or all-or-nothing ways?

   - Are the words and phrases I am using extreme and exaggerated (such as *always, forever, must, should, ought, have to*).

   - Am I making excuses?

   - Is the source of information for my belief reliable?

   - Am I thinking in terms of probabilities (shades of gray) or certainties (black and white)?

   - Are my judgments based on feelings, not facts? Do I consider a feeling to be a fact?

   - Is this belief my own, or does it come from or belong to someone else?

   - Does it fit in with my priorities, values, and judgments?

   - Does it make me feel bad?

   - Is it hurtful to me?

   - Is it hurtful to others?

   - Is it appropriate in the demands it makes on me?

   - Is it appropriate in the demands it makes on others?

   - Is it considerate of me?

Exercise: Challenge My Beliefs

Use the technique given in the "Identifying My Core Beliefs" exercise above to identify two or more of your core beliefs. (You may use your journal or notebook to identify the additional core beliefs.) Then answer the questions above for each core belief. Use your journal, as well, if you need more space to answer.

Core belief 1 _____

Answers to the questions: _____

_____

_____

_____

_____

_____

_____

_____

Core belief 2 _____

Answers to the questions: _____

_____

_____

_____

_____

_____

_____

What do the previous three exercises say about your beliefs about power? _____

_____

_____

* * * * *

Journal Exercise: My Power Shield

One way to develop your personal power is to draw it in the form of a power shield. You may draw a shield in your journal or notebook in any shape that suits you. Divide the shield into six parts and, in each section, draw, write, or attach something that is a symbol of the power you have or of potential sources of your power. You might use words, or pictures to symbolize your skills, abilities, resources, accomplishments, or support systems. If you have problems filling in all six sections using your present reality, think of yourself as you would like to be one year from now, after doing all the work in this workbook, and then draw a shield based on that vision. You may draw both a shield based on your present and one based on your hopes for the future. Some sources of your personal power might be:

- a symbol of your life's motto (for example, It can be done, Live life to its fullest)

- a symbol of your knowledge

- a symbol of your ability to communicate

- a symbol of those you love or who love you, care for you, and accept you

- a symbol of things for which you have passion and commitment

- a symbol of things over which you have some control
- a symbol of your life
- a symbol of the energy from which you draw strength and find your will to survive
- a symbol of your personal resources
- symbols of those to whom you owe allegiance
- symbols of those who are your mentors
- a symbol of a promise to yourself
- a symbol of a promise to others
- symbols of life experiences that have given you strength
- symbols of beliefs that protect you
- a symbol of your support network
- a symbol of your safe place
- a symbol of your ability to change situations
- symbols of your self-care strategies

You may also revisit your personal bill of rights in chapter 8 and incorporate more statements about power. One example of such a bill of rights follows.

- I have needs and can take steps to meet them or try to meet them.
- I have the right to express my feelings as I feel them.
- I have the right to make mistakes.
- I have the right to change my mind (and what I believe).
- I have the right to change who I am.
- I have the right to ask for help.
- I have the right to set a boundary.
- I have the right to be alone if I want to be.
- I have a right to let go of the past.
- I have the right to seek support from myself.
- I have the right to seek support from others.
- I have the right to set goals and then prioritize them.
- I have the right to give myself a compliment.
- I have the right to forgive myself when I am not perfect.
- I have the right to stop making unrealistic demands on myself.
- I have the right to stop blaming myself for things for which I was not responsible.
- I have the right to believe that I can succeed.
- I have the right to judge myself appropriately.
- I have the right to care for myself before giving to others.

* * * * *

Journal Exercise: My Story of Personal Power

If you are still unsure about your personal power, you may write a fable about your own journey as a hero. This technique is adapted from Ayalon (1992). This story is a metaphoric work that helps you identify your coping and power resources. You can write it or draw it in your journal or notebook. There are six parts to the story:

1. Imagine yourself as a hero in certain surroundings of your choice.

2. Set yourself a task.

3. Decide who will help you, the hero, get the task done if you need help (you might not—you decide).

4. Look at who or what prevents you from completing your task or trying to.

5. Look at how you cope with the obstacles put in front of you.

6. Decide what happens then and how the story ends.

Through doing this story, you can look at the ways you cope with a stressful situation.

* * * * *

Self-Esteem

If you are going to overcome at least some of the negative impacts of the traumas that happened to you, it is important for you to learn to nurture yourself and to develop a positive sense of who you are, what you like about yourself, and what you see as your strengths. Trauma can challenge your good feelings and beliefs about yourself and lead to negative thoughts and emotions of unworthiness, badness, contempt, and disillusionment. You may believe that you are flawed, bad, or damaged. You may also think that your presence contaminates others or will doom them to a life of pain just by your presence. A poor sense of self-esteem is associated with feelings of self-loathing, despair, cynicism, and general withdrawal from others.

If you see yourself as having worth as a person, you have good self-esteem. A part of good self-esteem is self-respect. If you see yourself as capable and competent, you will be more able to cope with stress and respond to crisis as a challenge. Doing something well leads to higher self-esteem. A higher sense of self-esteem and a sense of being able to do things leads to accomplishments. In other words, these three things (activity, a sense of being able to do something, and having high self-esteem) are related (Schiraldi 1999).

The major way to build self-esteem is to picture and develop high self-esteem affirmations. You worked on building affirmations in chapter 7. What affirmations did you create then? Do you believe them now? Have you been practicing them over time?

When you develop high self-esteem affirmations, it is important for you to begin the exercise with relaxation (see chapter 2). Once you have relaxed your body, visualize a success that you have had—or other problem, crisis, that you resolved, about which resolution you had good feelings. Experience those good feelings as you remember them.

Exercise: My Self-Esteem Affirmations

Choose four or five affirmations. Relax your body, then state your first self-esteem affirmation out loud or to yourself while visualizing it in detail, as if it were totally true.

Some affirmations you might use include:

- I have worth.

- I like myself for myself, without comparing myself to others.

- I can do good work at my job.

- I do my best.

- I care about others.

- I make a difference in my own life.

- I make a difference in the lives of others.

- I am worthy of love from myself.

- I am worthy of respect from myself.

- I am worthy of love from others.

- I am worthy of respect from others.

- I respect my own and others' boundaries.

- I am lovable and capable.

- I love myself unconditionally.

- I am capable of changing and growing.

- I am willing to accept love.

- I am proud of my body.

- I am no longer a helpless child.

How does this exercise work for you? _____

_____

_____

* * * * *

Ways to Raise Your Self-Esteem

There are other ways you can raise your self-esteem. You may want to: improve your communication skills, find a hobby that you can do, or do something for others. You may also want to look at the beliefs you have about self-esteem. (One way to do this is to do the next two exercises.) It is important that the beliefs you hold about yourself are realistic, accurate, and honest (Schiraldi 1999). Self-esteem is built on feelings of unconditional worth and unconditional love for yourself, which is really self-acceptance.

Journal Exercise: My Questions about My Self-Esteem

In your journal or notebook, answer the following questions as fully as you like.

- What do I like or value about myself?
- What do I do to take care of my physical self (my body)?
- How do I take care of myself emotionally?
- What do I do (if anything) to reward myself, and when and how do I do it?
- When and how do I devalue myself or cut myself down?
- What are my hopes and dreams?
- What are my realistic expectations for myself?
- What are my unrealistic expectations for myself?
- In what situations do I have a sense of humor?
- When and how do I show love and affection?
- Where do I find hope?
- Under what circumstances am I open and honest about my feelings?
- Do I help others feel good about themselves even when I feel bad about myself?

* * * * *

Journal Exercise: Identifying My Core Beliefs about Self-Esteem

Turn back a few pages and complete the exercises called "Identifying My Core Beliefs" and "Challenging My Beliefs." Do them in your journal, using the question about your self-esteem you just answered.

What does completing this exercise teach you about yourself? _____

_____

* * * * *

By recognizing which of your beliefs you want to challenge (and perhaps even change), you begin to improve self-esteem. Other ways to improve your self-esteem include the ability to:

- Be aware of your negative thoughts.
- Stop your negative thoughts by using the thought-stopping technique (chapter 6).
- Practice your affirmations.
- Set realistic goals you can achieve.
- Develop a variety of interests and participate in related activities.

- Maintain a high level of energy while pacing yourself.

- Take appropriate risks.

- Trust in yourself and the decisions you make.

- Stay who you are rather than changing to fit a situation or another person's ideas of you.

- Live in the present while being aware of your past history, and having realistic future goals.

- Turn any mistakes into lessons.

Exercise: Life Lessons

Write down what you believe are the two main lessons you are to learn in this life.

1. _____

2. _____

* * * * *

Coping with and Solving a Problem

You may be faced with situations that need you to make a decision or solve a problem. In the past, if you felt helpless and out of control, you may not have tried to solve problems or make decisions on your own. Instead, you may have just let things happen around you, or continued to keep a victim role. Solving problems by *doing something*—by taking deliberate action—is a functional way of coping with a situation and eliminating some sources of stress for you. Developing realistic goals for solving a problem can make a crisis more manageable. Tedeschi and Calhoun (1995) describe the functions of coping with a problem as follows:

- a way to work through trauma

- a way to make a crisis manageable

- a way to reverse negative changes

- a way to appraise the degree of threat of a situation

- a way to use spiritual beliefs positively

- a way to learn through the experience of others

- a way to vent emotions

- a way to seek support when you need it

- a way to look at the impact of coping on your schemas

If you are able to cope successfully, you probably have:

- persistence, determination, confidence, flexibility, and tenacity

- the ability to connect emotionally with others

- the ability to accept your limitations when necessary

- an internal locus of control

- the perception you can do what you need to do (self-efficacy)
- optimism
- a problem-focused style
- hardiness (which involves commitments, a belief in your ability to influence life events, and the ability to respond to challenge brought by the normal changes of life)

Exercise: How I Cope

How do you generally cope with a challenging situation, whether or not it involves a crisis? Check which of these apply to you, and give an example of when you use it:

_____ I deal with my feelings. I name them, accept them, express them. An example of when I cope in this way is: _____

_____ I adjust my attitude. An example of how I cope in this way is: _____

_____ I make choices using a decision-making plan (like the one described just below). An example of when I cope by problem-solving is: _____

_____ I accept my own imperfection and the mistakes I have made (and do make) (Schab 1996). An example of when I cope in this way is: _____

_____ I take action. An example of when I cope in this way is: _____

_____ I use language to build rapport and then translate the language spoken to an action plan. An example of when I cope in this way is: _____

_____ I set realistic limits. An example of when I cope in this way is: _____

_____ I remain calm and empathize with others. An example of when I cope in this way is: _____

_____ I negotiate and compromise. An example of when I cope in this way is: _____

_____ I distance myself from a situation without dissociating. An example of when I cope this way is: _____

_____ I seek social support. An example of when I cope this way is: _____

_____ I educate myself and get information. An example of when I cope this way is: _____

_____ I use another method: _____

_____

_____ An example of when I cope this way is: _____

_____

✱ ✱ ✱ ✱

Facing a Difficult Situation

Suppose you are going to go to your cousin's wedding and know that your father, who molested you, will be there. You have told your cousin you do not want to sit next to your father at the wedding. In fact, you really don't even want to go, but you and your cousin are very close emotionally. She does not know about the abuse (yet) and just wouldn't understand if you didn't come. You have not spoken to your father in three years—not since you wrote him a letter of confrontation. He wrote a simple letter back that said, "Let's be a family again." You need to develop a plan about how you'll react when you see him. How can you plan how you will react?

First, you might consider which emotions you think you will have and what you will do as they arise. What triggers will hit you upside your head? What can you do to calm yourself ahead of time? Then you could visualize yourself going to the wedding and then to the reception. Imagine that at the reception you have assigned seats and your father is across the table from you. What would you do? In short, imagine what might happen in the difficult situation and decide what resources you will need to cope with what might happen. This strategy is adapted from McKay and Rogers (2000). It is adaptable to any situation that resembles your prior trauma, when you have unexpected or even expected contact with your perpetrator, or if you have to deal with unsupportive others. Another way to prepare yourself in advance for a difficult situation is to refer to the story of the hero that is found just above in the section "Journal Exercise: My Story of Personal Power" and do that exercise using the situation, writing yourself in as the hero.

Exercise: Coping with a Difficult Situation

1. Fill in the blanks using the wedding situation described above.

The triggers that I will have to deal with are: _____

_____

I need cues around me to help me to cope. These might include my list of affirmations, a crystal, a stuffed toy, a small angel, or a miniature of my power shield. My cues are:

_____

_____

Aspects of timing I need to be able to cope are (e.g., some time alone, a time to go out of the room and throw things): _____

_____

The coping strategy (from those listed in the section above, "Coping with and Solving a Problem") that will help me best is:_____

The relaxation strategies I will use to soothe and calm myself are: _____

_____

The self-talk that I can use includes: _____

_____

2. Now, think of a problem that you are having or will have and apply the same strategy to yourself.

The situation I am facing is: _____

The triggers that I will have to deal with are: _____

_____

I need cues around me to help me to cope. These might include my list of affirmations, a crystal, a stuffed toy, a small angel, or a miniature of my power shield. My cues are:

_____

_____

Aspects of timing I need to be able to cope are (e.g., some time alone, a time to go out of the room and throw things): _____

_____

The coping strategy (from those in the section above, "Coping with and Solving a Problem") that will help me best is:

_____

The relaxation strategies I will use to soothe and calm myself are: _____

_____

The self-talk that I can use includes: _____

_____

* * * * *

Formulating a Decision-Making Plan

Another strategy for coping with a tough situation is to use the following decision-making plan.

1. Describe the problem:

- What is the problem situation?
- What is wrong?
- Why is it a problem now?

- Who is responsible for the problem?

- What circumstances are responsible for the problem?

- What will happen if the problem is not solved?

- How likely is it that what you believe will happen will happen? Circle the number that best describes it (1 = not likely; 10 = it will happen)

  1   2   3   4   5   6   7   8   9   10

- When did the problem start? What happened then? Who caused the problem?

- Might the situation change, and what would it change into? What would happen then?

- What needs to change if the problem is to be resolved?

- What are you thinking right now? How do you perceive the meaning of the problem? (Miller et al. 1989)

- What are you feeling? What spontaneous internal physical responses are you aware of having (from the past as well as the present) that can give you information?

- What are you hearing? What sensory data from the present and triggered from the past are coming in? What intuitive sensations are you having?

- What are you doing? What actions are you taking or are you going to take, and what commitment to action are you willing to make?

- What do you want or intend to do? What are your core values now? What do you want to accomplish? What is motivating you to act?

- How does this problem relate to your earlier traumas? If so, which ones? What was the outcome of those traumas?

2. Understand the problem:

   - Have you asked yourself about the problem and why it is a problem?

   - Have you asked yourself what needs to happen?

   - Have you "sat" with the problem (that is, just spent some time with it without trying to resolve it)?

   - Have you considered if you want to avoid the problem? This may or may not be a feasible solution, but it may be an alternative to consider at this time.

3. Make a decision to solve the problem:

   - What five reasonable things could you to do resolve the problem for yourself? What are the pros and cons of each?

	Pros	**Cons**
1.	_____	_____
2.	_____	_____
3.	_____	_____
4.	_____	_____
5.	_____	_____

Which of the five possible solutions seems to have the most pros for trying it?

4. It is up to you to decide if you will try your chosen strategy to help solve the problem. If you do, you may want to make a contract that

- formulates a plan of action and sets a reasonable goal

- considers alternatives, their likely costs, and their possible outcomes

5. Once you have tried your chosen strategy, look at its results. Ask yourself:

- What happened?

- What about this strategy needs to change?

- Is there another solution that might also work?

Journal Exercise: My Decision-Making Plan

In your notebook or journal, you may use the description on the pages just above to formulate your own decision-making plan, use it to solve a problem you are having, and describe the results.

Basically, the decision-making plan asks you to:

- State your problem.

- Gather information.

- Brainstorm about possible solutions.

- Evaluate the pros and cons of each.

- Decide which to use.

- Do whatever you have decided to do.

Evaluate the strategy you chose and make any needed changes. Another simple problem-solving model developed by Peterson (1968) is to use the following prompts to describe the problem and its possible solutions:

- My problem is: _____

- The severity of my problem is: _____

- The frequency that the problem occurs: _____

- The problem bothers me because: _____

- The last time this problem occurred was: _____

- The changes I need to make are: _____

- To improve the situation I must: _____

- I would like _____ to happen because _____

- I can get help with the problem by: _____

- If I decide not to make changes to solve the problem, then the impact will be: _____

_____

* * * * *

Whatever problem-solving model you choose, remember not to try to solve problems without taking the time to look at a number of possibilities and considering the consequences for each. Making impulsive, radical changes can be unhealthy and can throw you into distress. Any plan will also be easier to follow if it is very specific.

Exercise: What I Learned from This Chapter

In this chapter, you have looked at ways to help you improve your personal power and your self-esteem. You have also looked at coping skills and problem-solving strategies. Remember, should you get overwhelmed at any time, you may take a break from doing the work, or refer back to the exercises for relaxation and safety in chapter 2. What has this chapter taught you about yourself? How have you changed or begun to change through the work you have done here?

* * * *

12

Dealing with Your Perpetrators

(Complex PTSD, Category 5)

The fifth symptom category of complex PTSD involves alterations in perceptions of the perpetrator. One major aspect of this category is adopting distorted beliefs held by the perpetrator as your own (these beliefs are called *introjects*). We have talked about introjects elsewhere in this workbook and will not deal with them again here. Another aspect is idealization of the perpetrator. Many times, victims continue to look up to and idealize a perpetrator because of the messages instilled in them, because they are "supposed" to do so, and for other reasons. If you use the levels of responsibility technique described in chapter 7, realistically looking at the percentages of responsibility for your trauma that you had and that your perpetrator had, your tendency to idealize your perpetrator will be less. A third aspect of this symptom category is preoccupation with hurting your perpetrator and getting revenge. Sometimes it is very difficult to let anger and fantasies of revenge go.

What about Forgiveness?

Many trauma specialists have written about the trauma victim's need to forgive his or her abuser. Forgiveness supposedly is a way to release the rage and hatred you have toward your perpetrator, as well as a way to release your desire for revenge. But many offenders do not deserve unconditional forgiveness. Many also do not even admit that they have done wrong; therefore, they don't seek or want forgiveness, because forgiveness is not necessary for something that was not bad.

If your trauma was perpetrated by a person, you may choose to forgive that perpetrator. Your forgiveness of that person does not mean that what she or he did was right or acceptable, or that your trauma has not had negative impacts on your life. It does not mean that you are now to forget what happened to you, as some people may say you are to do (Schiraldi 2000).

According to Enright and Fitzgibbons (2000) forgiveness is the willful abandonment of resentment and the willingness to respond toward your perpetrator with compassion, generosity, beneficence, and moral love. Big words, but what do they mean? This definition does not mean you are to go back into a relationship with an abuser, or that you will trust or reconcile with that person. It does not mean you condone or excuse what was done to you or what happened in your world. It does mean a change in your own internal response. If you forgive, you do a willful act that is for your benefit alone. Enright and Fitzgibbons say that forgiveness has degrees that range from slight to complete, surface to deep. In addition, forgiveness develops over time as you sort out what happened to you and as you consider whether or not you are willing to forgive.

You may forgive on a variety of levels. You may forgive emotionally (you feel compassion for the perpetrator), cognitively (in your statements or thoughts), or spiritually (by turning to a higher power or god to help you with the act of forgiving). A focus on forgiving is a coping strategy that may help you improve your psychological functioning, these authors say.

They also say what forgiveness is not. Forgiveness is not just having the perpetrator apologize and accepting that apology. Forgiveness does not restore your situation to what it was prior to the traumatic event or offense. An apology says that the perpetrator has regret; it also may mean that you still have limitations to the amount of healing you have done because accepting a quick, superficial, or even emotionless apology as an "endpoint" does not allow for later expression of sadness or anger. Instead, if other emotions arise after an apology is accepted and forgiveness is given, you may blame yourself for being uncaring. Forgiveness by you also does not depend upon the existence of remorse in your perpetrator. Forgiveness is not about granting your perpetrator pardon, leniency, or mercy; it does not mean you excuse the trauma, forget the offense, or abandon resentment. If you quickly tell your perpetrator "I forgive you" without a great deal of thought, the perpetrator may believe that he or she is off the hook with a quick fix and then move on, while you may still continue to be stuck in your trauma.

Self-Forgiveness

Forgiving your perpetrator may allow you to let go of your anger and rage to some degree. However, it is more important that you forgive yourself for any perceived complicity in what happened, whether through something you did or something you did not do. You need to forgive yourself if you lost control, feel guilty for what happened, were unable to fight back, or were unable to stop what happened. Forgiving yourself can also help you to let go of your rage and thoughts of revenge; it can help you decrease your fears, lessen the amount of obsessive thoughts you have about your perpetrator, and help you access additional memories of what happened to you. Letting go of anger through forgiveness also can help you let go of at least some of the power your offender has had over you.

Exercise: Forgiveness

How much anger do you still hold against yourself for what happened? _____

_____

What do you need to do for yourself if you are to forgive yourself? _____

_____

How do you think forgiving yourself can help you to heal? _____

_____

Do you want to forgive your abuser? _____

If so, what will you do? _____

_____

* * * * *

Journal Exercise: Forgiveness Ritual

Using the format for constructing a ritual that is found in chapter 7, develop a ritual to help you let go of any unjust self-blame, shame, and guilt that you may still hold. This is a forgiveness ritual.

* * * * *

Exercise: Warnings about Forgiveness

In this short chapter, what have you learned about forgiveness? What have you learned about yourself? _____

_____

_____

* * * * *

13

Alterations in Your Relationships with Others

(Complex PTSD, Category 6)

The sixth category of symptoms used in the description of complex PTSD describes the impact of trauma on your interpersonal relationships. The three main aspects of this category are inability to trust, revictimizing yourself, and victimizing others. Enduring and surviving traumatic experiences can lead to problems with attachment, intimacy, and interpersonal relationships that were not present before the trauma (Wilson, Friedman, and Lindy 2001). Among the problems that may occur are:

- feelings of alienation from others in social, emotional, and personal areas of life

- mistrust and guardedness

- detachment, isolation, and withdrawal

- a loss of pleasure in life and of your capacity to feel joy

- a loss of the ability to feel sensual and sexual or have sexual feelings

- a loss of your capacity to have healthy connectedness to others

- repetitive self-destructive relationships

- discontent with self-comfort and an inability to receive nurturing (and even touch) from others and yourself

- problems with setting or maintaining boundaries

- problems with communicating your wants, needs, and feelings

- feelings of abandonment and loss that may or may not be based on fact

If you have identified with any of the problems listed above, the exercises found in this chapter may help you build trust and, eventually, may help you establish some level of intimacy in relationships. Trust and intimacy are two of your five basic psychological needs.

In many instances, trauma survivors find it difficult to trust others, the world, and themselves, after a traumatic event has occurred. This is particularly true if their traumas were because of human intention or error. Over time, these survivors can become isolated and alone.

Trust and Betrayal

A betrayal in the past may lead you to have difficulties with trust in the present. In the past, have persons in close relationships with you ever betrayed you? If so, you may use the following exercises modified from those developed by Matsakis (1998, 62).

Journal Exercise: People Who Have Betrayed Me

For each person who was in a close relationship with you and betrayed you, complete the following sentences (do the first one here, and the others in your journal):

I was betrayed by _____

As a result, I _____

One example might be: I was betrayed by my father, who molested me. As a result, I have very few memories of my childhood and have never been able to trust men.

* * * * *

According to constructivist self-development theory (McCann and Pearlman 1990), *trust* involves your need to feel confident about your own perceptions and judgments about yourself, others, and the world, and to be able to depend upon others to meet your emotional, physical, and psychological needs. It is important for you to examine your own beliefs about trust if you are going to be able to set boundaries, communicate effectively, and know when and how to rely on yourself and others. One way to find and challenge your beliefs about trust is to complete the following two exercises.

Journal Exercise: My Beliefs about Trust

Ask yourself the following questions and record your answers in your journal or notebook.

1. What does it mean to me to be able to trust?

2. In what situations do I trust my own thoughts?

3. In what situations do I trust my own judgments or conclusions about a person?

4. About a situation?

5. How would I define the word *intuition*?

6. When do I feel that my intuition speaks to me? When do I notice my intuition?

7. How else do I become aware of my feelings, impressions, and beliefs about others or situations?

8. Am I a trustworthy person?

9. When do I keep promises? When do I not keep them?

10. Do I develop trust in someone gradually or all at once?

11. What persons or groups do I trust? Which do I distrust?

12. When I have to depend on another person I feel:

13. I ask others for help with tasks when:

14. I ask others for help with my emotional needs when:

* * * * *

Exercise: Identifying and Challenging My Core Beliefs about Trust

Choose one answer from the questions in the preceding exercise, and answer the following questions about it:

The answer: _____

1. What does that answer say about me? _____

_____

2. Now what does *that* answer say about me? _____

_____

3. And what does *that* answer say about me? _____

_____

Question 3 gives you your core belief. What is it? _____

_____

In order to challenge or examine that belief, you can ask yourself the following questions:

1. Does this belief belong to me or to someone else? _____

_____

2. Does this belief fit with my priorities and goals? _____

_____

3. Does this belief fit with my values and judgments? _____

_____

4. Does this belief make me feel better or worse (about myself, others)? _____

_____

5. Is this belief hurtful to me in any way? _____

_____

6. Does this belief put appropriate demands on me (at home, work, or play)?

_____

* * * * *

Intimacy and Connectedness

Intimacy is the capacity to feel connected to yourself and others. Enduring trauma may lead to disconnects between you and others or within yourself, as we have noted. The aim of this chapter is to help you learn ways to set boundaries, communicate with others, and build healthy attachments that do not make you feel vulnerable, that do not repeat trauma-related patterns of interaction, and that are based on new or modified belief systems. These beliefs include beliefs of empowerment and self-acceptance. The following questions may help you identify a belief or beliefs about intimacy that you might want to examine or challenge.

Exercise: My Beliefs about Intimacy

1. Answer the following questions or complete the following thoughts (use your journal or notebook if you need more room).

Do I feel connected to others? If so, to whom? _____

_____

To me, an intimate relationship means I _____

_____

At this moment in time, I have an intimate relationship with _____

_____

I believe that the word "love" means _____

_____

I am able to express love safely with _____

_____

From whom and where do I get support? _____

_____

From whom and where do I get love? _____

_____

Do I feel more distant from others now, after the trauma (or after I have begun to work on the trauma)? _____

_____

How do I express love and caring to others? To myself? _____

_____

Am I able to have an intimate sexual relationship with another? _____

_____

2. Which of the following statements describes you? Check all that apply.

_____ I stay away from people.

_____ I avoid certain social activities (such as _____).

_____ I want to spend my time alone.

_____ I am afraid to talk to others.

_____ I am afraid to be physically close to another.

_____ I try to force others to have physical contact with me.

_____ I say *"no"* to any suggestion of sexual contact with someone I love or for whom I have loving feelings.

_____ I overdo taking care of others.

_____ I have no one to take care of me.

_____ I am generally hostile toward others.

_____ I feel afraid to depend on others.

_____ I believe others will always let me down.

_____ I fear touch of any kind.

_____ I am unable to play.

_____ I am unable to make friends.

_____ I am unable to keep friends.

_____ I have no friends.

_____ I am unable to disclose my real self to others.

_____ I am unable to go out to meet others.

_____ I do not trust that I am okay.

_____ I am unlovable and undeserving of love.

_____ I don't believe anything nice that others say about me.

_____ I cannot make decisions.

_____ I continue to get in disastrous relationships (modified from Leehan and Wilson 1985).

The more statements you checked, the more you need to look at ways to challenge and change your beliefs about intimacy and trust. You also need to look at your boundaries and communication skills.

* * * * *

Matsakis writes that "it has been established that the single most important predictor of who develops long-term PTSD or other traumatic reactions is the ability to derive comfort from another human being" (1998, 110). Van der Kolk (1988) agrees, and notes that two primary factors can lessen the negative effects of trauma: the presence of a support system and a strong belief system that is positive and allows you to trust, set boundaries, and be intimate.

An important reason for you to establish and maintain good relationships with at least one or two significant others is so you can ask for and receive help from them when you need support or are in crisis. Identifying who can be the most supportive to you (in a safe way) and then building relationships with them (if those relationships do not already exist) can be taxing and exhausting. However, even though you may not believe this statement now, the end goal is worth the energy drain.

Looking More at Boundaries

We looked at what is meant by the word *boundary* in chapter 8. A boundary is the way you let yourself know where you end and where someone else begins. A boundary is like a container; if your boundary container is too open or too closed, you will have problems setting, maintaining, or dissolving relationships. Your physical boundaries set the limits of physical space that you keep between yourself and others, even in intimate relationships that may involve sexual contact. Your emotional boundaries encompass your needs for and rights to internal safety. If your emotional boundaries are overprotective, you may not let anyone or anything into your space. If you lack good emotional boundaries, you may not be able to see yourself as a separate person and may even lose your sense of personal identity.

June was a survivor of sexual abuse. She married Bernie because she believed no one else could possibly ever love her. Bernie was very cruel and was only interested in himself and having his own needs met. He began to decide how June would dress, talk, and behave. June believed that she had to do what Bernie suggested because she was his wife. When she did try to set any boundary or say no to him, he became very angry and would threaten to leave her. June was terrified to be alone. It was not until June had a child that she began to challenge his authority: she realized that she had no access to money unless Bernie gave her some (so she was unable to buy anything for her baby without his permission). Bernie became violent and verbally abusive. June feared for the safety of her child (not herself) and left. She went to a shelter, and there she began to learn about her ability to set boundaries.

Exercise: My "I Am's"

One way to learn about boundaries is to view yourself as an individual. In the space below, list twenty statements that start with the words "I am." You may find that it is easy to write the first ten. Don't stop there. Keep on going. If you have a good friend, ask that person to do the same exercise and then compare your lists (Mundahl, Parks, Gray, and Fields 1995). What did you find that was similar about the two of you? What was different.

1. _____
2. _____
3. _____
4. _____
5. _____
6. _____
7. _____
8. _____
9. _____

10. _____

11. _____

12. _____

13. _____

14. _____

15. _____

16. _____

17. _____

18. _____

19. _____

20. _____

What did completing this exercise teach you about yourself? _____

_____

How hard was it to do? _____

_____

* * * * *

Physical Boundaries, Revisited

If you have very tight physical boundaries, you may feel very uncomfortable if someone touches you, even in a social situation (e.g., if someone puts a hand on your shoulder). You may avoid physical closeness, keep a very stiff body posture, and try to keep a "stone face." If you have very loose physical boundaries, you may touch others without asking permission, may let others touch you even when you do not want to be touched, may invade the private conversations and spaces of others, may personalize (take what others do as being a personal attack on you), and may overreact to others. If you have a healthy physical boundary, you know the limits of your own personal space and make your boundary clear to others.

Exercise: My Physical Boundaries

What amount of space between you and another person is necessary for you to feel comfortable or safe?_____

_____

Do you always need or want the same amount of space between you and others? _____

_____

How can you keep that space? Does keeping it make you tired? _____

_____

How do you let others know if they get too close to you—in words or in actions? If you don't let others know, what stops you?_____

_____

If someone gets too close to you physically, what happens to you inside? What feelings do you have? What messages do you say to yourself?_____

_____

* * * * *

Exercise: Defining My Personal Space

Mundahl et al. (1995) suggest that you do the following exercise with another person whom you think you might trust:

1. Ask the person to stand about twenty feet away from you and stay still. Now slowly walk toward that person with your arms held out in front of you. Keep walking toward the other person until you begin to have any feelings of discomfort and lack of safety. Then stop. This is your personal space. How large is that space? When we work with children in elementary school and teach them about "good touch" and "bad touch," we teach them that the personal space they are entitled to have is the distance between them and another person if both persons have their arms outstretched. Is your personal space more or less than this distance? How did doing this exercise make you feel? What did it teach you about yourself? _____

_____

_____

2. Now, repeat the exercise with your friend or support person. Let that person walk toward you. How does his or her personal space compare with yours? How did you feel in this role? _____

_____

_____

* * * * *

A healthy physical boundary means respecting your own personal space and that of others. You ask permission before touching others or invading their personal space. You also are respectful of their boundaries and needs. If someone begins to invade your personal space, you have various choices of ways to react. You may back up or put an object (e.g., a chair or table) between you and the other person. You may say, "I feel uncomfortable because you are so close to me physically." If you were physically or sexually abused as a child, your boundaries were invaded in many ways and you may find it difficult to set boundaries now. Practice these suggestions; be assertive in saying what you want from others and how you want them to respect your physical space. You have the right to be safe and to feel safe. You do not have to allow others to get closer to you than your personal space zone (usually eighteen inches to four feet). If you want others to have closer contact, you have the right to say when and with whom and for how long.

Emotional Boundaries, Revisited

If you have emotional boundaries that are too tight, you may be emotionally numb. You may seem to be insensitive, unaccepting of others, and not interested in others. You may avoid reacting or showing your feelings to others and have problems asking for or giving help. If you have emotional boundaries that are too loose, you may be unable to contain your feelings and you may overreact to yourself or others. You may tell others too much about yourself, may depend too much on others to meet your needs, and may trust too quickly or get into intimate, sexual relationships too fast. You may also agree to do things when you really want to say "no." If you have boundaries that are too loose emotionally, you may also give too much to others, take too much from others, and not respect your own or others' personal rights.

How do you separate your own feelings from the feelings of others? If you are in a good mood and someone else around you is having a bad day, does your mood immediately change or are you able to maintain your happiness or contentment? If you feel good about yourself and something happens in one part of your life to challenge that feeling (e.g., your boss treats you rudely), do you feel bad about every part of you? Do you allow your boss's unfair comments to ruin how you feel about every part of yourself and your world?

Your emotional boundaries are impacted by your beliefs. If your beliefs tell you that anything that upsets your emotional boundaries is correct and that you do not deserve to maintain a healthy boundary, then it is important for you to challenge those beliefs. Your beliefs are the filters through which you see the world and help determine whether you react defensively, appropriately, or without a boundary.

Exercise: My Boundary Script

When others invade your emotional boundaries and impact you, you might say something like this to them:

When you _____ (talk rudely to me in front of others), I feel _____ (embarrassed, humiliated, unfairly treated, judged). I need _____ (for you to treat me with the respect you treat others in the office). If you (continue to) _____ (be so rude to me), I will _____ (go to your supervisor, file a complaint, etc.).

If you use this exercise, try to make sure that your end options of behavior are realistic and will not bring you undue harm, or criticism.

* * * * *

If you have healthy emotional boundaries, you are able to share how you feel with others in direct, appropriate language and body language. You are able to be assertive and make appropriate choices between possible actions. You also are able to admit your mistakes and then correct them, if at all possible, without seeing yourself as a totally horrible, awful person. You also are able to accept others' opinions and views, even though you may not agree. You can look at the pros and cons of others' views, and decide how to act in response. If you have appropriate emotional boundaries, you are a caring, feeling person who is empathic and sensitive, without being either overly distant or overly involved. You do not assume that you know how others think or feel or what they need. You respect their rights as well as your own. You ask for help when you need it but don't depend on others alone to meet your needs or to give you constant support and reassurance. You can keep your own values and morals.

Exercise: My Emotional Boundaries

1. I believe my emotional boundaries are rigid, loose, or healthy because: _____

_____

_____

2. Look at the following checklist and mark which of these statements are true about you.

I have good boundaries in the following areas:

_____ I tell others only what makes me comfortable to disclose.

_____ I do not have an intimate, sexual relationship immediately or shortly after beginning a relationship.

_____ I take my time to learn to know someone before I decide to trust that person.

_____ I do not change my behavior and values to please others.

_____ I am sexual only when I want to be.

_____ If someone tries to invade my personal space, I will tell that person that I am uncomfortable or back away.

_____ I do not accept touch from others when I do not want it.

_____ I make choices about my own life and the direction in which it is going.

_____ I do not expect others to anticipate my needs.

_____ I do not expect others to fulfill my needs.

_____ I do not fall apart to get others to take care of me.

_____ I am not self-abusive; if I did self-abuse, I have stopped doing so.

_____ I consciously try not to repeat patterns of abuse that happened to me in the past.

_____ I expect realistic assistance from others.

_____ I have realistic expectations of myself.

3. How many of these did you check? Ideally, you checked all of them. If your boundaries are good, you checked at least twelve or thirteen of these statements. If you left any blank, write that sentence below and look at the belief that lies behind why you did not check it. Then consider what you might do to challenge that belief.

The statements I did not check include:

1. _____

2. _____

3. _____

The beliefs that stopped me from checking each statement are:

1. _____

2. _____

3. _____

What I am willing to do to challenge those beliefs is:

1. _____

2. _____

3. _____

What did completing these exercises about physical and emotional boundaries teach you about yourself? _____

_____

* * * * *

You may also go back to your personal bill of rights (in chapter 8) and list statements about your rights to maintain healthy physical and emotional boundaries. Remember that you have the right to set limits on your physical and emotional space and ask others to respect those limits.

Maintaining Good Relationships

By setting appropriate boundaries, you have a better chance of maintaining good relationships with others. If you have a good relationship, you and the other person respect each other and accept each other as you are. You are able to communicate with the other person—including communication about what has changed, what could change, what needs to change, what you each want to change without demanding or disrespecting. The next section of this chapter looks at communication skills.

If a relationship is to last in any form (between friends, partners, coworkers), it is important that each party accepts change and adjusts to change in the other person, if that change is healthy for you both. If the other person changes in such a way that the change puts you at risk (emotionally, physically, spiritually), then you have the right to end the relationship or change its boundaries. Remember, you have the right to get out of a relationship if you are not happy in it or with it. You do not have the right to try to change the other person to fit your idea of what is a good relationship, and that person does not have the right to try to change you. Your relationships in the past may have been shaped by those who hurt or abused you through their actions and the beliefs they put into your head. Their repetitive traumatic abuse of you may have brainwashed you and led to your feelings of terror and helplessness. You may have learned from them that the only way to survive was to be helpless, or you may have been so terrified of their rejection and abandonment that you were submissive and bonded with them so tightly that it has been hard to break away. You no longer have to be enslaved by those beliefs or by your abusers' earlier threats, actions, and control. You have the right to be your own person and to set your own personal boundaries. If you need to remind yourself of your rights in any relationship, you and the person in that relationship may choose to fill out, sign, and agree to follow the following contract:

Exercise: Our Relationship Contract

This contract is made between _____ and _____ and becomes valid on the date we sign it. It will remain valid for _____ (period of time).

1. We care about this relationship and want it to succeed.

2. We admit that we are each responsible for half of the success or failure of this relationship.

3. We can improve our relationship by doing the following four things, upon which we agree:

   a. _____

   b. _____

   c. _____

   d. _____

4. We are willing to make compromises on the following four things:

   a. _____

   b. _____

   c. _____

   d. _____

5. We will not abuse one another in this relationship in any way.

6. We will not bring up problems that we had with our relationship in the past.

7. We will take time to participate in this relationship on a regular basis by:

   a. _____

   b. _____

   c. _____

   d. _____

8. We will set time to communicate about our relationship if either one of us needs to talk, as long as that talking follows good rules of communication.

Signed _____ Date _____

Signed _____ Date _____

* * * * *

Communication Techniques

Effective communication involves talking directly with another person when something needs to be said. When you communicate effectively, you use clear messages that say what you mean; make statements when a statement is needed (rather than asking a question); clearly state your wants and feelings; do not intend to hurt the other person; and listen actively as well as talking.

Active Listening

When you listen actively, you listen with openness as you try to see the other person's point of view, with empathy as you try to understand the other person's emotional state or feelings, and with awareness, as you try to be aware how what the person says fits with your known facts. As you listen, keep eye contact, maintain safe physical boundaries, and ask questions if you need to do so. Active listening also involves paraphrasing. When you *paraphrase* what another person says to you, you make a statement that reveals what you understand the other person's comment to mean. It is not just an echo of what the other person says, but asks a question through which you test your understanding. If you paraphrase, you may say some variation of the following statement:

"If I hear you correctly, you're saying that you really don't want to go to the party tomorrow night because your ex-wife may be there. Am I right?"

Your paraphrase may include an example, a general idea of what you have heard, or a specific idea you believe you heard from the other person. When you paraphrase what the other person says, you really want to know what he or she means and show you are interested in what he or she is saying. Your paraphrasing can help that other person to hear how he or she is being heard and can then help that person correct any misunderstandings or inaccuracies. The object of paraphrasing is to get clarity as you tell the other person how you have heard him or her and ask for feedback. Paraphrasing also can help you cool down a situation and can help you get more information before you react.

Asking Questions

If you want to communicate with another, you may want to ask probing questions to get better information about how that person thinks or feels. *Probing questions* ask the other person to think and become more aware about what he or she has just said, and to clarify it. Asking a probing question does not mean that the other person was "wrong." In asking for clarification, you may ask the other person to explain something particular, or you may say, "Just what do you mean by what you said?" You may ask the other person to refocus his or her answer or to increase his or her awareness of the meaning of his or her words ("What are your reasons for saying that?") You may also ask the same question of other persons in order to compare the answers.

Describing Feelings

Another basic communication skill is to describe your feelings by making an "I" statement, such as "I feel happy when I am with you." The aim of making such a statement is to start a conversation that will improve your relationship. If the other person is to take you and your feelings into account as worthy of consideration, that person needs to know how you feel. Describing feelings reports on your inner state, and gives information that can help build communication and a relationship.

Describing Behavior

Behavior description is another basic skill for improving communication. If you use this skill, you report the specific, observable actions that the other person has done without valuing them as right or wrong, bad or good: "I noticed that every comment I have made in the past two days has been countered with a rude statement or a negative look." The aim of behavior description is also to open up discussion about how each person affects the other and about their relationship. It is important that you describe the behavior clearly, using evidence and actions that are open to the observation of others. When you use this skill, it is important to avoid trying to infer beyond what is observed.

Using Humor

Using humor can help communication by relaxing tension, reducing bad feelings, increasing a feeling of fellowship, or reinforcing a point. Humor also can help you express feelings more openly and spontaneously. You may use exaggeration, irony, wordplay, or other types of humor. People who have been traumatized may use *black humor*, humor that makes jokes about what happened to themselves or others and that is frequently misunderstood by those who have not been traumatized (or who do not work in the trauma field). Humor should not be a way to attack the other person. It should be used with playfulness and should not evoke ridicule or sarcasm designed to hurt the other. Humor can make a situation more joyful and can improve a relationship. Laughter is good for the immune system, it reduces stress hormones, and, over a prolonged period of time, burns calories. It seems there are many reasons to laugh.

"I" Messages

An "I" message is a specific, nonjudgmental message that focuses on the speaker, not the person listening. "You" messages are hostile and blaming and focus on the listener. When you use an "I" message, you describe what is affecting you without blaming the other person. An I message states how you feel about what the behavior leads to in you and then states a consequence. The "I" message includes three parts:

1. When you _____ (state the behavior),

2. I feel _____ (state the feeling),

3. because _____ (state the consequences).

For example, instead of saying, "Why are you always so rude to me?" You could say, "When you talk rudely to me in front of my coworkers, I feel angry and humiliated because I don't deserve to be talked to in that manner, and it makes me not want to be around you."

Exercise: Practicing Communication Techniques

1. Which of the communication techniques on the preceding pages are you willing to try in the next week? With whom? _____

_____

_____

2. What is the purpose of trying those techniques? _____

_____

_____

3. After a week of trying one or two of them, in the following space, write the results of your attempts at good communication. Did your relationship with the person improve?

_____

* * * * *

Developing Your Sense of Humor

Have you ever wanted to choke the person who told you to "lighten up" or to "get a sense of humor"? Not so easy, when the world seems to be closing in and your stress level is rising. But developing a sense of humor in the face of adversity can be done.

As with any other skill, developing a sense of humor takes some attention and practice. The following steps can help you focus on your sense of humor, defining what is amusing to you and deciding how you can use humor to cope.

Know What Makes You Laugh

You may have lost touch with your playful side. Research has shown children laugh on average 400 times a day, but adults laugh only a few times. Think about the things that make you smile (e.g., TV comedies, the comics, jokes, morning coffee, a sunny day, etc.) and list them here:

_____

_____

_____

_____

Know People Who Can Make You Laugh

Do people in your life fill you with joy or are they real downers? Which people are the negative influences in your life and which are the positive? List these people (use extra paper if you need to):

Positive People   **Negative People**

_____   _____

_____   _____

_____   _____

_____   _____

Are you spending too much time with people who drain your energy? Are you letting others help you or are you carrying the weight of the world on your shoulders? Look at your list of positive people and think of ways to develop these relationships. Spend more time with the people who add to your life and decrease the time with people who leave you feeling used up.

Use Jokes and Collect Them in a Humor Log

It doesn't matter if you are not a good joke-teller. It only matters if *you* find a joke to be funny. Jokes, anecdotes, and funny quotes are everywhere. Radio, TV, the Internet, and printed media are full of them. Bookstores have entire sections on comedy, so get out of the self-help section and find what's funny to you. Write down jokes or amusing stories in a humor notebook. You might even want to paste in your favorite fortune cookie predictions.

Laugh at Life

Never miss an opportunity to enjoy yourself. Remember the "someday we will laugh about this" philosophy and use it immediately. Look for the ironic, the ridiculous, and the absurd in situations that trigger you or lead to feelings of anxiety. Once you see things as not so awful, you can overcome them.

Laugh at Yourself

We all make mistakes. When you make a mistake, having the ability to laugh at yourself is as important as being able to laugh at life. This does not mean you need to be critical of yourself, but rather to see yourself in a more forgiving light, recognizing your humanness.

Never Miss an Opportunity to Play

Be spontaneous. Take a moment to read your humor log, tap along to your favorite song (or be really daring and sing), make love with your spouse or partner, call or write to a positive person on your list, or have ice cream or frozen tofu—especially if you just had a particularly difficult day.

Schedule Fun Time

Your fun time is just as important as your work schedule. Look at your calendar and make appointments with yourself and your positive people. Mark off your vacation time or plan days off in advance so you don't book other appointments in those slots. Write all of your fun time activities in your calendar using bright gel pens, not in the blue or black you use to write in your business appointments and other obligations. When you look back over the previous month, are there several fun activities? Did you keep all of your fun appointments or did you skip them? Reevaluate what you scheduled and decide if you need to start simpler or change priorities. Fun time does not have to be long. Surely you can find time to take the kids to the park, go for a walk along a scenic trail, read a book, take a cooking class, see a movie, or just dance!

Celebrate Successes Big and Small

When was the last time you said "ta-da!" after you completed a goal? When life is stressful, even small accomplishments become big ones. Create a reward system for yourself. Don't wait for someone else to reward your good work or accomplishments, reward yourself. Sometimes just making it through a difficult day is reason enough. Set realistic goals and work toward them. Break the goal down into steps, so you can see your successes and celebrate each one. Use the following planning sheet as a guide.

Exercise: Goal Planning Sheet

Goal: _____

Planned completion date: _____

Step	Reward	Date Completed

* * * * *

Treat Yourself

If you enjoy it, do it! Use your fun time schedule to add enjoyable activities and people to your life. You may tend to feel guilty or self-indulgent when you celebrate yourself. But ultimately, you will be a better person if you treat yourself with care and compassion. Don't be afraid to have lunch with a friend after a promotion, soak in a tub after step aerobics, or stop for ice cream after completing a major report.

Don't Wait to Be Happy, Do It NOW

This is part of celebrating life's successes. The quicker you say "ta-da," the better you will feel. If you bargain with yourself over your reward, you diminish your achievement. If you want to buy a new dress, don't tell yourself you will do it after you lose weight. Buy it in the size that fits and wear it as soon as you can.

Smile, Smile, Smile

Seems simple enough, right? Yet you may not always practice this behavior. When tension builds, humans have a tendency to stiffen facial and other muscles and clench their jaws; tension then results in headaches and other ailments. Loosen up your tensed muscles by taking deep breaths and then smiling. It helps to use a mirror so you can see how you look as you become more relaxed. When talking to other people, smile at them. You will notice that they too will start smiling. This helps prevent or reduce discomfort during difficult discussions.

Practice all these activities over the next week or two. Then return to this page of the workbook and write down how your efforts have made you feel and how they have impacted your relationships with others.

How has working on your sense of humor felt? What changes has it made in your relationship? _____

Styles of Communication

Miller et al. (1989) note that there are four styles of communication. After reading the description of each, think of when you use that style and with whom.

Small Talk

Small talk tends to be used in social situations in order to build rapport and keep in touch. It is generally relaxed, cordial, and playful and includes greetings, stories, and talk about conventional topics or daily routines. It may also include talking about special events that have occurred or will be occurring. *Shop talk* is a form of small talk that occurs on the job and is designed to gather or give information and monitor work-related activities and schedules. It may include a team meeting that asks who, what, where, when, and how questions in order to report on and describe what is going on. If you use shop talk, you are showing others how competent, informed, and productive you are.

When do you use small talk, and with whom? Shop talk? _____

_____

_____

Control Talk

Control talk is used to lead, direct, persuade, evaluate, instruct, reinforce, show authority, get compliance or agreement, sell, or caution. The intent of control talk is to show that you are in charge while also being both helpful and persuasive. It uses statements, questions, "shoulds," and assumptions. Control talk can become *fight talk* when you want to force change on or defend yourself against another. It then includes statements that are demanding, attacking, blaming, threatening, or intimidating. The aim of fight talk is to justify yourself, hide your own fear or vulnerability, put the other person down, or use abuse to control. Fight talk often includes "you" statements and "why" questions. Another form of control talk is *spite talk*. Spite talk is used to make someone else feel guilty, to get even, to protect yourself, to cover over your hurt, or to stop change from occurring. It can include gossiping, complaining, sulking, keeping silent, or showing defiance. How do you use control talk and with whom and when? Fight talk? Spite talk?

_____

_____

_____

_____

Search Talk

The third type of communication style is *search talk*. If you use search talk, you are trying to get insight, clarify what has happened, look for options or causes, evaluate alternatives, or ask questions. You want to explore, brainstorm, and expand upon what you already know.

Your mood in using this style is calm, supportive, and inquisitive, and you are open to possibilities. When do you use search talk, and with whom?

_____

_____

_____

Straight Talk

The final communication style is *straight talk*. Straight talk is open, direct, honest, assertive, responsive, and respectful. If you use straight talk, you aim to disclose information, connect with others without trying to control them, collaborate with those others, and look toward the future. Straight talk includes observing, using active listening and the other communication techniques described above, and has a "now" orientation. When do you use straight talk, and with whom?

_____

_____

_____

Final Thoughts on Communication

Remember, communication is inevitable. You cannot **not** communicate. If you do not respond verbally to someone or something, you are still communicating. Communicating is a continuous process that occurs even during sleep (particularly if you sleep with a person or an animal). Communication is irreversible. Once you have communicated a message, it cannot be "taken back" or erased. It can be challenged, modified, or reexpressed, but the original message is out there.

Communication has many levels: the words said, the setting, the style and technique of the communication, the level of trust that exists between the giver and receiver of the message, and the perceptions of each all play roles. The sender and receiver of a communication never share the same perception completely and, therefore, there is always room for communication error. Communication is most effective when what is sent in words (verbally) and what is sent in action (nonverbally, through body language) are the same or reinforce one another. Communication also is most effective when the listener gives feedback to and interacts with the speaker. One major purpose for communicating is to build more communication—and, hopefully, better communication. Finally, communication is a very personal process that is impacted by who you are; it is impossible for you to separate totally what you say and give out from who you are as a person.

Before you look at what you have learned about yourself by completing the exercises in this chapter, consider the Ten Commandments of Good Listening:

1. Be quiet and stop talking.

2. Put the person who is speaking at ease through your attention and body language, eye contact, and respect.

3. Show that person you want to listen to him or her.

4. Remove possible distractions if you are having anything more than a superficial conversation (noise, television).

5. Show empathy through body language and vocalizations (sounds you make such as "oh," "wow," "hmm").

6. Have patience with the person talking and let him or her take time to get out what it is he or she wants to say.

7. Keep your anger under control.

8. Try not to argue or criticize.

9. Use the communication techniques listed above, including asking probing questions, paraphrasing, and observing emotion and behavior.

10. Stop talking (adapted from Virginia State CISM 1998).

Exercise: What I Learned from This Chapter

What did you learn about yourself by completing the exercises in this chapter?

_____

_____

_____

_____

_____

_____

_____

_____

_____

* * * * *

14

Finding Meaning

(Complex PTSD Category 7)

We have said many times in many different ways throughout this workbook that traumatic events have the ability to change anyone who experiences them. You have been changed in some or many ways by your experiences of prolonged, repeated trauma, and those changes may be soul-deep. Still, if you are to heal, it is important for you to find some sense of meaning from what has happened to you. If your basic psychological needs for safety, trust, power or control, esteem, and intimacy cannot be met adequately by yourself, the world, or others, then finding that meaning may be a difficult task. You also may believe that you are destined to live a very short life and that you will never live long enough to find peace or joy. This is called *belief in a foreshortened future*, and it is one of the benchmark symptoms of PTSD and complex PTSD.

Working Through a Traumatic Event

The person who works through a history of trauma and comes out the other side as a (somewhat) whole person, has certain character traits and abilities that can be learned or developed by using many of the exercises in this workbook (the appropriate chapter number is listed after each ability). That person has the ability to:

- tolerate or lessen the intensity of painful feelings (chapters 5, 6, and 8)

- recognize self-blame and shame and then counter it (chapter 7)

- stay connected with persons who are both present and absent (chapter 13)

- be alone without being lonely (chapter 8)

- self-soothe when upset (chapter 2)

- anticipate consequences of actions and events (chapter 11)

- set and maintain appropriate physical and emotional interpersonal boundaries (chapters 8 and 13)

- provide mutual self-support with supportive others (chapters 11 and 13)

- have willpower (chapter 11)

- take initiative (chapter 11)

- have empathy for others (chapter 13)

- have a sense of humor (chapter 13)

Which of these do you have? Which do you want to develop? _____

_____

_____

_____

_____

You may also want to try to develop what Covey (1999) lists as the "seven habits of highly effective people." Those habits are:

1. Be proactive—decide what you want to do and do it. This is personal vision.

2. Begin with an end in mind (your legacy) and then make every decision and take every action with that final legacy in mind. This is personal leadership.

3. Put first things first and concentrate on what is important, though not always urgent, to do. This is personal management.

4. Think win-win. Seek solutions to problems that benefit everyone involved. This is interpersonal leadership.

5. Seek first to understand and then to be understood. Listen to others with the goal of understanding them and their position. This is empathic communication.

6. Synergize through teamwork. This is creative cooperation.

7. Commit to improving yourself constantly. This is balanced self-renewal.

The key to implementing these seven habits is to make a choice each day to try to live by them. Choosing to do so with awareness means you have that end result in mind. As you choose, look at the results of each choice you make. If you like those results, then keep up your good work. If you do not like the results, then learn from your mistakes and try again (Power 1992a).

Continuing to Heal

Healing from trauma occurs when you are able to have at least some level of power or authority over your memories, when you can manage any emotions connected with those memories, and when you can manage intrusive and avoidant PTSD or complex PTSD–related symptoms. Healing occurs also when you are able to control your own behavioral responses (e.g., choosing when and how to express anger). To be healed means you are able to take care of yourself emotionally, physically, interpersonally, and spiritually. It also means that you respect yourself and have relationships with yourself and others that are safe (Matsakis 1998).

We have given you many suggestions and provided many exercises that will help with this healing. We have shown you how to deal with your own messages about what happened to you as well as the messages others instilled within you (your introjects). We have given you strategies to deal with your deserved and undeserved guilt. We have helped you learn self-care and gain boundaries (Matsakis 1999). It is our expectation that your healing will continue long after you finish this workbook, even if you come back to it on occasion for a brushup. Challenging and even possibly changing some of your beliefs about those five basic needs has given you strength to continue to grow. You also have given voice to what happened to you consciously, with the intent of healing and bringing any intrusive memories, thoughts, or nightmares under more control. You have learned to set boundaries and are better able now to keep your traumatic experiences contained, letting out what happened to you only to those who need to know. You have developed strategies to resolve your grief and deal with your losses. Also, you have learned to be satisfied with taking small steps toward healing and are learning to accept yourself as you really are (Schiraldi 2000).

Speeding Up Healing

Power lists a number of ways to speed up healing without retraumatizing yourself (1992a, 92, 104). You may:

- become more and more aware of each choice you make

- choose to work for a "common good" that gives you a sense of meaning

- utilize self-management techniques to control or minimize the impact of flashbacks

- implement ways to be more functional on a daily basis

- look for what makes you resistant to doing your work, and then do something to modify that resistance

- manage your pain in constructive ways (exercise a "normal" amount, not to the point of injury or exhaustion, for example)

- remind yourself consistently that you survived "the worst"—your original traumas—and that you now exist in this present time

- learn the names of your feelings, find out what those feelings feel like, and practice them

- practice turning the volume up and down on various feelings

- seek out positive experiences and enjoy them and the positive emotions that accompany them

Exercise: The Ladder

Another way to look for meaning in your healing is use the ladder exercise developed by Busuttil et al (2002). The aim of this exercise is to identify short- and long-term goals that can be presented to others. In your journal, draw a ladder with several rungs. On the top rung, write in your long-term goal for healing or finding meaning. On the bottom rung, write in the lowest point of your life. On the intervening rungs, fill in the steps you want or need to take in order to achieve your ultimate goal. You will want to include many life dimensions as you climb the ladder, such as your marriage or other long-term relationships, social activities, spiritual endeavors, occupational and financial goals or pursuits, and your values. If you seek feedback from important persons in your life, you may change what you have put on your rungs.

* * * * *

Thoughts about Finding Meaning

How do you find meaning in life? One way is to pursue some type of activity or project that grows out of your traumatic experiences. Mothers who have lost children to drunk drivers often become active in MADD. Family members of those lost in major airline disasters have formed support groups and have advocated for changes in airline regulation. Through this process, you will again recognize your abilities and your limitations. You may become a mentor to others or start your own organization or project. You may write poetry or throw pottery or draw. You may decide to enter a helping profession (once you are healed enough that your baggage does not influence how you practice your professional skills). Through these or similar activities, you give something back to the world.

You may also find meaning by developing your own self further or by enjoying some of the beauty and pleasures of the world (Schiraldi 2000). You may become a photographer of nature. You may develop a new loving, intimate relationship or foster the relationship you presently have. You may develop friendships or you may commit to personal growth that helps you to understand yourself and others.

It is quite possible that you will never know exactly why you were a victim; on the other hand, you may have some knowledge about what lay behind your abuse, torture, or trauma. Bad things do happen to good people (Kushner 1981). At times, growth comes from suffering. How have you grown as you have done the work in this workbook? Have you changed?

_____

_____

_____

_____

It is possible to grow through trauma. If you have been responsible to any degree, through negligence or intent, for the event or events that happened to you or around you, and you own up to your responsibility, you have grown. When you realized and accepted that you were betrayed, violated, victimized, and abused and that what happened to you was due to the actions of others and was not of your own doing or causing, you have grown. If you no longer blame yourself for what was not your responsibility, you have grown. When events were due to chance and you can accept just that—that you were a victim of a random act of trauma—you have grown. As Tedeschi, Park, and Calhoun (1998) recognize, you grow when your trauma is no longer an incomprehensible present but becomes, instead, a comprehensible part of your past.

Spiritual Development

One way many person find meaning is through pursuing some form of spiritual development. Developing spirituality can be a lifelong pursuit as you learn to ask questions about how you view a Higher Being, Creator, God. Perhaps you may decide that you want to learn to pray or you want to use prayer more. Prayer can be a way to get understanding and clarity if you open up to whatever "comes in" as you pray. Through prayer, you have a tool to give voice to your pain and listen in the present to what messages are given to you. Do you pray for answers? For relief? Or do you pray for specific interventions or material goods? It is important to decide just what you are praying for.

Brussat and Brussat (2000) discuss many prescriptions for spiritual practice in their book *Spiritual Rx*. One prescription is to search for beauty; beauty is truly everywhere around you, but noticing it can be difficult when trauma and traumatic symptoms overshadow your ability to see. They also examine the prescription of faith, stating that "faith [is] not something you have but . . . something you are in—a relationship. It involves an awareness of and an attunement to God's presence in your everyday experiences" (81). When you have faith, you can choose and then remain true to a vision or an aspiration, e.g., the vision of yourself as healed from your traumatic past. In order to follow that vision, you need some level of trust (one of the five psychological needs) in yourself, in Providence, and in others. If you pray and have a conversational relationship with a Higher Power, you can ask for guidance in following that vision.

We have spoken of forgiveness in chapter 12. One aspect of a spiritual journey is to examine forgiveness in three contexts: forgiveness of self, allowing release of guilt and shame; forgiveness of others (to the extent that is possible); and forgiveness of God, which you may seek depending on your spiritual practices. Through your spiritual quest, if you choose that route to try to find meaning in what happened to you, you may look at what you want to do to forgive yourself and others or to seek God's forgiveness if you believe that is essential to your growth.

Another spiritual prescription involves keeping hope. The Brussats believe that hope can be learned and that it is the major ingredient of optimism. What does the word hope mean to you? Do you have hope in your future—that you will be healed as much as you can be? Do you have hope now, in the present, in your ability to heal? _____

_____

_____

_____

Do you have any or all of the following three attitudes that help you to have hope?

- patience—the ability to accept that healing takes time, and often occurs on a time line other than your own

- courage to pursue healing without knowing what lies ahead, particularly if you still have memories that you have not faced

- persistence—the ability to keep going on with your healing, even after you finish this workbook

Another spiritual practice involves seeking joy or allowing yourself to have feelings of happiness and pleasure. You may find that you find joy by doing for others, as you try to find meaning in your life. When and where do you feel joy? How can you share joy with others or help others find joy? _____

_____

_____

_____

According to the Brussats, "many people . . . define spirituality as the search for meaning and purpose . . . (that) involves both seeking and making" (2000, 172). Think of a time when you suddenly changed what you were going to do and as a result met someone you needed to meet or were presented with a new opportunity. There are many possible paths open to you at all times. Is finding a purpose a difficult task for you? How do you show yourself that your life really does matter—to yourself, if not to others? _____

_____

_____

_____

You alone know whether you view your God or Higher Power as anthropomorphic (having human qualities) or beyond human in attributes, and where you see God. You alone know if your connection to that Higher Power or God is personal or distant. Bourne (1998) notes that you may see God in:

- natural beauty
- creative inspiration
- premonitions
- synchronicities (coincidences that are not coincidences)

- deep insights or truth
- love given or received
- miracles
- other visionary experiences

Exercise: Ways to Improve Your Spirituality

Bourne (1998) suggests a variety of ways to improve your spirituality. If you answer these questions, try not to do so merely with "yes" or "no," but write about when you use each way to improve your spirituality, if you do.

1. Do you pray as a way to communicate with your Higher Power or to request something from him or her? _____

_____

_____

2. Do you turn over problems to that Higher Power for solutions? _____

_____

_____

3. Do you meditate in order to get in touch with deeper parts of your self through quieting your mind? _____

_____

_____

4. Do you read literature that is spiritual in nature? This might include the Bible or other works. _____

_____

_____

5. Do you meet with others in a "spiritual fellowship" whether through church attendance, vision quests, workshops, or other activities? _____

_____

_____

6. Do you do some type of compassionate service for others? _____

_____

_____

* * * * *

If you are seeking what Bourne describes as "a more optimistic and tolerant view of life" (1998, 282), you may use some of the following suggestions and revelations to guide your quest.

1. Life is a school with the primary purpose of growth in consciousness and wisdom and the capacity to love.

2. Adversity and difficult situations are lessons designed for growth rather than random, capricious acts of fate. In the larger scheme of things, everything happens for a purpose. This may be difficult to accept but, if you have used your experiences to find your life purpose, you may have helped many others in many ways. Through your experiences, you have hopefully learned compassion and empathy.

3. Your personal limitations (including disabilities and illnesses) can point up the lessons you have to learn in life and can be challenges to be used for growth.

4. Your life has a creative purpose and mission, something that you must do in order to feel complete.

5. You have a higher source of support and guidance available to you in your Higher Power if you ask.

6. You can contact your Higher Power directly through your personal experience.

7. The power of intention can promote what Bourne calls "miraculous consequences" if your intention is for the highest good.

8. Evil is the misuse of your creative power.

9. Love is stronger than fear and can overcome fear.

10. Death is a transition. Some part of your being transcends and survives beyond death.

Do you believe any of these principles? If so, which ones: _____

_____

_____

_____

Are there other statements or principles you can turn to that will help you on your healing path? _____

_____

_____

_____

What did you learn about yourself by completing these exercises about developing spirituality? _____

_____

_____

_____

Connecting with Nature

Another way to seek meaning and purpose is to connect with nature. Eitner (2001), president of the Masters Group (a group focused on developing expanded consciousness) and a Reiki master, has used and taught various methods to achieve advanced states of consciousness that shift and change old trauma-bound patterns, fears, and defenses. She has found that healing of trauma and related negative addictive behavior patterns can be done effectively in nature. Project Nature Connect, also called "the natural systems thinking process or reconnecting with nature," provides safe, easy, and supportive experiences to restore the senses wounded by traumatic experiences. Through the use of these exercises, persons who have been traumatized can become part of and build connections to the "web of life" or supportive natural community. Project Nature Connect, in a series of interactions experienced in nature, restores these connections and senses to their natural state. The exercises she uses in her work emphasize natural attractions, positive feelings, and appreciation, building a framework for you, as a survivor, to become connected to what is specifically positive and supportive for you. You can obtain more information about Project Nature Connect from the Web site, www.ecopsych.com, or from Project Nature Connect, P.O. Box 1605, Friday Harbor, WA 98250.

The first two of the three exercises below for connecting with nature were designed by Dr. Michael Cohen, an educator and environmental psychologist. The third of these was initially designed by Christina Brittain and has been modified by Eitner.

Exercise: Gaining Permission

This exercise begins to set the pattern to help you ask for and receive permission to interact with nature. You will also be able to begin distinguishing between what is naturally attractive and welcoming and what is not. As you complete this exercise, you will begin to notice differences in your interactions with other people as well as with nature.

1. Go to an attractive natural place like a wood, park or backyard, or even to an indoor plant. The key factors are that the area should be natural, attractive, and safe.

2. You will find that something in this natural place will stand out and look very attractive, and you will be drawn to it.

3. Ask permission of that plant, tree, bush, or whatever to interact with it. This is generally done nonverbally and always respectfully.

4. Obtain its permission in some way. If you receive that permission, you will find yourself feeling acknowledged and connected. This will be a positive experience.

5. If you don't receive this permission, identify another attractive something, and obtain permission to interact with it.

6. Sense the connection; feel what gift this natural attraction has for you.

7. When you are finished with the experience, thank the natural attraction for interacting with you.

I tried this exercise when I: _____

_____

_____

_____

The results of my trying this exercise in nature were: _____

_____

_____

_____

* * * * *

Exercise: Establishing Trust

This closed-eye experience begins to establish your trust in the person you choose to lead you and in nature itself through using your senses.

1. Ask someone you like and trust and with whom you feel comfortable to be your nature guide. Go with that nature guide to an attractive natural place like a backyard, wood, or park.

2. Ask the area for permission to interact, as described above.

3. Take your guide's hand, close your eyes, and explore the area. Be open and receptive to gathering information through your other senses. Walk along and ask your guide to place your hand on natural things, like a tree, rock, or leaf. As you touch it, be receptive, noticing what you feel, smell, sense, or hear. Do you notice changes in temperature, hear more sensitively, feel more distinctly? Are you comfortable with the connections?

4. After interacting with each leaf, tree, rock, etc., thank it for sharing itself with you. Thank your guide for leading you.

I tried this exercise when I: _____

_____

_____

_____

My experiences with this exercise were: _____

_____

_____

_____

$$* \quad * \quad * \quad * \quad *$$

Exercise: Sharing Your Troubles with Nature

Sometimes, when nothing feels safe, you still need to tell your troubles to someone or something. Nature can provides connection and comfort and a place where you can share (and look for) meaning.

1. Go to a natural attractive place like a backyard, park, or wood. An indoor plant will do if needed.

2. Ask the place for permission to visit. Nature welcomes you when you see or feel something that attracts you. Sit down beside it, or where you can easily see and interact with it.

3. Now think about what is troubling you.

4. Tell the attractive part of nature what is troubling you.

5. Feel nature sharing your troubles; this sharing can make them easier to bear.

6. Continue to sit still and feel nature sharing your troubles with you.

7. When you feel your troubles getting lighter, express your appreciation to nature. Nature is always there to comfort you.

As you share with nature, you may find that you see beauty around you and feel connected with something greater than yourself. Perhaps your Higher Power is some type of connection with nature. Allow yourself to take in whatever nature offers you.

I completed this exercise by: _____

_____

_____

_____

What it taught me about letting go of my troubles (and traumas) was: _____

_____

_____

_____

* * * * *

Exercise: Affirming Positive Qualities

1. Go to an attractive natural place like a backyard, park, or wood, or to an indoor plant.

2. Find something that is attractive to you, and ask for permission to interact with it.

3. When you receive permission, identify what it is about the natural attraction that you like. (For instance, "I like that flower because it is pretty and graceful.")

4. Recognize that you have those same (or similar) qualities and say to yourself, "I like myself because I am pretty and graceful." Be sure to choose realistic qualities of both nature and, potentially, of yourself.

5. Continue the same process with other attractions.

6. It might be helpful to ask another person to assist you to discover things you like about yourself (particularly if you have not worked through your self-esteem or psychological need issues).

I completed this exercise by: _____

_____

_____

_____

What I learned through completing this exercise was: _____

_____

_____

_____

* * * * *

How did it feel to you to try to connect with nature in this way? Remember to check out the Web site for more information about the program.

This chapter has looked at ways to find meaning in your life. Finding meaning for what you endured and survived can be a very difficult task. Keep the three attitudes in mind as you do so—keep your courage, try to be patient, and persist as you keep in mind that healing is possible.

If you are able to let go of those aspects of trauma that are not positive in your life, if you are optimistic, if you are a self-starter and are hardy, you will have a better chance to grow. We will discuss the concept of resilience in more detail in the final chapter of this workbook. Before you go to that chapter, what have you learned about yourself in this one? How have you let go of what happened to you? How have you grown? How do you reach out to others who are hurting? When and how do you show your appreciation of life? Have you bonded with other survivors? Have you joined any support groups or created a new group? How have you used your personal energy to survive?

15

Final Thoughts and Exercises

Now that you have worked through most or at least some of the exercises in this workbook, whether dealing with PTSD of complex PTSD, you have learned a great deal about trauma and about how trauma has transformed you. Hopefully you have also learned about yourself.

Trauma often transforms those persons who experience it. You may have heard this statement before and you have read similar statements in this workbook. Your exposure to trauma has changed you in some way. You may have gone from a familiar everyday existence of comfort and predictability to an unfamiliar world of post-traumatic stress with its intrusions, avoidances, and physiological reactions. You may have experienced a lifetime of abuse and terror and now have many or all of the symptoms of complex PTSD. As you have made a journey by completing the exercises in this workbook, you also may have changed and, hopefully, have learned to trust yourself and your intuitions more often or even most of the time. You may have been schlogging along, putting one foot in front of the other, but you have kept on going. Now it is time to look at where you are today and where you hope to be tomorrow or the next day or the next.

Your Real Self

Masterson (1988) has proposed several characteristics that describe a real self. After each of the characteristics that are listed below, write a short description of how you meet this capacity now and what you might do to fulfill it even further.

- I have the capacity to experience deeply a wide range of feelings including joy and excitement in a spontaneous way. _____

_____

_____

- I have the capacity to expect that I will get the things to which I am appropriately entitled. _____

_____

_____

_____

- I have the capacity to be assertive in expressing my wishes, dreams, and goals once I have identified those that are appropriate to my life. _____

_____

_____

_____

- I have a good sense of self-esteem because I have coped with my traumatic experiences in a positive, creative way. _____

_____

_____

- I am able to soothe my own feelings, even when they are painful, without wallowing in misery. _____

_____

_____

- I am able to make and stick to commitments, in spite of obstacles and setbacks.

_____

_____

_____

- I am able to be creative in seeking new ways to solve my problems. _____

_____

_____

_____

- I am able to have intimate relationships with others without being overcome by anxiety or, if anxiety comes up, I have the ability to self-soothe. _____

_____

_____

_____

- I have the capacity to be alone with myself without feeling abandoned or despairing, without having to fill up my life with meaningless activity or bad relationships.

  _____

  _____

  _____

- I have a core self that persists through time and I am aware of that core and of who I am. _____

  _____

  _____

  _____

- I have the capacity to develop or maintain the other capacities listed above. _____

  _____

  _____

  _____

Blessings

What are the blessings you now have in your life? Can you identify any? You may have more than you imagine. Do you have children, peace of mind, enough food on your plate at night, a job, physical relief, understanding of your symptoms, safety (in all its aspects or just in one or two aspects), prosperity, or other gifts? Do you have the respect of others for your survival and strong spirit? Do you have spirituality, the absence of fear, and an intimate relationship? All of these things and others are blessings. In the space below, write down any blessings you can name. _____

  _____

  _____

  _____

  _____

Health

Do you now consider yourself to be a healthy person? As a healthy person (or even a person on the road to health), how do you respond to the following statements:

I am aware of the trauma or traumas I experienced. _____

  _____

  _____

  _____

I am aware of the feelings the trauma led to. _____

_____

_____

_____

I have a sense of my own identity as it is now, after the trauma, and how that identity has changed over time, even as I worked in this workbook. _____

_____

_____

_____

I know and trust the following feelings that working through the trauma has led me to.

_____

_____

_____

I have communicated about the trauma and my feelings with: _____

_____

_____

_____

I am empathetic with other victims and sensitive to them. I have showed this to others by:

_____

_____

_____

I recognize that the trauma or traumas impacted me in the following ways and hold myself in high regard because I have survived. _____

_____

_____

_____

I have kept good boundaries or learned to keep good boundaries in (behaviors, activities):

_____

_____

_____

I am now autonomous and do not need the approval of _____ to survive (list your specific traumas): _____

_____

_____

_____

I believe my perception of the traumas and their impacts are reality based upon objective information of: _____

_____

_____

_____

I am now willing to take the following risks and want to continue to grow: _____

_____

_____

_____

I am committed to life, and I show this commitment by: _____

_____

_____

_____

Life has meaning to me; I have hope that: _____

_____

_____

_____

I advocate for myself by: _____

_____

_____

_____

(adapted from Caruso 1986)

Resilience

As you have done the work in this workbook, you have learned a great deal about yourself, what happened to you, and what can help you heal. One major characteristic of persons who heal most is their ability to be resilient. Just what does it mean to be resilient?

The following checklist contains numerous characteristics that combine to form resilience. Check off which of them you believe now describe you. The more you check, the more resilient you may be.

_____ I have a good self-concept.

_____ I have good self-esteem.

_____ I am sensitive to others' needs.

_____ I am generally cooperative with others.

_____ I am socially responsive.

_____ I have a good sense of humor.

_____ I am able to postpone getting my needs met (I can delay gratification).

_____ I am generally flexible.

_____ I can control my impulses when I need to do so.

_____ I believe in the future and plan for it.

_____ I have a good support system.

_____ I recognize that I have many opportunities in life available to me.

_____ I respect individual human beings.

_____ I respect appropriate authority.

_____ I am able to look for more than one solution to a problem.

_____ I am able to plan ahead.

_____ I have hobbies and interests beyond my traumas.

_____ I have a positive view of life and see life's joys (as well as its sorrows).

_____ I can problem-solve and have a strategy which I use.

_____ I have a sense of spirituality.

_____ I celebrate myself regularly.

_____ I celebrate others regularly.

_____ I believe that I have some level of control over myself and others.

_____ I would rather take action than wait for something to happen to me.

_____ I am able to find meaning even in bad things.

_____ I am someone others like and love.

_____ I am able to find someone to help me when I need it.

_____ I can ask questions in a creative way.

_____ I have a conscience that allows me to see my own goodness.

_____ I have a "knowing" about things that happen to and around me.

_____ I can disengage and separate from others if they are not good for me.

_____ I can attach to others and connect.

How many of these traits were you able to check? If you find that you still can check only a few, you may want to redo some of the exercises in this book. If you want to build your resilience, you need to monitor and observe how you interact in the world. See just when and how (or if) you use humor. When you are presented with a problem, try to come up with at least two solutions, and then weigh the pros and cons until you can make an appropriate choice between the solutions. You may want to try new hobbies or activities to broaden yourself. You also may want to seek out your spiritual side to a greater degree or become more connected with nature.

Looking at the Purpose of Your Life

Do you now have a purpose in life? Bourne defines life purpose as "something you need to do in order to feel whole, complete, and fulfilled in your life . . . that expresses a particular talent, gift, skill, or desire that you hold most dear . . . something that reaches beyond the limited needs and concerns of your own ego [and is] 'other-directed' . . . an important activity or service you could have come into this world to accomplish" (1998, 246).

Exercise: My Life Purpose

If you are sure of your life purpose, then write it here: _____

_____

_____

_____

If you are not sure, you may ask yourself the following questions and see where the answers lead you.

How do you feel about the work you are doing? Is it fulfilling? _____

_____

_____

_____

Do you want to continue your education and, if so, in what area or areas? _____

_____

_____

_____

Do you have hobbies or interests you want to learn or follow? If so, what are they? _____

_____

_____

_____

If you were to write a motto for your life right now, what would it be? _____

The motto of my life is: _____

_____

If you could accomplish anything in your life, what would you hope to accomplish within the next year? _____

_____

_____

_____

The next five years? _____

_____

_____

_____

The next ten years? _____

_____

_____

_____

What values are most important to you and give you the most meaning? Do you value wealth? Material possessions? Good health? Close relationships? Family? Friends? Closeness with a supreme being? _____

_____

_____

_____

If you were to make a commitment to change one thing in your life that would make it easier for you to achieve your life purpose, what would it be? _____

_____

_____

_____

As Bourne (1998) notes, it is important to counter negative belief systems that might interfere with your trying to reach your dreams and goals. If you truly are on a path to achieve your life purpose, it is important to stick to the task and look for opportunities to achieve it whenever possible.

What are your reactions to completing this exercise? _____

_____

_____

_____

* * * * *

Journal Exercise

Earlier in this book (chapter 1), you did an exercise that asked you to respond to a series of five suggestions for drawing. Now that you have completed the exercises in this workbook, has your view of yourself and your world changed?

In your journal, you may again draw these five pictures: of yourself, your space, your road, your family, and, again, of yourself. How do your new drawings, when compared to your first drawings, show you have changed?

Psychological Wellness

The goal of working in this workbook has been to help you build psychological wellness. If you are psychologically well, you are able to maintain a healthy lifestyle that has balance in its physical (fitness, nutrition), social (relationships, support systems), emotional (self-worth, hardiness), vocational and educational (productivity), and spiritual (purpose, meaning, ethics, values) aspects. In which of the five areas do you feel balanced? Unbalanced? Why? _____

_____

_____

_____

_____

_____

How comfortable are you with yourself and your life? _____

_____

Do you like your present standard of living? _____

_____

Do you like your home? _____

_____

Do you like the pace of your life? _____

_____

Are you satisfied with your employment? Your education? _____

_____

Are you clear with yourself as to who you are and what you are? _____

_____

Do you have an inner sense of purpose for your life? _____

_____

Do you keep the balance in all five areas of your life that we listed above? _____

_____

How do you balance between private and social time? Between personal and professional time? Between exercise and relaxation? _____

_____

_____

_____

* * * * *

Resourcefulness

A healthy person has learned to be resourceful and has a sense of coherence. Antonovsky (1987) defined coherence as personal beliefs that life (including stressor situations) is comprehensible, manageable, and meaningful as well as structured and predictable. You know that bad things happen. In all likelihood, the rest of your life will not be trauma-free. However, the way you approach traumatic experiences may be changed by the work you have done in this workbook. You now may be able to approach new stressors and potential traumas (unless they are so incredibly overwhelming that there is no way to make sense of them) as challenges for which meaning is to be sought. If this is the case, you will be willing to invest your (depleted) energy to work through those experiences, even if your energy is depleted. If so, hopefully you will be able to maintain some sense of balance, use action-oriented coping skills, realistically adapt the way you approach or avoid the new situation, and thrive as you become stronger than before.

Dunning (1997) has developed a list of thirteen characteristics that she calls the "Thirteen C's of Salutogenesis." *Salutogenesis* means learned resourcefulness, or the ability to use stressful situations for self-direction and growth. This wellness model focuses on retaining control, even through traumatic events, and finding the benefits and meaning in what has happened to you. How many of these "C's" are you able to apply in stressful situations?

1. control: a sense of autonomy and an ability to influence what happens around you in your environment

2. cohesion: connecting or belonging with concerned others who care about you, your feelings, and your experiences

3. communication: expressing positive self-discovery and growth with others through words and writings

4. challenge: using stressor events as opportunities for growth and development and seeing hardships as something to overcome or change in some way (however small)

5. commitment: remaining active in the pursuit of meaning

6. connection: forming a bond of trust with others to help healing

7. clarification: accepting that the event and its reasons for occurring go beyond your influence while still looking at what you can change or control

8. coherence: making your trauma story logical and consistent with your past, present, and future

9. congruence: seeing the event through the eyes of others, looking at external forces, accepting that every trauma you (or others) have experienced can lead to feelings of self-blame, responsibility, and failure, and doing the appropriate exercises to combat these feelings

10. commemoration: developing ritualistic closures to events in order to memorialize them and to put them in the context of history

11. comfort or consolation: developing feelings of relief and encouragement while accepting how things have changed

12. culture: understanding how your cultural context and history impacts your healing

13. closure: achieving a sense that the traumatic event has truly ended, even though you will probably never be the same; understanding the differences between your "before" and "now" selves

Are you a salutogenic person? Which of the C's apply to you? _____

_____

_____

In spite of it all, no matter how hard you work to deal with your trauma-based memories or how much you try to avoid the traumas that have befallen you, you remain a human being who has been through traumatic events. If you are fortunate enough to be a thriver who has walked through trauma toward healing, or who has become an educator to help others on their healing paths, you have possibly found meaning in your life and have new goals.

Exercise: My Healing Alphabet

Take a few moments, based on all the work you have done, and develop your own healing alphabet. This exercise asks you to take each letter of the alphabet and come up with one to three words that describe you and your healing. For example:

A. accountability, achievement, anxiety

B. balanced, burned out

C. compassionate, caring

D. dignified

... and so on. Develop your own alphabet.

A _____

B _____

C _____

D _____

E _____

F _____

G _____

H _____

I _____

J _____

K _____

L _____

M _____

N _____

O _____

P _____

Q _____

R _____

S _____

T _____

U _____

V _____

W _____

X _____

Y _____

Z _____

What do you see in the words you have chosen? Are there patterns to how you have healed?

_____

_____

_____

* * * * *

We want to thank you for making the commitment to heal and for doing all the hard work you have done in this workbook. Please remember that you can turn back to any of the exercises in this workbook at any time for a "refresher." You will find a questionnaire following this chapter that was developed by Williams (1990) to measure or identify some of the characteristics of complex PTSD. You may have completed it earlier in your work. If so, compare your answers with ones you would give now. If you have not done it earlier, please take the time now to complete it.

To conclude, the following Rules for Being Human were provided to one of the authors; their source is anonymous. Keep them in mind as you continue to work on healing.

Rules for Being Human

1. You will receive a body. You may like it or hate it, but it is yours for the entire period of time you are here.

2. You will learn lessons. You are now enrolled in the full-time informal school called Life. Each school day will give you opportunities to learn lessons. You may like the lessons you have to learn or you may believe that your lessons don't really fit you and are stupid.

3. You will make no mistakes; rather, you will learn through your lessons. You will experiment and do trial-and-error learning. Some (if not much) of what you do will end in failure; this is part of the process called Life.

4. Your lessons will repeat themselves until you learn them. Each lesson you are to learn will be presented to you (or will present itself to you) in various forms until you learn it.

5. As long as you are alive, you will have lessons to learn.

6. "There" is no better than "here." There is no geographical cure. If you move, your "there" will become a "here" and you will look for a new place to go.

7. What you love or hate in another person often is a mirror of you. When you love or hate something about another person, it reflects something you love or hate about yourself.

8. What you make of your life is up to you. You have the tools and resources, skills and information; how you use them depends on the choices you make. Remember, the choice is yours—to succeed, fight, or give up.

9. Your answers to your life's questions lie inside you. Look, listen, trust your own internal self and intuition to tell them to you.

10. You probably will forget these rules as you live life.

11. You can come back to these rules whenever you need or want to do so.

Remember, *IT CAN BE DONE.*

Complex PTSD Questionnaire for Trauma Survivors

If you would like results of this questionnaire please send SASE and your completed questionnaire to Dr. M. B. Williams, 9 N 3rd St. Suite 100, #14, Warrenton, VA 20186.

Fill out the items below. Higher scores are more indicative of Complex PTSD. All seven dimensions are included.

Number/Name _____

Year(s) your trauma(s) occurred _____

How long did it (they) last? _____

Your Date of Birth _____

Length of time you have been in therapy and what years: _____

_____

When did the trauma(s) have the most impact on your life? _____

_____

What is the event (what are the events) that you consider traumatic? _____

If you have more than one, which event is most distressful? _____

Please use that event as reference point for completing the questions in this questionnaire.

What is your assessment of the present impact of that traumatic event on your current life? Please circle the appropriate answer:

1. No impact

2. Little impact

3. Some impact

4. A lot of impact

5. Severe impact

For the following questions, unless you are given additional directions, please CIRCLE the answer that seems most appropriate. The choices for 1, 2, 3, 4, and 5 are as follows:

1. Absent, no effect, an effect does not exist

2. Subthreshold—only a little but not enough to bother me a great deal

3. This happens to me sometimes

4. This happens often

5. This happens most of the time to me

1. Do small problems get you more upset than they used to? Do you   1 2 3 4 5
   get much more angry now at a minor frustration?

2. Do you cry more easily than you used to, for example, at a sad movie? 1 2 3 4 5

3. Do you get more nervous now about things you have to do?   1 2 3 4 5
   Do you overreact to minor incidents?
   If you answered 2, 3, 4, or 5 to any of the first three questions,
   how much do you overeact?

   1. not at all

   2. a little

   3. I get extremely upset sometimes

   4. I often am extremely upset and may even have tantrums

4. Do you find it hard to calm yourself down after you become upset?   1 2 3 4 5
   If you answered 2 or 3 or 4 or 5, can you give an example?

   Please circle which applies to how long you stay upset?

   1. seconds

   2. minutes

   3. hours

   4. days

5. Do you find that things that used to put you back on track   1 2 3 4 5
   (like playing music, going out with friends) don't seem to work anymore?

6. Have you been in many accidents or near accidents, including   1 2 3 4 5
   |little accidents at home, since the trauma ended?

7. Do you find you are now more careless about making sure that   1 2 3 4 5
   you are safe (e.g., avoiding unsafe places and people; locking doors
   and windows)?

8. Have you deliberately tried to hurt yourself (e.g. burning or   1 2 3 4 5
   cutting yourself)?
   If you answered anything but 1, please respond. This happened as:

   1. one minor episode or accident

   2. more than 1 minor accident or superficial episodes

   3. at least 1 serious accident or frequent superficial episodes

4. more than 1 serious accident, several potential near-misses or frequent and serious episodes

9. Have you ever thought of killing yourself?   1 2 3 4 5
   If you answered other than 1, what have you thought of doing?
   How often is killing yourself on your mind?

   2. rarely

   3. occasionally

   4. frequently, regularly

   5. almost always

   6. always

10. Have you actually tried to kill yourself?   1 2 3 4 5
    If you answered other than 1, how?

11. Do you feel angry much/most of the time?   1 2 3 4 5
    If you answered other than 1,

    1. my anger doesn't bother me or interfere with my life

    2. I feel quite angry but can shift my anger to other matters

    3. anger interferes with my paying attention to daily tasks

    4. anger dominates my daily life

12. Do you have thoughts or images of hurting someone else?   1 2 3 4 5
    If you answered other than 1, would you give an example of
    whom and how?

13. Are you less able to control anger now than before?   1 2 3 4 5

    If so, then do you

    2. snap at people

    3. yell or throw things

    4. attack people physically

14. Are you so worried about upsetting others or losing control that   1 2 3 4 5
    you try not to show anger at all?

15. Do you make an active effort to keep yourself from thinking about sex?   1 2 3 4 5

16. Are you actually disgusted about the idea of sex?   1 2 3 4 5

17. Does it bother you to be touched?   1 2 3 4 5

18. Do you avoid sexual involvements with previous partners?   1 2 3 4 5

19. Do you avoid new sexual involvements?   1 2 3 4 5

20. Do you find yourself thinking about sex too much of the time?   1 2 3 4 5
    If you answered other than 1, how does this affect your life?

21. Are you sexually active in ways that may cause you problems or   1 2 3 4 5
    put you in danger (sex with people you do not know very well,
    unprotected sex, for example)?
    If you answered other than 1, what behaviors do you do?

22. Do you get into situations that might be dangerous to you,   1 2 3 4 5
    e.g., going to places that are not safe, driving too fact, involving
    yourself in dangerous sports, selling drugs, gambling?
    If you answered other than 1, in which do you participate?

23. Since the traumatic event happened, was there a period of time   1 2 3 4 5
    when you could not remember it, were confused about what
    happened (e.g., couldn't remember certain aspects of it, including
    when it began or how long it lasted) or weren't sure it really happened?

    If you answered other than 1,

       2. some details are missing

       3. a few lapses of memory

       4. entire missing episodes

       5. no memory for months or years of my life

Exactly which of these occurred and to what degree?

24. Do you have difficulty now accounting for periods of time in your   1 2 3 4 5
    daily life?

25. Are you confused about names of familiar people or places?   1 2 3 4 5

26. Do you find yourself in places without knowing how you got there?   1 2 3 4 5
    If you answered anything but 1, to questions 24, 25, or 26,
    how much of a problem is this to you?

       1. no problem

       2. somewhat of a problem

       3. this is a major problem for me

27. Do you find you lose track of time?   1 2 3 4 5
    If you answered other than 1, what is that like for you?

28. Not counting when you use (used) drugs or alcohol, do you   1 2 3 4 5
    sometimes feel so unreal that it is as if you were living in a
    dream or not really there?
    If you answered other than 1, does this cause problems in your
    work or social life?

29. Do you sometimes feel like there are two or more totally   1 2 3 4 5
    different people living inside yourself who control how you
    behave at different times?

30. Do you have trouble getting the event or the trigger off your mind?   1 2 3 4 5

31. Are you able to stop thinking about the event when you are   1 2 3 4 5
    working or doing something that requires your attention?

32. Have you lost your confidence in being able to deal with   1 2 3 4 5
    everyday situations (daily chores, work, paying bills, driving,
    paying attention to your children)?
    If you answered other than 1, could you please give examples?

33. Do you believe there is something "wrong" with you because of   1 2 3 4 5
    the event, something that can never be fixed?
    If you answered other than 1, can you describe what you feel is
    wrong with or "different" about you?

34. Do you feel guilty about not having done more to prevent the   1 2 3 4 5
    event from happening?
    If you answered other than 1, could you describe what you now
    think you could have done then?

35. Do you try to hide your traumatic history from others or fear   1 2 3 4 5
    what may be exposed about you if the trauma is revealed
    (e.g., if other learn of your past)?

36. Do you avoid talking about the trauma with people?   1 2 3 4 5

37. Do you keep your trauma history a secret?   1 2 3 4 5

38. Do you feel embarrassed if you talk about the trauma? If so, why?   1 2 3 4 5

39. Do you have the belief that nobody else could possible   1 2 3 4 5
    understand what you went through during the trauma?

40. Do you believe that your trauma history does not really   1 2 3 4 5
    bother you? Do you think that others sometimes make too
    much of a "big deal" about it?

41. Do you sometimes think that the event happened for very good reasons?   1 2 3 4 5
    If you answered other than 1, what are those reasons?

42. Do you sometimes think that the perpetrator of the event   1 2 3 4 5
    (if the event was caused by a person) is special?
    Do you admire him or her?

43. Do you think about getting revenge against the perpetrator   1 2 3 4 5
    of the event?
    If you answered other than 1, what would you want to do
    and how often?

44. If the event was caused by an act of God or nature, are you angry at God?   1 2 3 4 5
    How do you explain the meaning of the event to yourself?

45. Do you feel safe in your life at the present time?   1 2 3 4 5

46. Do you have difficulties trusting others?   1 2 3 4 5
    If you answered other than 1, would you list examples of mistrust.

47. Has your ability to relate to other changed?   1 2 3 4 5
    If you answered other than 1, specifically

    2. I have fewer relationships

    3. I am more distant in relationships with others

    4. I set more careful boundaries

    5. I have fewer boundaries

    6. I spend less time with others

If you spend less time with others (free time) now than before, to what extent?

    1. a little bit less

    2. somewhat less

    3. much less

    4. a lot less time

48. What other events have happened to you since the originally
    named traumatic event occurred?

    I have been _____

    I have been raped ____ times

    I have been mugged/robbed ____ times

    I have been in ____ natural disasters (examples)

    I have witnessed ____ traumatic events (examples)

    I have been battered (hit) ____ times

49. Have you hurt others in ways similar to how you were traumatized?   1 2 3 4 5
    If you answered other than 1, what have you done?

50. Have you felt helpless and/or pessimistic about the future?   1 2 3 4 5

    How, specifically, has your view of the future changed?   1 2 3 4 5

51. Have your feelings changed about your ability to find happiness   1 2 3 4 5
    in love relationships so that you no longer find happiness in
    these relationships?

52. Do you now find more happiness in your relationships?   1 2 3 4 5

53. Do you find more satisfaction in your work now?   1 2 3 4 5

54. Do you find less satisfaction in your work now?   1 2 3 4 5

55. Has it been hard to find a reason to go on with life?   1 2 3 4 5

56. Have your ethical and/or religious beliefs changed because   1 2 3 4 5
of the trauma that happened to you?
If you answered other than 1, could you give examples?

Resources

The American Counseling Association (ACA) has a Statement of Understanding with the American Red Cross (ARC) to provide a pool of qualified mental health professionals (Licensed Professional Counselors) who have the Disaster Mental Health Services required course to respond to disasters. In addition, ACA has a variety of resources to assist members and the people they serve deal with the aftermath of both man-made and natural disasters. ACA is the largest professional counselor association in the world and represents professional counselors who provide services including clinical, educational and work settings. ACA also works to influence public policy on issues that impact various client populations. Contact ACA at our website: www.counseling.org or by phone at 1-703-823-9800 or fax at 1-703-823-3760.

References

Adams, E. 1994. *Understanding the Traumas of Childhood Psycho-Sexual Abuse.* Bedford, Mass.: Mills, Sanderson Publisher.

Alderman, T. 1997. *The Scarred Soul: Understanding and Ending Self-Inflicted Violence.* Oakland, Calif.: New Harbinger Publications.

———. 2000. Helping those who hurt themselves. *The Prevention Researcher* 7(4):5–8.

American Psychiatric Association. 1994. *Diagnostic and Statistical Manual of Mental Disorders,* 4th ed. Washington, D.C.: American Psychiatric Association.

Antonovsky, A. 1987. *Unraveling the Mystery of Health: How People Manage Stress and Stay Well.* San Francisco: Jossey-Bass.

Astin, M. C., and B. Rothbaum. 2000. Exposure therapy for the treatment of post-traumatic stress disorder. *Clinical Quarterly* 9(4):50, 52, 55.

Ayalon, O. 1992. *Rescue: Helping Children Cope with Stress.* Ellicott City, Md.: Chevron Publishing Corporation.

Ayalon, O., and A. Flasher. 1993. *Chain Reaction.* London: Jessica Kingsley Publishers.

Baker, G. R., and M. Salston. 1993. *Management of Intrusion and Arousal Symptoms in PTSD.* San Diego: Association for Traumatic Stress Specialists (International Association for Trauma Counselors).

Bandler, R. 1985. *Using Your Brain—for a Change.* Moab, Ut.: Real People Press.

Benson, H. 1975. *The Relaxation Response.* New York: William Morrow.

———. 1984. *Beyond The Relaxation Response.* New York: Berkeley Press.

Bloom, S. 2000. Personal interview using trauma center protocol for the Sanctuary Program. In *Creating a Comprehensive Trauma Center: Choices and Challenges,* edited by M. B. Williams and L. A. Nurmi. New York: Plenum Publishing.

Bourne, E. 2001. *Beyond Anxiety & Phobia: A Step-by-Step Guide to Lifetime Recovery.* Oakland, Calif.: New Harbinger Publications.

Branscomb, L. 1990. *Becoming Whole: Dissociation and Me.* Decatur, Ga.: Lodestar Productions.

Brittain, J. C. 2001. *Keepsake Stories.* Washougal, Wash.: Beyond the Bounds.

Brussat, F., and M. A. Brussat. 2000. *Spiritual Rx: Prescriptions for Living a Meaningful Life.* New York: Hyperion.

Busuttil, W. 2002. The development of a 90-day residential program for the treatment of complex PTSD. In *Simple and Complex PTSD: Strategies for Comprehensive Treatment in Clinical Practice*, edited by M. B. Williams and J. F. Sommer. Binghamton, N.Y.: Haworth Press.

Caruso, B. 1986. *Healing: A Handbook for Adult Victims of Child Sexual Abuse*. St. Louis Park, Mo.: Beverly Caruso.

Catherall, D. 1992. *Back from the Brink: A Family Guide to Overcoming Traumatic Stress*. New York: Bantam.

Cohen, B. M., M. Barnes, and A. B. Rankin. 1995. *Managing Traumatic Stress Through Art: Drawing from the Center*. Lutherville, Md.: Sidran Press.

Cohen, M. J. 1977. *Reconnecting with Nature*. Corvallis, Ore.: Ecopress.

Cole, P. M., and F. W. Putnam. 1992. Effect of incest on self and social functioning: Developmental psychopathology perspective. *Journal of Consulting and Clinical Psychology* 60(2):174–184.

Collings, M. 2001. *Reasons Not to Kill Yourself*. www.ctsserve.com/~svship, March 28.

Courtois, C. A. 1988. *Healing the Incest Wound: Adult Survivors in Trauma*. New York: W. W. Norton.

Covey, S. 1999. *The 7 Habits of Highly Effective People*. New York: Simon & Schuster.

Curro, E. 1987. Assessing the physiological and clinical characteristics of acute vs. chronic pain. *Dental Clinics of North America* 31(4):xiii–xxiii.

Davidson, J. R. T. 1996. *Davidson Trauma Scale*. North Tonawanda, N.Y.: Multi-Health Systems, Inc.

Davis, M, E. R. Eschelman, and M. McKay. 1995. *The Relaxation and Stress-Reduction Workbook*, 4th ed. Oakland, Calif.: New Harbinger Publications.

Dolan, Y. 1991. *Resolving Sexual Abuse: Solution-Focused Therapy and Eriksonian Hypnosis for Adult Survivors*. New York: W. W. Norton.

Dunning, C. 1997. *The 13 Cs of Salutogenesis*. Tuscaloosa, Ala.: Traumatology Certification Training Program, University of Alabama.

Eitner, G. 2001. Letter to author.

Engel, B. 1995. *Raising Your Sexual Self-Esteem*. New York: Fawcett Columbine.

Enright, R. D., and R. P. Fitzgibbons. 2000. *Helping Clients Forgive: An Empirical Guide for Resolving Anger and Restoring Hope*. Washington, D.C.: American Psychological Association.

Figley, C. R. 1989. *Helping Traumatized Families*. San Francisco: Jossey-Bass.

Figley, C. R., B. E. Bride, and N. Mazza, eds. 1997. *Death and Trauma: The Traumatology of Grieving*. Washington, D.C.: Taylor & Francis.

Friedman, M. J. 2000 *Post-Traumatic Stress Disorder: The Latest Assessment and Treatment Strategies*. Kansas City, Mo.: Compact Clinicals.

Garrick, J. 2001. Letter to author.

Gatchel, R. J., and D. C. Turk. 1996. *Psychological Approaches to Pain Management*. New York: Guilford Press.

Greenberger, D., and C. A. Packoly. 1995. *Mind Over Mood: A Cognitive Therapy Treatment Manual for Clients*. New York: Guilford Press.

Grand, L. C. 2000. *The Life Skills Presentation Guide*. New York: John Wiley & Sons.

Grant, M. 1997. *Pain Control with Eye Movement Desensitization and Reprocessing*. Wyong, N.S.W., Australia: Wyong Medical Centre.

Herman, J. L. 1992. *Trauma and Recovery*. New York: Basic Books.

————. 1999. Complex PTSD: A syndrome in survivors of prolonged and repeated trauma. In *Essential Papers on PTSD*, edited by M. J. Horowitz. New York: New York University Press.

Ilardo, J. 1992. *Risk-Taking for Personal Growth: A Step-by-Step workbook*. Oakland, Calif.: New Harbinger Publications.

International Society for Traumatic Stress Studies. 1997. *Childhood Trauma Remembered: A Report on the Current Scientific Knowledge Base and Its Applications*. Northbrook, Ill.: ISTSS.

Janoff-Bulman, R. 1992. *Shattered Assumptions: Towards a New Psychology of Trauma*. New York: The Free Press.

Kelly, F. D. 1999. *The Psychological Assessment of Abused and Traumatized Children*. Mahweh, N.J.: Lawrence Erlbaum Associates, Inc., Publishers.

Kobasa, S. C. 1982. The hardy personality: Toward a social psychology of stress and heal. In *Social Psychology of Health and Illness*, edited by J. Suls, and G. Sanders. Hillsdale, N.J.: Lawrence Erlbaum Associates, Inc., Publishers.

Kushner, H. S. 1981. *When Bad Things Happen to Good People*. New York: Avon.

LeDoux, J. 1997. Emotion, memory, and pain. *Pain Forum* 6(1):36–37.

Leehan, J., and L. P. Wilson. 1988. *Grownup Abused Children*. Springfield, Ill.: Charles C. Thomas, Publisher.

Levine, P., and A. Frederick. 1997. *Walking the Tiger: Healing Trauma*. Berkeley, Calif.: North Atlantic Books.

Linehan, M. M. 1996. *Cognitive Behavioral Treatment of Borderline Personality Disorder*. New York: Guilford Press.

Linley, P. A. 2001. Positive adaptation to trauma: Wisdom as both process and outcome. Unpublished manuscript.

Louden, J. 1997. *The Women's Retreat Book: A Guide to Restoring, Rediscovering, and Remembering Your True Self—in a Moment, an Hour, a Day, or a Weekend*. New York: HarperCollins Publishers.

Masterson, R. 1988. *The Search for the Real Self: Unmasking the Personality Disorders of Our Age*. New York: The Free Press.

Matsakis, A. 1994a. *Post-Traumatic Stress Disorder: A Clinician's Guide*. Oakland, Calif.: New Harbinger Publications.

————. 1994b. *Post-Traumatic Stress Disorder: A Complete Treatment Guide*. Oakland, Calif.: New Harbinger Publications.

————. 1998. *Trust After Trauma: A Guide to Relationships for Survivors and Those Who Love Them*. Oakland, Calif.: New Harbinger Publications.

————. 1999. *Survivor Guilt: A Self-Help Guide*. Oakland, Calif.: New Harbinger Publications.

McCann, I. L., and L. A. Pearlmann. 1990. *Trauma and the Adult Survivor: Theory, Therapy, and Transformation*. New York: Brunner/Mazel.

————. 1992. Constructivist self-development theory: A theoretical framework for assessing and treating traumatized college students. *Journal of American College Health* 40(4):189–196.

McCrae, R. R. 1992. June. The five factor model: Issues and applications. *Journal of Personality*. 60(2):329–361.

McDermott, D., and C. R. Snyder. 2000. *The Great Big Book of Hope: Help Your Children Achieve Their Dreams*. Oakland, Calif.: New Harbinger Publications.

McKay, M., and P. Rogers. 2000. *The Anger Control Workbook*. Oakland, Calif.: New Harbinger Publications.

Meichenbaum, D. 1994. *A Clinical Handbook/Practical Therapist Manual: For Assessing and Treating Adults with Post-Traumatic Stress Disorder.* Waterloo, Ont.: Institute Press.

———. 2000. Treating patients with PTSD: A constructive narrative approach. *Clinical Quarterly* 9(4):55, 58–59.

Metropolitan Washington Council of Governments Health Care Coalition. 2001. Getting a good night's sleep. *Total Wellness: Becoming a Total Person* 9(4):1.

Miller, S., D. Wackman, E. Nunnally, and P. Miller. 1989. *Connecting Skills Workbook.* Littleton, Colo.: Interpersonal Communication Programs, Inc.

Mundahl, P., D. Parks, D. Gray, and J. Fields. 1995. *The Women's Specialized Program Patient Workbook.* Brattleboro, Vt.: Brattleboro Retreat.

Muss, D. 1991. *The Trauma Trap.* London: Doubleday.

Pearlman, L. A., and K. W. Saakvitne. 1995. *Trauma and the Therapist: Countertransference and Vicarious Traumatization in Psychotherapy with Incest Survivors.* New York: W. W. Norton.

Pennebaker, J. W. 1997. *Opening Up: The Healing Power of Expressing Emotions.* New York: Guilford Press.

Pennebaker, J. W., and R. S. Campbell. 2000. The effects of writing about traumatic experience. *Clinical Quarterly* 9(2):17, 19–21.

Peterson, D. 1968. *The Clinical Study of Social Behavior.* New York: Appleton Century & Crofts.

PILOTS. 2001. Published international literature on traumatic stress. White River Junction, Vt.: National Center for PTSD.

Power, E. 1992a. *Managing Ourselves: Building a Community of Caring.* Brentwood, Tenn.: E. Power & Associates.

———. 1992b. *Managing Ourselves: God in Our Midst.* Brentwood, Tenn.: E. Power & Associates.

Prend, A. D. 1998. *The Model for Transcending Loss.* Charleston, S.C.: ATSS Annual Meeting.

Resick, P. A. 1994. Cognitive processing therapy (CPT) for rape-related PTSD and depression. *Clinical Quarterly* 4(3/4):1, 3–5.

Rosenbloom, D., and M. B. Williams. 1999. *Life After Trauma: A Workbook for Healing.* New York: Guilford Press.

Rothschild, B. 2000. *The Body Remembers: The Psychophysiology of Trauma and Trauma Treatment.* New York: W. W. Norton.

Saindon, C. 2001. Good sleep hygiene. *Self Help Magazine.* www.shpm.com/articles/trauma/trsleep.html, February 14.

Schab, L. M. 1996. *The Coping Skills Workbook.* King of Prussia, Penn.: The Center for Applied Psychology.

Schiraldi, G. R. 1999. *Building Self-Esteem: A 125-Day Program.* Ellicott City, Md.: Chevron Publishing Company.

———. 2000. *The Post-Traumatic Stress Disorder Sourcebook: A Guide to Healing, Recovery and Growth.* Los Angeles: Lowell House.

Scurfield, R. M. 1994. War-related trauma: An integrative experiential, cognitive, and spiritual approach. In *Handbook of Post-Traumatic Therapy,* edited by M. B. Williams, and J. F. Sommer. Westport, Conn.: Greenwood Press.

Shapiro, F. 1995. *Eye Movement Desensitization Reprocessing.* New York: Guilford Press.

Smyth, L. D. 1999. *Clients' Manual for the Cognitive-Behavioral Treatment of Anxiety Disorders.* Havre de Grace, Md.: The Red Toad Company.

Solomon, R. 2001. Dynamics of fear. Unpublished manuscript.

Spring, D. 1993. *Shattered Images: Phenomenological Language of Sexual Trauma.* Chicago, Ill.: Magnolia Street Publications.

Suyemoto, K. L., and X. Kountz. 2000. Self-mutilation. *The Prevention Researcher* 7(4):1–4.

Tedeschi, R. G., and L. G. Calhoun. 1995. Trauma and transformation: Growing in the aftermath of suffering. Thousand Oaks, CA: Sage Publications.

———. 1996. The post-traumatic growth inventory: Measuring the positive legacy of trauma. *Journal of Traumatic Stress* 9(4):455–471.

Tedeschi, R. G., C. L. Park, and L. G. Calhoun, eds. 1998. *Post-Traumatic Growth: Positive Changes in the Aftermath of Crisis.* Mahweh, N.J.: Lawrence Erlbaum Associates, Inc., Publishers.

Tennen, H., and G. Affleck. 1998. Personality and transformation in the face of adversity. In *Post-Traumatic Growth: Positive Changes in the Aftermath of Crisis,* edited by R. G. Tedeschi, C. L. Park, and L. G. Calhoun. Mahweh, N.J.: Lawrence Erlbaum Associates, Inc., Publishers.

Terr, L. 1994. *Unchained Memories: True Stories of Traumatic Memories Lost and Found.* New York: Basic Books.

Trautman, K., and R. Connors. 1994. *Understanding Self Injury: A Workbook for Adults.* Pittsburgh, Penn.: Pittsburgh Action Against Rape.

Van der Kolk, B. A. 1988. The biological response to psychic trauma. In *Post-Traumatic Therapy and Victims of Violence,* edited by F. Ochberg. New York: Brunner/Mazel.

———. 1996. The complexity of adaptation to trauma: Self–regulation, stimulus discrimination, and characterological development. In *Traumatic Stress: The Effects of Overwhelming Experience on Mind, Body, and Society,* edited by B. A. van der Kolk, A. C. McFarlane, and L. Weisaeth. New York: Guilford Press.

———. 1997. The body keeps the score: Memory and the evolving psychobiology of post traumatic stress. In *Essential Papers on Post-Traumatic Stress Disorder,* edited by M. Horowitz. New York: New York University Press.

Van der Kolk, B. A., A. C. McFarlane, and L. Weisaeth. 1996. *Traumatic Stress: The Effects of Overwhelming Experience on Mind, Body, and Society.* New York: Guilford Press.

Virginia State CISM Team Members. 1998. *Telecommunication Stress Workshop.* Critical Incident Stress Management Annual Training, Virginia Beach, Va. June.

Weekes, C. 1986. *More Help for Your Nerves.* New York: Bantam Doubleday Dell Publishing Group.

Williams, M. B. 1990. *Creating a Self-Report Scale for DESNOS: A New unpublished Instrument.* Warrenton, VA: Author.

Williams, M. B. 1994. Establishing safety in survivors of severe sexual abuse. In *Handbook of Post-Traumatic Therapy,* edited by M. B. Williams and J. F. Sommer. Westport, Conn.: Greenwood Press.

Williams, M. B., and J. F. Sommer. 1994. *Handbook of Post-Traumatic Therapy.* Westport, Conn.: Greenwood Press.

Williamson, G., and D. Williamson. 1994. *Transformative Rituals: Celebrations for Personal Growth.* Deerfield Beach, Fla.: Health Communications, Inc.

Wilson, J. P., M. J. Friedman, and J. D. Lindy. 2001. *Treating Psychological Trauma and PTSD.* New York: Guilford Press.

Zampelli, S. O. 2000. *From Sabotage to Success: Ways to Overcome Self-Defeating Behavior and Reach Your True Potential.* Oakland, Calif.: New Harbinger Publications.

Some Other
New Harbinger Titles

Do-It-Yourself Eye Movement Technique for Emotional Healing, Item DIYE $13.95

Stop the Anger Now, Item SAGN $17.95

The Self-Esteem Workbook, Item SEWB $18.95

The Habit Change Workbook, Item HBCW $19.95

The Memory Workbook, Item MMWB $18.95

The Anxiety & Phobia Workbook, 3rd edition, Item PHO3 $19.95

Beyond Anxiety & Phobia, Item BYAP $19.95

The Self-Nourishment Companion, Item SNC $10.95

The Healing Sorrow Workbook, Item HSW $17.95

The Daily Relaxer, Item DALY $12.95

Stop Controlling Me!, Item SCM $13.95

Lift Your Mood Now, Item LYMN $12.95

An End to Panic, 2nd edition, Item END2 $19.95

Serenity to Go, Item STG $12.95

The Depression Workbook, Item DEP $19.95

The OCD Workbook, Item OCDWK $18.95

The Anger Control Workbook, Item ACWB $17.95

Flying without Fear, Item FLY $14.95

The Shyness & Social Anxiety Workbook, Item SHYW $16.95

The Relaxation & Stress Reduction Workbook, 5th edition, Item RS5 $19.95

Energy Tapping, Item ETAP $15.95

Stop Walking on Eggshells, Item WOE $15.95

Angry All the Time, Item ALL 13.95

Living without Procrastination, Item LWD $12.95

Hypnosis for Change, 3rd edition, Item HYP3 $16.95

Toxic Coworkers, Item TOXC $13.95

Letting Go of Anger, Item LET $13.95

Call **toll free, 1-800-748-6273,** or log on to our online bookstore at **www.newharbinger.com** to order. Have your Visa or Mastercard number ready. Or send a check for the titles you want to New Harbinger Publications, Inc., 5674 Shattuck Ave., Oakland, CA 94609. Include $4.50 for the first book and 75¢ for each additional book, to cover shipping and handling. (California residents please include appropriate sales tax.) Allow two to five weeks for delivery.

Prices subject to change without notice.